WALKS &

# WALKS & MORE

by
Andrew Johnson & Stephen Punter

With original drawings
by
Ken Hutchinson

LOGASTON PRESS 1990

LOGASTON PRESS
Little Logaston Woonton Almeley
Herefordshire HR3 6QH

First published by Logaston Press 1985
Completely revised and published by Logaston Press 1990
© Copyright Andrew Johnson & Stephen Punter 1990
© Copyright (illustrations) Ken Hutchinson 1990

Extracts from *Kilvert's Diaries* are reproduced with the
kind permission of Mrs. Sheila Hooper, William Plomer
and Jonathan Cape Ltd. (publishers)

Extracts from *The Journey Through Wales* by Gerald of Wales,
are reproduced with the kind permission of Lewis Thorpe
and Penguin Books Ltd. (publishers)

Sketch maps are based upon the Landranger Ordnance Survey
1:50 000 maps with the permission of the Controller of
Her Majesty's Stationary Office, Crown Copyright reserved

ISBN 0 9510242 6 4

Photoset in 10/12 pt New Baskerville by Logaston Press
Printed in Britain by Billings and Sons Worcester

# CONTENTS

*Also from Logaston Press*

*Aspects of Herefordshire, by Andrew Johnson and Stephen Punter*
*Aspects of Worcestershire, by Andrew Johnson and Stephen Punter*
*Ludford Bridge and Mortimer's Cross, by Geoffrey Hodges*
*The Humble-bee Its Life History and How to Domesticate it, by F.W.L. Sladen*
*The Happy Farmers, by Sheila Wenham*

# INTRODUCTION

Welcome to the new Walks and More.

So popular did the first edition prove that it is now out of print. And in response to an obvious need, we're happy to bring you a new edition.

However we have some good news for those of you who have the first edition on your bookshelves: the second edition will make an excellent companion for your well thumbed friend. This is no warmed through offering, nor does it come to you merely tidied up around the edges. The new Walks and More is completely revised, revamped and over hauled. And yes there are 80 walks this time, the majority of them brand new. For a start the new Walks and More covers a wider area. At its centre is still the old county of Herefordshire. But we've added to it part of Worcestershire from the Malvern Hills to the Severn; and more of southern Shropshire and eastern Powys. In all it is indisputably an area of some outstanding unspoiled countryside, comparatively little known, though rich in both history and custom.

Visitors to the area, or in fact anyone with limited time, needs to have a reliable guide to be able to explore a cross section of the wealth that's available. And as one of the best ways to get the most out of a visit is to travel on foot, we've selected the 80 walks that we feel do justice to the countryside. Our approach has been to look for those walks which are circular, broadly of about two hours duration, and only those that are completely on public rights of way. Not only are all of the walks we've chosen on routes registered on definitve footpath maps compiled and maintained by the county councils, but all of them were passable when walked within the eighteen months of going to print.

But the book is more than just a walkers' guide. Walks and More divides into three sections. Apart from the walks themselves we've chronicled the main historical events in the surrounding countryside in one of a series of introductory essays; there's also an account of the area's agriculture; its customs and folklore; its cider and apples; its beer and hops; its literature, art and music.

The second part of the book is made up of a directory of more than 150 entries covering villages, towns, and other places of interest, and not just the well-known sites! Private places which can be seen from public paths or roads without disturbing the owner's privacy have been included. Our notes on churches have been kept short deliberately so as not to duplicate those easily available in the churches themselves.

And to give you a flavour of the amazing variety of places to visit, from the smallest chapel to the largest castle, and of the countryside, local artist Ken Hutchinson has contributed many drawings.

Walks and More: even bigger and better than before.

Andrew Johnson and Stephen Punter
Spring 1990

# HISTORY

### Early History till the Construction of Offa's Dyke

The first inhabitants were hunter gatherers living on the edge of the dense oak forests or on the pastoral areas that lay at around 1,000 feet above sea level. The area has few remains from this period, just the occasional standing stone and Arthur's Stone, a neolithic tomb on Dorstone Hill.

From about 1000 B.C. groups of Celts started to settle in Britain. The clutch of hilltop settlements in the west of Herefordshire, including those of Croft Ambrey and Credenhill were built by the Dobunni, whilst the Silures carved out the British Camp and Midsummer Hill on the Malverns. Excavations at Croft Ambrey have proven that these settlements were inhabited for a span of several hundred years from around 400 B.C. The population of the major settlements could have been counted in their thousands rather than hundreds, but numbers alone were not able to stem the Roman Invasion of 43 A.D. This period saw the emergence of Caractacus and his heroic resistance, a story which was part myth and part history. Over time one historian or another has claimed most of the larger hillforts of the area as the site of his last battle.

By 74 A.D. Agricola's campaigns had brought the whole area into conflict with the Romans. Many of the isolated Roman marching camps were established at this time. So were the Legionary fortresses of Deva (Chester) and Isca (Caerleon) which were used to control the borderland. These were linked by a road running due north-south which used existing tracks where possible. Their construction on raised banks in the river valleys made them passable in winter. Leintwardine, Roman Bravonium, was established in about 160 A.D. and was occupied till the middle of the fourth century. Ariconium, to

1

the east of Ross, was an industrial site where iron ore from the Forest of Dean was forged and refined.

With the withdrawal of the legions for the defence of Rome various Romano-British kingdoms were created. Maximus, an officer of Count Theodosius, the ruler of Britain in the late fourth century, is thought to have founded the kingdom of Powys, its name derived from pagenses, the Latin for 'people of the countryside'. This kingdom dominated the northern and middle Marches from the Dee to the upper Wye, whilst smaller kingdoms lay to its south.

The kingdom of Brycheiniog lay to the south of Powys, and is traditionally believed to have been founded by Brychan, son of an Irish chieftain called Anlac. Irish settlements to the south-west formed the nucleus of the kingdom of Dyfed.

A smaller princedom lay close to the Wye called Erging by the Welsh and Archenfield by the English. (The English name was derived from Ariconium, the Roman town in the Forest of Dean.) Its eastern border lay along the Wye and its western was formed by the Monnow and Black Mountains.

Throughout the British Isles these kingdoms and princedoms owed a loose allegiance to an overall ruler. During the fifth century this leader was Vortigern, king of Kent. With Britain under attack from the north and west he invited over Saxon mercenaries to help keep the Irish and Picts at bay. As Saxon numbers increased and their own home territory was threatened from the east, the Saxons challenged their former hosts. A balance of power was achieved whilst Arthur led the British in the sixth century, but continued Saxon immigration and British emigration to Brittany, coupled with a plague that only affected the western, British held part of the island, opened the way for continued Saxon expansion westwards.

In 603 the borderland was still firmly in Celtic hands, for Saint Augustine, who had been sent over to convert the Anglo-Saxons, held a meeting with the British bishops at which the Severn was regarded as the boundary between the lands of the English and British. But this position was not to last for long. The Battle of Deorham in 577 had cut off the Celts of Wales from their compatriots to the south-west, and in 616 the Battle of Bangor on Dee split Wales from the British kingdom of Strathclyde. At the Battle of Chester in 614 Cynddylan, King of Powys, was killed. Powys also lost its fertile lands in the Severn valley to the advancing Saxon kingdom of Mercia.

A temporary buffer state of Maegonsaete was formed about 650 as a Saxon principality ruled over by Merewalh, third son of Penda, King of Mercia. The Maegonsaete (a name probably derived from Maund or Magana near Leominster) were a mixture of Celtic and Saxon people, and certainly many of the place names within the old principality appear to be corruptions of Celtic names, for example Dinmore from Din Mawr, meaning great hill. To the north there was formed a similar princedom of the Wreocencaete, centred on the Wrekin and north Shropshire.

Westward Saxon encroachment continued along the river valleys where a large number of Saxon place names are found. (Places ending in -ing, -ham, and -ton denote some of the Saxon settlements.) Despite this Archenfield was still observing Celtic laws and customs in 1086 and Brycheiniog was to remain free from Saxon intrusion till the tenth century.

But further east the country had passed firmly into Saxon hands. By 670 a group of West Saxons called the Wiccas or Hwiccas had settled on the site of a small Roman station called Vertis, the future Worcester. As trade developed the town grew rapidly, since for many centuries it possessed the only bridge across the Severn between Gloucester and Bridgnorth.

In 731 Aethalbald of Mercia was recognized as the overlord of the whole of England south of the Humber and the princedom of the Maegonsaete was ended. Offa was Aethalbald's successor as King of Mercia, and he marked the border between the predominately Saxon areas and the Celtic areas with the dyke named after him. Four areas

*Offa's Dyke above Norton*

3

of Saxon settlement were left to the west of the dyke, one being to the south of Radnor Forest where the Saxon villages of Kinnerton, Downton, Evenjobb, Harpton, Walton and Womaston are located.

The dyke was built between 757 and 796. It was never designed as a permanently fortified border, but as a boundary which allowed those on its east, the English, to keep watch on those to its west, and thus gain forewarning of any Welsh raids. Apart from marking the border the dyke appears to have controlled trade by directing movement to certain crossing points. It also appears to have been constructed piecemeal by each landowner along the border taking responsibility for building a particular section, the length being dependent upon the size of his holding or the amount of labour available to him.

Later records reveal that Offa's laws provided for a joint English and Welsh board to explain the laws to their respective citizens; laws which included a code for the recovery of stock rustled across the border, and another for the safe conduct of either Welshman or Mercian when on the other side of the dyke by a specially appointed guide.

The line of the dyke runs for a distance of 149 miles, though the earthwork itself is traceable for only 81 miles. It consisted of a bank ditched usually only on the west side, though occasionally on both.

Only short sections of the dyke are seen in the Herefordshire Plain. The reason may be that the forest provided a natural barrier with the dyke only necessary where tracks crossed the agreed border. Or possibly the area posed no great threat as Archenfield was already fairly anglicised. In other places there are shorter dykes which precede Offa's Dyke in construction, and which would seem to be protective screens at the head of valleys, and these may have afforded sufficient protection.

**Offa to the Norman Invasion**

In England Offa was all powerful. However on his death his kingdom declined, and with the defeat of his son Cenwulf at the Battle of Basingwerk so began the ascendancy of the kingdom of Wessex.

Powys, meanwhile, had been in decline since the Battle of Chester in 614. After Cynddylan little is known of the dynasty until the 800's, apart from Elised who is remembered in the Eliseg Pillar, erected sometine around 750 in the valley of the Dee. From 844 till 878 Powys and Gwynedd passed under the rule of Rhodri Mawr, Rhodri the Great, after who's death the kingdom was shared between his two sons

Anarawd and Cadell. In the face of their combined pressure the kings of the lesser Celtic kingdoms turned to King Alfred for support and swore allegiance. It was upon these voluntary acts of submission during 878 to 881 that later English kings were to base their claims to the overlordship of Wales.

In the tenth century the English West Mercia was ruled by Ethelflaed, a daughter of King Alfred. During her reign the area was raided by the Danes. The Danes had been troublesome for many years, using the Severn to sail into the depths of the country and pillage the lands and to take slaves from the monastic settlements. Several monasteries in the Severn valley were so devastated that they ceased to function. Worcester was the objective of at least one raid, for on one occasion a raider tried to make off with the cathedral's Sanctus bell. However its weight slowed him down and the returning citizens, who had fled at the Danes' approach, caught and flayed him, nailing his skin inside the cathedral's west door. In 915 the two Danish jarls Otto and Harold came up the Severn and captured the Bishop of Llandaff. However the men of Herefordshire and Gloucestershire combined to defeat them.

In 939, in the reign of Athelstan, the Welsh princes were made to do homage at Hereford, and the Wye was then fixed as the western boundary of Mercia, re-establishing the limits that had earlier been decreed by Offa.

After a period when England was divided between Saxon and Dane, the country was united again under Edward the Confessor. During his reign he installed several Norman relatives in positions of power, some of them on the Welsh Marches. The first stone castle keeps were built, notably that by Richard le Scrob at Richards Castle, twenty miles north of Hereford.

The intention was to keep in check a resurgent Wales under Llewelyn, but Llewelyn defeated an Anglo-Norman army at Leominster in 1051, and a further raid reached Hereford in 1055. Ralph, Earl of Hereford and the Confessor's nephew, was replaced with Harold Godwinson, later Harold II, who pushed the Welsh back to the west, beyond Offa's Dyke. Harold took for himself several manors in the north-west of Herefordshire, including those of Eardisley, Tupsley, Kington, Huntington, Titley, Presteigne and Old Radnor.

On the eve of the Norman Conquest Wales was divided into cantrefs, based on a hundred or a township. In each Gwlad or State each king exercised certain privileges at his Llys or Court. In each cantref there was a lesser court which the king visited twice a year. The three main Gwlads at this time were Gwynedd in the north with 12 cantrefs, Powys with 6 and Deheubarth in the south with 29. In England the Saxons had created a system of shires, each divided into hundreds, an area of land that contained, at their formation, around a hundred free families. Within the hundred there developed the townships, or parishes as they became known once Roman ecclesiatical rule had been accepted by the British church. The business of the hundreds was conducted in a moot attended by the freemen, with the reeve as president or chairman and the tithingman as constable. The Shire Moot was ruled over by the earldorman, the king's representative, and the overall body of shires was governed by the witenagemot, literally the meeting of wise men.

## The Norman Conquest to rebellion in 1260

After the Norman Conquest several of William the Conqueror's aides were given lordships on the Welsh border. Among these were numbered William Fitzosborne who was made Earl of Hereford; Ralph de Todeni—William's standard bearer at the Battle of Hastings, who was created Lord of Clifford on the Wye; and Ralph de Mortimer who was granted the lordship of Wigmore further north, once he had defeated the Saxon earl Edric of Salop who held out against the Normans.

These lords became known collectively as the lords marcher, the name March deriving from the Saxon kingdom of Mercia, itself derived from the 'mearc' or border between two nations. William the Conqueror created these baronies to keep the Welsh under control, and whilst restricted to the east, they could carve out their own territory to the west. They owed allegiance to the crown, but were in essence independent, for they were able to appoint their own chancellors and judges; their land was not shire ground, meaning they could harbour refugees from the Crown; and they were able to execute criminals, though only those caught on their own territory and only after they had been tried in the royal towns of Shrewsbury or Hereford. The head of the executed criminal had then to be sent back to prove that the execution had been carried out.

Most of the Crown's control over the lords marcher was exercised through threat of forfeiture of lordships that were held elsewhere in England. Later on control was increased by making the lords members of parliament, thus causing them to be in London and divided from their power base.

However the Norman kings also planned against the eventuality that the marchers and Welsh would combine to threaten England. During the eleventh and twelfth century much of the Severn valley was low lying marshy land and on the eastern bank of the Severn, itself crossed by few bridges, they constructed castles.

At the crossing at Worcester they built upon the strength of the bishopric by endowing monastic settlements at Worcester itself, Evesham, Pershore and the surrounding area, so creating a host of tenants and retainers owing allegiance to the bishop.

This additional line of defence was tested in 1088 whilst Wulstan, later St. Wulstan, was bishop. Many of the marcher barons were in revolt supposedly in support of Robert of Normandy, the Conqueror's brother, who had claimed the throne. Bath was stormed and Ralph de Mortimer, Bernard Newmarch, Roger de Lacy, Osborn Scroop and Roger, Earl of Shrewsbury, marched on Worcester. Wulstan, so his chronicler Florence relates, called the church tenants and retainers together with its citizens and his bodyguard to defend the city. The Norman garrison in the castle asked the bishop to move from the monastery to the castle for greater protection and he consented, but before he did so he ordered his motley force to go and meet the enemy on the other side of the river. From his vantage point Wulstan could see that the rebel forces had set fire to some of the monastery's barns and farms, and he was asked to pronounce a curse on the enemy. He did, and Florence then records that a miracle occurred— the opposing forces appeared to become paralysed, scarcely being able to carry their arms and see what they were doing. The foot soldiers were routed and the knights were taken prisoner.

However William II seems to have forgiven Ralph de Mortimer for his part in this revolt, for when on a punitive expedition against the Welsh, he granted Ralph the area that was later to become Radnorshire. For the next hundred years the Mortimers, often with the support of the king, were in constant warfare with the Welsh over the disputed territory.

Further south the marches suffered from the civil war in the 1130's between the Empress Matilda, also known as Maud, and King Stephen. Matilda had much support in the area, her most prominent supporter being Milo Fitzwalter, Constable of Gloucester whom she made Earl of Hereford. Bredwardine castle was probably built at this time as one of many unlicensed castles. Further to the east Stephen had made one of his supporters Waleran de Beaumont Earl of Worcester in 1139, but when Waleran was absent in 1140 Matilda and the Earl of Gloucester sacked the city. Stephen and Waleran took revenge the following year when they ravaged Gloucester. In 1145 Waleran seemed to tire of the conflict and went on a pilgrimage, returning to found a cistercian abbey at Bordesley with Matilda, whom he now decided to support. However Stephen gradually asserted royal control, and in 1149 took and burnt Worcester, after which Waleran fled to an exile in Normandy.

Milo Fitwalter had five sons, Roger, Walter, Henry, William and Mahel. Each succeeded to their father's inheritance, except William, and each died without issue. The last, Mahel, 'was even more notorious for his inhuman cruelty' according to Gerald of Wales and was killed at Bronllys Castle near Talgarth in 1175 when a stone fell on his head during a fire. After Mahel's death, Brecknockshire passed to William de Braose through his mother Bertha, another child of Milo Fitzwalter.

In 1175 de Braose became known as the 'Ogre of Abergavenny', after he had invited a number of neighbouring Welsh chieftains to a banquet in the middle of which he had them all killed. This was supposedly to revenge the death of his uncle, Henry Fitzwalter. The Welsh retaliated by storming the castle and killing the governor and garrison, but by 1200 the de Braoses were Lords of Radnor and Buellt by conquest and Lords of Brecon and Abergavenny by marriage.

Meanwhile Gwynedd had been left free to become the prominent Welsh kingdom, which in 1199 was in the hands of another Llewelyn. Llewelyn allied with King John when he became king in 1199 and gained supremacy in Wales, after which, in 1208, John broke off the allegiance. With the loss of Normandy early in John's reign, and the murder of his nephew Arthur which was attributed to him, his rule started to completely fall apart when he also took on the pope. He had quarelled with Pope Innocent III over the appointment of the archbishop of Canterbury, when he refused to agree to Innocent's choice. In 1212 Innocent, tired of endless haggling with John, excommunicated him and released Llwelyn from his vows of allegiance to John on condition that he helped Philip of France to depose him. John turned the tables on his enemies by succumbing to the pope's demands and placing the kingdom in his care. However Philip of France continued with his aggressive intentions, now himself in opposition to the pope, and sent an army to England under the command of his son Louis. The country essentially divided into an eastern and northern area largely in support of Louis, whilst the west remained loyal to John. Worcester however declared for Louis, but the Earl of

Chester captured the castle for John, John meanwhile busying himself on the Marches, capturing Hay Castle in 1216. When John died later that year, he was buried in Worcester Cathedral between the shrines of St. Oswald and St. Wulfstan, a wish stated in his last will.

On the accession of John's son Henry III, the factions on the border split and reformed, as was to happen throughout the twelfth and thirteenth centuries. Now, under the leadership of William Marshall, Earl of Pembroke, many of the barons came together to support the young Henry and a fresh start. The strengthened army marched east and defeated Louis at Lincoln. In 1231 war again broke out on the border, the spark provided by the murder of several Welsh prisoners, and Llewelyn lay waste to much of the border. Henry came to campaign from a base at Painscastle and peace was eventually restored in 1234.

Llewelyn was succeeded by his son David and the English sought to divide the Welsh kingdom by sowing dissension. War commenced yet again in 1244 and David died in 1246. He in turn was succeeded by his sons who were forced to accept the humiliating terms of the Treaty of Woodstock in 1246, under which the rulers of Powys and Deheubarth severed their link with Gwynedd and transferred their allegiance to the English crown. Any unsuccessful rebellion by them would henceforth result in their land being forfeited to the king.

## Rebellion in 1260 to The Civil War

David's youngest son, yet another Llewelyn, having gathered support from the disgruntled Welsh, displaced his brother Owain as ruler. In 1255 he regained parts of Gwynedd and then gradually extended his control to all of Wales. By 1263 he was co-operating with Simon de Montfort gainst Henry III in a new outbreak of war between the barons and the king.

Simon de Montfort had risen to lead a faction of the barons against Henry's continual non-observance of Magna Carta and failure to honour promises to reform his lax and bankrupt government. As the kingdom was still pledged to the pope, Henry had used this as a way of continually delaying decisions and of manipulating allegiances. In the end Simon de Montfort, Henry's brother-in-law, was forced to choose between exile or war, and chose the latter. Through over confidence in the larger royalist army and his own superior generalship, he defeated the king and Prince Edward at Lewes in Sussex and took both men prisoner. However gaining control of the king created further problems. In the thirteenth century the king was accepted as ruler, the question was only as to the extent that the absolute power of the king was influenced by the wishes of his magnates. After Lewes, government was still carried on in the king's name, but it was Simon's de facto rule. Believing that de Montfort had now overstepped the mark, many of his original supporters found their position untenable and drifted away, with his party coming to be based on his family and the more ardent, often younger, supporters of his cause for better government. As the royal forces regrouped and the Earl of Gloucester wavered in his support for Earl Simon, the latter moved west to Hereford. Then some of those who had escaped from Lewes to France landed at Pembroke. The Earl of Gloucester joined them and Roger Mortimer, a long time opponent of de Montfort's, freed Prince Edward from his light guard at Hereford. Simon was soon cut off on the west of the Severn, though he managed to cross it whilst Edward defeated de Montfort's son, also Simon, outside Kenilworth Castle. Now the senior de Montfort found himself trapped between Edward, the Earl of Gloucester and Roger Mortimer at Evesham. After a fierce but hopeless fight he and many of his supporters were killed. But the kingdom remained troubled for the next two years. In 1267 Henry III agreed to recognize Llewleyn as King of Wales to remove one thorn from his side. In Henry's dotage, government passed to Prince Edward, a wiser and more respected man. Pardons were granted to de Montfort's surviving supporters, rule of law was re-established and peace returned.

But Henry's acceptance of Llewelyn as king of Wales meant he consequently refused to pay homage to Edward I when he became king. When conditions permitted, Edward invaded Wales advancing on three fronts—one in the south, one in the centre, and one in north Wales supported by a fleet. Llewleyn was killed in a skirmish in 1282 on the River Ifon near Builth.

With Llewelyn's death, resistance soon ended. By the Statute of Rhuddlen, Edward I divided Wales into shires and introduced many English laws and customs. This meant that there were no new lands to conquer for the lords marcher, who now numbered 141. The strongest of these lordships were held by the Mortimers in central Wales and the de Bohuns based in Huntington and Brecon. Edward tried to reduce their right to wage private wars, but died before he fully achieved his aim. The powerful Roger Mortimer rebelled against Edward I's ineffective son Edward II and was imprisoned, only to

*The remains of the Mortimer stronghold at Wigmore Castle*

escape to France where he joined Edward's queen, Isabella, the so-called 'she wolf of France'. Later he returned to England, was pardoned and spent much time in the queen's company. On the murder of Edward II, in which he played a leading part, Roger Mortimer became king in all but name, as he was joint custodian, with Isabella, of the young Edward III. He was created Earl of March.

When Edward III reached the age of 18, he arranged for the seizure of Mortimer at Nottingham, where a session of parliament was being held. Mortimer was speedily condemned for his part in the murder of Edward II and taken to London, where he was hanged at Tyburn on 29 November 1330. His son Edmund died a few months later and the Mortimer estates were put in the care of the Earl of Nottingham during the minority of the young Roger Mortimer. When Roger was 23 he received a restoration of the title from Edward III, and was later to become commander of the English forces in Burgundy.

His son, another Edmund Mortimer, became Lieutenant of Ireland and married Phillipa, the daughter of Lionel, Duke of Clarence, a

11

younger brother of Edward III, and was selected by Richard II as heir to the throne.

Whilst the Mortimer fortunes waxed, those of the Welsh waned. After Edward I's conquests, the various offices of Welsh government were put out to the highest bidders, who in turn exacted the most profit possible from their position. New systems of law enforcement and castle building were introduced under the English system, and the old Welsh custom whereby land left without an owner became common land was changed, and instead the land passed to the king. With the advent of the Black Death, large areas of land passed to the king in this way. This and other changes to the law were largely unpopular. The spark for revolt and a new Welsh resurgence was provided by a dispute in 1400 between Owain Glyndwr and Lord Grey of Ruthin over the boundary between their land.

Glyndwr sought to conspire with the English nobles who were disenchanted with Henry IV's usurption of the crown from Richard II—especially Mortimer who was Richard's declared heir—and Percy of Northumberland. Percy attempted to link up with Glyndwr but was defeated at the Battle of Shrewsbury in 1403 before he could do so.

The three formed a tripartite pact in 1405, and Glyndwr also arranged a treaty with France. A French army landed at Milford Haven in 1405 and advanced on Worcester, where it encountered some resistance and retreated. It wintered in west Wales and then re-embarked for France, promptly suffering losses at the hands of an English fleet.

Glyndwr's forces suffered defeats at Grosmont and at Usk in 1405, after which his power gradually declined until 1413 when Wales was once more in submission to England.

In the meantime the Mortimer fortunes were about to reach their climax. The last Mortimer was Edmund, son of the Edmund who had been declared heir to the throne by Richard II. He was kept under close watch by the usurper Henry IV, but was nevertheless given a command in France by Henry V. He died in 1425 aged 24. His sister Anne became the representative of the family, and married Richard Plantagenet, son of the duke of York and grandson of Edward III.

The defeat in France and lack of justice under Henry V's son Henry VI, led to general discontent in the country. In the periods of Henry's mental incapacitation, the protectorship of the realm passed by turn and turn again between Somerset and the Duke of York, the Mortimer heir apparent. The rivalry between these two men soon led to the First Battle of St. Albans which was little more than a brawl. It did however signal the start of the Wars of the Roses.

After this brawl York became Protector once more, but Margaret of Anjou was determined to restore Henry to full control and York was soon replaced again. When the queen and her supporters called a council at which it was clear action was to be taken against the Yorkists, the latter once more resorted to arms, collecting an army on the Welsh Marches. But Henry's superior force, York's bad generalship and finally treachery by his best force—the battle seasoned garrison of Calais—led to his army disintegrating at Ludford Bridge outside Ludlow. York fled to Dublin, whilst his son Edward and the Earl of Warwick, who now became effective leader of the opposition, retired to Calais.

Warwick soon seized his opportunity, landed in Kent and marched into London. Margaret of Anjou promptly gathered an enormous force in the north and lured the Duke of York and the Earl of Salisbury to defeat and death at the Battle of Wakefield. This great army then marched south to meet the Earl of Warwick, whilst another assembled at Pembroke under Jasper Tudor and the Earl of Wiltshire to march on York's son Edward who was in the Marches, based on Ludlow and Wigmore. Edward was a much finer general than his father and planned his ground and campaign carefully before meeting Jasper Tudor's force. This he did on 3 February 1461 at Mortimer's Cross south of Wigmore where he routed the Lancastrian army. With the Mortimer inheritance and success in its homeland, he now gathered a larger force and advanced on London. Warwick was defeated at the Second Battle of St. Albans on 17 February, though he managed to retire westwards with much of his army. Margaret of Anjou failed to advance on London and Edward entered the city on 4 March and claimed the crown as Edward IV. Before his coronation, he set off northwards in pursuit of the Lancastrian horde, catching it up and first defeating it at Ferrybridge before winning a bloody victory over it at Towton two days later. (The Mortimers were finally extinguished with the death of Richard III at Bosworth, where the Welsh supported Henry Tudor.)

With the accession of Edward IV, roughly a third of the marcher lordships became crown property and the position of the Warden of the Marches was replaced by the Court of the Lord President and Council of the Marches of Wales, which co-ordinated the arrangements for policing and defence. Much of the marcher power was destroyed, and over succeeding years the marcher lordships continued to lose their power eventually enabling William III to abolish the council.

With the Act of Union under the Tudors in 1536 and then the Reformation, church reforms and monastic confiscation extended into Wales. English laws further influenced Welsh custom, and English became the official language. Monmouthshire was placed on an English legal footing and dues were paid direct to the King's Exchequer rather than to those in Wales. The old Welsh laws of inheritance were replaced by those of primogeniture. New forms of estate farming started to remove the scattered hamlets from the map. Wales began to lose its separate identity, and the border its meaning. But the changes helped establish a prolonged period of peace right up until the English Civil War.

**The Civil War to the present day**

When parliament finally decided to exert its authority over Charles I, the Earl of Worcester was put in charge of assembling the royalist forces in the west country. Worcester itself saw one of the first military engagements of the Civil War when a parliamentarian force tried to capture a carriage taking some of Charles's wealth to safety, but was defeated and driven off by Prince Rupert. Once the royal army had gathered, it advanced on London, fought the inconclusive Battle of Edgehill en route and reached Turnham Green before retreating.

Gloucester and Bristol were held by parliament and sorties from Gloucester gradually extended parliamentary control to Monmouth, Chepstow and later Hereford. The success was short lived though, for the royalist forces co-ordinated their strength, recaptured Hereford and then took Bristol in 1643, before closely investing Gloucester.

July 1643 saw the zenith of royalist fortunes, before indecision and then defeat at Naseby, allowed parliament to slowly gain permanent control. King Charles fled to Hereford at the end of June 1644, and thence to Abergavenny and Raglan, the main centre of resistance in the west in the latter part of the war. In July 1645 Fairfax and Cromwell were given command of the parliamentary forces and the war was pursued more rigorously. Fairfax broke the siege of Plymouth and advanced northwards capturing Bridgewater, Bath and Bristol, whilst a Scottish army advancing south besieged Hereford, but failed to take it. However John Birch, who had been a trader of presbyterian persuasion in Bristol before joining the army once his business enterprise had been ruined by the conflict, launched a surprise attack on the city in the depths of winter and captured it. With parliamentary control ever increasing, Charles became a wanderer travelling around south Wales, Oxford and Raglan trying to raise a further army. But Oxford fell in June 1646. Raglan was then besieged and eventually surrendered as again there was no hope of relief. Oliver Cromwell was to settle many of his ex-soldiers in Radnorshire, which is supposed to have contributed to the area's later non-conformism.

The economy of the area was still almost exclusively agricultural. Industry was not to develop till the 1800's with more intensive iron working in the Forest of Dean, and lead workng around Shelve in south-west Shropshire. The infrastructure serving this infant industry also grew. For centuries the Severn had provided a trade route, the Severn bore and tides providing natural assistance in travelling upstream as far as Worcester. As the years progressed the numbers of barges and trows increased. The latter was a vessel specifically designed for the lower Severn, with its shifting sands and shoals. It had a rounded bilge, a shallow draught and usually a flat bottom, though some had an inverted keel. The largest trows were 60 feet long, had a main and mizzen mast and could carry up to 60 tons of cargo. In the 1200's the cargo had included wine destined for storage in Worcester's priory and castle, and by 1600 the Severn had become the second busiest river in Europe after the Meuse. The variety of cargo had increased to include oranges, raisins, soap and oil.

But as industry developed, so too did the need for better transport. The first canal scheme was launched in 1677 by Andrew Yarranton, a local writer and engineer. Over succeeding years improvements were made by canalising sections of rivers. However still greater development was required, for in 1752 around 100,000 tons of soft clod coal alone was carried from collieries near the Iron Bridge Gorge to the salt works at Droitwich and for household use at the major cities and towns along the river. Other traffic included salt carried from Droitwich, corn from Tewkesbury and the Vale of Evesham, cheese from Cheshire and Warwickshire, and fruit, cloth and wool from the midlands. Packhorses met the barges and trows and the goods were often transferred to sea-going vessels at Bristol. As the volume increased, so did the need for bulk transport from source to market, and only then did the idea of canals really take hold.

The first local act of parliament for canal construction in Worcestershire was passed in 1766 to enable a canal to be built from or near Bewdley to the Trent, to link up with a further canal which was designed to join the Trent and Mersey. Because of the hills near Bewdley the canal, known as the Staffordshire and Worcestershire, was constructed from near the junction of the rivers Stour and Severn. In 1771 the development around this junction provided the impetus for the new town of Stourport.

In 1767 an act of parliament provided for a canal linking the Severn to Droitwich and a further one for linking the Severn and various coal mines with Birmingham. The Droitwich Canal was started in 1768 and its six mile length was opened in 1771 and was used in the main for carrying coal and salt. Whilst canal building exploded in Worcestershire, progress in Herefordshire was much slower. In 1790 an act was passed proposing to link Stourport to Leominster and Kington. Similar plans were laid for a canal to connect Hereford with the Severn at Gloucester, and by 1798 the section from Gloucester to Ledbury was open. The last part was not completed until 1840-1845 when Aylestone Hill was tunnelled under. However the lateness of its construction meant its opening coincided with the coming of the railways, and consequently it saw hardly any use.

In any event physical obstructions had prevented canal construction on a large scale in the west, and here the horse drawn tramway had played a more important role. The best known of these was the Hay tramway which was built for the purpose of carrying limestone from a quarry in the Usk valley below Brecon over to the Dulas valley and on to Hay. By use of the tramway and the Brecon canal, coal could be brought to Hereford, avoiding some of the more treacherous stretches of the Wye.

A tramway was also planned to connect Kington, Burlingjobb (where there was a lime quarry) and Brecon. One of its promoters was James Watt who owned land at Burlingjobb. It was used for almost forty years before the railway took over, incorporating some of the route of the tramway.

The Golden Valley railway line was laid in 1881, but was constantly on the brink of closure. It was taken over by the Great Western Railway in 1901 and for a while it made a small profit, bringing tourists to Abbey Dore, but the advent of the bus and the car soon caused it to decline again.

Many of the branch railway lines were closed in 1960 under the Beeching 'axe', leaving only the main north-south border route, and the central Wales line, to the west of Worcester.

Today transport within the area is almost exclusively by road, and the routes that the armies of old had to footslog for days on end, can be completed within hours. Fortunately the area retains a little of its previous pace of life.

# AGRICULTURE

Britain was originally very sparsely populated and rural settlements usually consisted of a few huts in a clearing with livestock grazing the neighbouring woodland. The Romans established villas and their estate farms. When the Saxons who followed settled in the country they often established new villages or took over and expanded derelict British ones. In the new settlements they ploughed just enough land on which to grow crops for the whole community, and then parcelled it out amongst the families that formed the village for planting up. After the harvest this first field was used as common grazing ground. The next year a second field was ploughed and shared out again, likewise for the third year, after which the first field was re-ploughed. This basic three field system was often varied, but after the fields had been established they were always worked in rotation, usually one year being planted with wheat or rye, followed by a crop of barley, oats, peas, beans or vetches followed by a fallow year. As the years went by the strips became permanently allocated to each family, rather than being parcelled out afresh each year, and this gave rise to the narrow and comparatively long fields that became common in later years; a pattern which can still be seen in some of the area's most ancient fields.

The woodland surrounding the fields was used for grazing, often by pigs, and there is a record that at Crowle a half square mile of woodland housed a hundred hogs. The woods also harboured wild bees' nests which were raided to provide honey.

The amount of land that could be ploughed by a team of oxen in one day became known as an acre. As this clearly varied with the type of soil and prevailing conditions the size differed from one part of the country to another. Nevertheless over the years 'an acre' became a standardised unit.

Tithes were imposed from around the 700's onwards. These originated as a tenth strip of land worked for the benefit of the church, but with the development of the Norman feudal system tithes became payable in kind. The feudal system created new duties owed to the owners of land, all land now being held from the king, often with an intermediary Norman lord. Even the Saxon freemen now owed these duties, duties which could involve military service, working land or helping at harvest time. Sometimes it involved paying a rent, but rents only really appeared with the spread of monasteries, as the extensive grants of land they received made it impossible for the monks to physically farm all the land under their control. So tenants were installed who paid a sum of money to help pay for the upkeep and extension of the monastic buildings.

Life was always hard, but cold stormy summers in 1308 and 1322 caused a shortage of food, though matters were even worse during 1315 and 1316 when there was widespread famine. In 1348 and the following year the country was hit by the Black Death and its population was more than halved. Depopulation meant that cattle strayed from the commons and roamed at will; whilst the price of labour rose due to its scarcity, until a royal ordinance in 1349 set out the wage rates to be applied. As land was left unworked, sheep were introduced to graze the abandoned ridges and furrows, so helping to found the wool and fleece industry.

During these years most stock was slaughtered in the autumn as there wasn't the feed to keep it through the winter. An ox and a 40lb wether lamb would fetch about the same price. All the stock ran together on the common land and selective breeding couldn't be practiced. Consequently breeding stock tended to decline in quality over the years. Liver rot, especially in wet years, was a major problem, and the first outbreak of sheep scab was reported in 1280. Pigeons were kept in large dovecotes for meat and for their dung, and apples, pears, cherries and quinces were grown. There were several vineyards in the county—thirty-eight were recorded in the vicinity of Evesham in the Domesday Survey—and these appear to have prospered in the summers of the twelfth and thirteenth centuries which were generally a few degrees warmer than they are now.

The Wars of the Roses between 1450 and 1485 saw a decimation of the old nobility and although the feudal system had managed in the past to adapt to changing conditions, it now finally fell apart. Rent paying tenancies became more common, and the land-owning labourer gained greater independence. However immediately after

*Dovecote at Luntley*

the accession of Edward VI in 1547, an act was passed to try to prevent vagrancy. This reduced the landless poor to slavery and forced them to work in chains. Fortunately this act was repealed two years later and was replaced by a system of parochial poor relief which was offered in return for work. Initially this was a voluntary code, but because the payment for work was not compulsory the system didn't work in practice. So in 1563 poor relief was made mandatory. Further acts under Queen Elizabeth I brought the various pieces of legislation together, establishing assessors or overseers in every parish to collect a poor rate, to organise the work of able bodied people and to relieve the lot of the old and infirm. This legislation, though amended from time to time, existed till the Poor Law Amendment Act was passed in 1834.

In Herefordshire the lack of decent navigation on the Wye—passage was fraught with difficulty because of shallows in summer and floods in winter—together with the absence of good roads, proved to be a barrier to the export of produce and hence to the most profitable development of agriculture. Consequently Bristol was the chief market for many years. Goods were sent down the Wye to

Chepstow or sometimes by packhorse to Monmouth first, if conditions demanded, then on by ship. Some produce was sent by sea from Bristol to London, most often the better quality cider. Cattle were frequently driven overland to London. Hops grown in the east of the county were sold mainly in Worcester, and production increased gradually till the Napoleonic Wars, after which it declined again. At this time the market also shifted to the growing industrial areas of the midlands and the north, and canals were planned to help ease the traffic, though those actually constructed remained few and far between. Those which were built enabled the sale of dessert apples that would otherwise have gone to make cider. These were sent to the north and west midlands and fetched twice the price that cider made from them would have done.

During the 1600's new crops were introduced, irrigation systems were experimented with, the ancient custom of liming was revived and renewed attention was paid to manuring and draining. During the 1700's landlords reorganised holdings, erected new barns of stone and slate and drained areas of wetland. Good farm buildings at the end of this century consisted of a house on one side of a square, the other three sides being formed by outbuildings including stables, barns with threshing floors, a cow house, feeding stalls, cider mill and a warehouse for alcohol, together with dovecotes, pigsties, sheep cots and a dairy.

As the 1700's drew on agriculture gradually became more prosperous for the owner-occupier farmer, but wages for the labourer did not rise in line with profits. The labourer worked long hours for low wages—these were especially low in Herefordshire due in part to its remoteness. During the Napoleonic Wars the average budget for a family with four children shows that annual earnings were just under £31, mainly generated by the man, though this was supplemented by hoeing, weeding, stone picking and bird scaring by the rest of the family. This amount did not cover the yearly outgoings of just over £35, of which over half was spent on bread, flour and oatmeal, around a tenth on bacon or pork and the rest on other foods, rent, wood, clothes, births, burials and sickness. The deficit of just under £5 could be made up in part by extra money earned at harvest time.

For generations labour was hired at a fair day of the patron saint of the parish. Failure by the labourer to abide by the terms of the verbal contract made at the fair was punishable by a fine, imprisonment or a beating. Lest residence of more than one year should lead to responsibility by the parish for the labourer in the event of him falling on hard times, the hiring period was normally for no more than eleven months.

Farmers argued for a good corn price to allow them to pay better wages and several attempts were made over the years to regulate its price as it varied enormously from year to year depending upon planting or harvesting conditions. These met with varied success. Then in 1776 Adam Smith published his *Inquiry into the causes of the Wealth of Nations* which advocated free trade between nations, and over the next century the story of creating a profitable agriculture is partly that of a tussle between protectionism and free trade. For the labourer, however, the battle remained the same: a fight for a decent wage.

But high-minded debate had to be set aside in the late 1700's as crop prices rose again, this time through a combination of bad weather and the war with France. Higher prices meant desperate times for the poor and in 1800 the dragoons were used to quell disturbances around the county. Sheep rustling became common again, even though it was punishable by death.

Depression followed the end of the Napoleonic Wars with tenants, who had taken on land at too high a rent, quitting and leaving the landlord to shoulder the burden. But from 1836 the recession started to ease and more investment took place, especially in land drainage. But the labourer's position had barely improved. His weekly wage was about 8 shillings, augmented in summer by extra piece and harvest work, sometimes by an allowance of cider, profit on the backyard pig which also provided much of the diet through the winter, and work carried out by his wife and children. Boys were set to work from the age of 8 upwards, whilst girls from the age of 12 or 13 were withdrawn permanently from school to help look after any other children, or they worked at gloving, earning between 1/6 to 3/6 for an eight to twelve hour day. At harvest time for hay, grain, hops and apples, which tended to overlap in many years, local labour was supplemented by gangs from Ireland or women who came out from the expanding towns to the north of the county. Approximately 3,000 women and children crossed Stourport Bridge each year to help in the hop harvest, sleeping on straw in the farms' outbuildings.

Fortunately agricultural profits temporarily rose after 1808 and the future looked bright. However it is said that the London auctioneer Christie, having an estate in Herefordshire to auction '... had as usual set it off by a flowing oration, but before concluding he said that he felt bound to observe that Herefordshire was a county that had two peculiarites, viz; turnpikes without end, and roads without bottom.'

Plainly prosperity had brought little or no improvement to the county's communications.

With the end of the recession more attention was paid to new machinery. Small steam engines were installed in many corn mills, and increasingly steam power was experimented with in threshing machines and later for ploughing.

Many of the wealthier landowners kept stock, though mortality rates were still high because of liver rot, distemper, foot and mouth and also losses through flooding. Of the cattle breeds kept the Shorthorn was the most favoured; the Durham and Improved Shorthorn breeds merged into the one in 1837. The Leicester was generally the most popular sheep breed, though the Shropshire was also prominent, and large numbers of this breed's rams were crossed on the Leicester. In fact the breed grew in importance throughout the nineteenth century and by 1878 was the most favoured breed in the county. The oldest recorded flock of pedigree sheep of any breed was the Stretton Court flock of Shropshires. This flock, at Stretton Sugwas to the west of Hereford, was finally dispersed in 1989. Pigs were kept only in small numbers.

*Shropshire sheep*

Agriculture has tended to be prosperous at times of war so that although the repeal of the protective corn laws in 1846 was expected to cause an agricultural recession, prices held up with the increase in demand caused by the Franco-Prussian, and the American Wars. The price of wheat rose again during 1867 and 1868, steadied then rose once more in 1871 and precipitated the formation of the national Agricultural Labourers Union in Warwickshire in February 1872. Membership quickly spread to Worcestershire and soon demands were being made for improved conditions. A resolution was passed calling for 'an increase to 2/6 per day with the same privileges as at present received, and where beer is not allowed 1/- per week extra; waggoners, cowmen and shepherds to be raised accordingly; the times to be as usual (6 a.m. to 6 p.m.) with the exception of Saturdays, when work will cease at 4 p.m. in winter and 5 p.m. in summer.'

Whilst some farmers accepted the demands, fundamental changes to the rural way of life were at work, altering landowners' requirements. The amount of agricultural labour was showing a rapid decline from the 1870's onwards, partly due to the bad harvests and lack of work, partly due to the loss of child labour with the 1876 Education Act, but mainly through mechanisation in the shape of reapers and threshers which dramatically reduced the need for labour at harvest time. This mechanisation coincided with the industrialisation in the cities so that villagers drifted to them to find work. Poor prices for agricultural produce and high returns for city businessmen, meant that many established rural familes had to sell out to the recently wealthy. These new stock farmers could buy feeding stuffs for over wintering stock, and the quality of cattle and sheep improved.

The thirty or so years between the disastrous years of the late 1870's and the First World War saw a great change in rural life. The Truck Acts of the late 1800's gradually encouraged farmers to pay wages in money, or 'coin of the realm', to differentiate it from tokens which could then be exchanged for goods in the employer's shop. However some food, a cottage and certain other allowances were still considered to be allowable as part of a man's wages. Cider and beer were not however, and these were replaced by additional wages.

With increasing mechanisation fewer people had reason to expect employment on the land, whilst expanding education, coupled with the advent of the bicycle and railways, widened the horizons of many rural dwellers. Labourers grasped at the opportunities to encourage their children to take jobs in the trades, professions, post office or on the railways. Some were encouraged to emigrate.

War once more was to give a boost to agriculture. The First World War saw such losses in the merchant fleet caused by German submarines, that the supply of American grain was largely cut off and the price of home produced wheat was forced up. With labour in short supply too due to the demands of the war, wage rates rose. But, as had happened before, the end of war saw the return of agricultural depression. To try to counteract this, in 1928 agricultural land was relieved of rates. Between 1931 and 1933 marketing boards were set up for milk, pigs, bacon, hops and potatoes. The Second World War saw much marginal land go under the plough, some of which was put down to permanent pasture once the war was over. Increased tillage, more grassland, the use of greater amounts of fertiliser and chemical controls, coupled with new and bigger machinery all contributed to greater efficiency at least in terms of the amount of food grown per acre.

With entry into the European Economic Community in 1973, Britain's marketing boards and quota system were replaced with intervention prices which set a minimum price level for most, but not all, produce. Output increased further, but with growing worries about the amount of food held in intervention stores and more recently over the quality of the food and the effect of intensive agriculture on the land, various measures have been taken to reduce agricultural surpluses by limiting production.

Such measures always hit the small farmer hardest, and in western England there are many family farms now struggling to survive. Most are being forced to look at ways of diversifying their farming activities. Whilst the focus of the debate may have shifted from free trade versus tariffs to food safety and the fight to reverse rural stagnation, the struggle to work in harness with nature continues. Recently, wet autumns have hampered potato harvesting and winter corn sowing, mild winters have allowed pests and diseases to survive in greater numbers, cold springs restricted grass growth, and wet summers meant bad hay. These worries will always remain whatever national politics achieve. It is the one certainty amongst the vagaries of farming life.

# CIDER AND APPLES

Cider is originally associated with the Celts, though it was not until the fifth century that serious cultivation of apples took place. Even then it was regarded as a poor man's drink made by floating pressed apples in water, a method called dépense.

By the seventh century however, imported Normandy cider was considered suitable to offer along with wine at a meal. A major improvement in quality seems to have resulted from the introduction of cultivated apple varieties, possibly from Spain or from eastern Europe, as the late ripening of some present day cider apples suggests that they may have originated in warmer climates. From the thirteenth century new varieties for cultivation were steadily imported from Normandy, with the first plantings taking place mainly in Devon. From Devon apple orchards spread in popularity: by 1212 cider is known to have been a source of income for Battle Abbey in Sussex, and by 1341 seventy-four of the eighty parishes in west Sussex were paying part of their tithes in cider.

In the United Kingdom orchards have tended to thrive best when grown in sheltered sites below about 400 feet above sea level, avoiding the higher winds and the lower temperatures and so reducing blossom damage and minimising the risk of frost. In addition with its moist climate and water retaining clays, Herefordshire is particularly well suited to apple growing.

Not so long ago when farms in Herefordshire were more mixed, it was quite common for each to have its own cider making facilities. Most had their own cider mill which consisted of a round stone called the runner. This was 3 feet 6 inches in diameter and 1 foot wide and, weighing over half a ton, was supported on its edge in a groove in a circular stone trough roughly 10 feet in diameter called the chase. This upright stone was pivoted in the centre of the trough and drawn

25

round by a horse or ox, and in this fashion it was possible to grind one hogshead or 110 gallons of cider a day. Traditionally the stone was a dark reddish grit from the Forest of Dean, and the trough would have only been partly hollowed out before the stone left the quarry, as a guard against damage during the journey. Calcerous stone was not suitable as the acid in the apple would have soon corroded it. About three-quarters of the weight of an apple is the juice, and much of this is expelled by the initial crushing, and would be run off into the fermenting barrels. The remaining apple pulp would have been wrapped in cloths, with one being stacked on the other until they were about eight or ten in number, so making a cheese. Then a large wooden block would be screwed down onto it to extract the remaining juice. These cider presses were often modified from an original olive oil press, and later still the cider press was in turn adapted to extract wood and other dye-stuffs, linseed oil and sugar from sugar cane. The relatively dry apple pulp left at the end of the pressing, called pomace, would not have been wasted but would have been fed to the farm's pigs or other stock. Whilst the juice from cultivated apples provided a drink, the orchards themselves gave shelter from the worst of the spring frost for livestock, proving to be good areas for lambing the sheep flock.

Nowadays, as with many other occupations, cider making has become more specialised and more mechanised, so much so that the more compact bush trees, which are productive within a shorter time, have supplanted the taller, the more stately and leisurely growing standard trees. It is impossible to run stock in orchards of bush trees and difficult to produce apples profitably from standards, so that over time the many smaller orchards, rich in local apple varieties, are giving way increasingly to the much larger contract plantations containing the handful of varieties of the industrial cider makers. A bush tree in full production in an average year will yield one and a third hundredweight of fruit, equivalent to about ten gallons of cider. With a planting density of between 130 and 200 bush trees to an acre as opposed to 40 standards, farmers are increasingly having to choose either to concentrate on cropping an orchard or running stock—apples and animals is much less of an option than it once was. Consequently Herefordshire is losing many of its most ancient apple varieties and all but a few of its cider makers.

Cider apples are quite different from dessert or culinary apples, not only are they much smaller and harder but they have other characteristics that make them unsurpassed for cider making. A seventeenth century writer noted that 'many think, so they be apples and ripe, it matters not what kind they are' but good cider is usually made from a blend of apples—one of the few apples that makes a good cider on its own is the Kingston Black which has the correct balance of acid and tannin. Both dessert and cooking apples can be used to make cider, but they ferment very quickly and don't have the same flavour. The old Herefordshire varieties include the Redstreak, Gennet-Moyle, Styre Apple, Leather Coat, Oaken Pin, Golden-Pippin, Hagloe-crab, the Red, White and Yellow Musks, Foxwhelp, Old Permains, Gillyflower, Whitesour, Dymock Red, and the Ten Commandments.

John Duncumbe writing in 1805 on Herefordshire agriculture said: 'The colours of a good cyder fruit are red and yellow, the colour to be avoided is green, as affording liquor of the harshest and generally of the poorest quality; the pulp should be yellow, and the taste astringent. Apples of a small size, ceteris paribus are always to be preferred to those of a larger, in order that the rind and kernel, in which principally consist the strength and flavour of the liquor, may bear the greatest proportion to the pulp, which affords the weakest and most watery juice.'

*Cider mill*

All the varieties have their own specific characteristics including differing dates of harvest; the earliest ripen at the end of August, and the latest up to the end of December. Traditionally most fruit was allowed to fall and then the trees were shaken to dislodge the remainder. The apples were gathered into tumps under the trees prior to bagging and carting to the cider press. It was found that the earlier varieties tended to rot if they were not washed, whilst the later ones were best stored for a while as they contained higher levels of starch which needed to break down into the simpler sugars before the yeasts could turn these to alcohol during fermentation.

Cider apples are divided into four groups, the sweets which are both low in acid and tannin, the bittersweets which are low in acid but high in tannin, the bittersharps which are high in both acid and tannin, and sharps which are high in acid, but low in tannin. The Kingston Black is a bittersweet, a member of the group having the best balance of acid and tannin. The tannin provides the 'bite' in cider and also acts as a preservative, whilst the acid prevents the taste from appearing flat. Cider fruit in general have less acid than dessert or culinary apples, but much more tannin which is why they are inedible on the tree—Barland perry pears are even said to be rejected as inedible by pigs, not normally known for their culinary fastidiousness. Thus in general a finished cider is made from a blend of varieties, the degree of tannin or acid, and therefore sweetness depending upon the blend, though nowadays sugar is often added after the completion of the fermentation to achieve the desired sweetness.

The apple juice naturally contains sugar, and yeasts that are present on the skin of the fruit will work on this sugar to convert it to alcohol. Some air is initially needed for the yeasts to grow, but then the conversion process takes place in anaerobic conditions. Usually a hole in the top of the cask is left open to allow air for the first vigorous ferment, which will carry out some of the suspended solids in the juice, and when it dies down a fermentation lock can be inserted to allow carbon dioxide formed by the fermentation process to escape without allowing air in. The casks are then kept topped up to prevent the vinegar bacteria working on the surface of the cider. After the fermentation the cider can be racked off into clean barrels and stored for later use.

It was the seventeenth century that witnessed the heyday of English cider, but all too soon the practice of watering down the apple juice was adopted, either directly, or by allowing the milled fruit to soak in water for a few days prior to pressing. The poorer cider, or small cider as it became known, was drunk more widely than the more expensive undiluted variety. Labourers were given six pints of small cider a day, increasing to between twenty and twenty-four pints at harvest time. And very often a young, frequently female, member of the household would have been responsible for filling the small wooden costrells and taking them into the fields for the farm hands. The costrells, which were slung over the horses' necks would have been refilled many times during a hot working day. However the growth in consumption at the turn of the seventeenth century led to many more cider apple growers and to conditions of oversupply. Soon, with the improvements in transport, it became more profitable to grow culinary and dessert fruit for the industrial areas and for London. And when pressure from the Napoleonic Wars led to land going over to the production of grain and livestock, the cider orchards became neglected. Duncumbe states that: 'The pruning of trees is too little attended to here, the redundancy of wood is very prejudicial, the tops being so close that scarce a bird can find its way through the boughs. Where one third of the branch is cut off, the tree would acquire additional vigour, and be enabled to bear more regular crops.'

Profitable cider production was soon faced with other problems. In 1763 Lord Bute, the Prime Minister, proposed to greatly raise the excise duty on cider and this was vigorously opposed. The Truck Acts at the end of the 1800's also hit cider production. They were intended to make payment for work in money rather than kind and encouraged the setting up of shops in areas where none existed. Whereas it was accepted that food and accommodation for agricultural labour were proper payment in kind, the provision of cider was not.

These setbacks quickly had an affect. In 1883 Herefordshire had 27,000 acres of orchard, Devon 26,348, Somerset 23,400, Kent 17,417 and Worcestershire 16,804. By 1936 with the increase in demand for culinary and dessert apples, and with the decline in cider production, Kent's acreage had increased to 68,206, far ahead of the next county, now Worcestershire with 25,460, then Devon showing a slight drop to 24,413 and Herefordshire to 22,413, of which about 14,500 acres was cider orchard. Somerset's acreage had also dropped to 19,516 acres. The acreage has continued to fall as standard apple trees are grubbed up, till today the combined county of Hereford and Worcester has some 12,600 acres of orchards.

Historically cider was considered to be beneficial as a medicinal product. Medical theories in the seventeenth century were based on an understanding of the four humours—blood, yellow bile, black bile and phlegm, and the four qualities—hot, cold, moist and dry. The logic was that for a hot and dry illness, for example, you took a cold and moist remedy. Cider was classified as a moist, but especially cold, item and was therefore recommended amongst other things to combat black bile, thought to be a cause of melancholy.

Nowadays cider comes in several forms, but whatever its ultimate style it will all have been given a period of storage after fermentation. Nevertheless modern cider is not stored for as long as wines, for being lower in alcohol content it is more liable to attack by micro-organisms. Although cider made from older varieties may have a specific gravity of between 1079 to 1085, or an alcohol content of 11 to 12 per cent, the newer varieties produce a cider with a specific gravity closer to 1044, or 6 per cent alcohol. Therefore these days cider tends to deteriorate markedly after a year of storage in wood.

Though cider is well known, its close cousin perry, the equivalent usually lighter drink made from perry pears is less so. As with cider, different varieties to the dessert and culinary pears are used in its production. Perry pear trees are much larger and longer living than their cider apple counterparts, lasting up to 150 years and giving maximum production between the ages of thirty and eighty years. The south-west midlands area is currently one of the few areas to grow these types of pears. Perry making is more idiosyncratic as the pears tend to need special treatment. Many are particularly high in tannin which can cause unsightly deposits after bottling, but if the milled fruit is left to stand for a while before being pressed this can reduce the problem.

By far the biggest cider maker in Herefordshire, indeed the world, is Bulmers which is based in the city, though much of their juice is now imported from France. And though they have encouraged the maintenance of the old orchards and varieties, most if not all of their own and their contracted orchards are of the high yielding bush type. Symonds Cider is the oldest cider maker in the country, and although it still trades under its own name, it was acquired by Bulmers in 1988. Westons is based at Much Marcle and makes just over a million gallons per year compared to Bulmers' 25 million. It also produces perry, as does Dunkerton's at Luntley near Pembridge where many of the old varietal ciders can still be found. Other small producers include Knight's cider at Crumpton to the north-west of the Malverns, and Old Oak Cider, named after the old oak tree in the village, which can be purchased from a few outlets near its home of Eardisley in north-west Herefordshire.

# BEER AND HOPS

Worcestershire and Herefordshire have been important hop growing areas for many years though, perhaps unfortunately, the hops have largely been exported to brewers outside the county which itself has no great tradition of beer making. Porter, a bitter dark-brown beer, was brewed in Worcester for a period and sold well, but when the premises burnt down the owners preferred to keep the insurance money rather than rebuild. A brewery in Hereford was started in Bewell Street in 1834 and merged in 1899 with one in Tredegar to become the Hereford and Tredegar Brewery. After a succession of further mergers and takeovers it eventually ended up as part of Ansells, which accounts for the number of their outlets in this area. Another brewery, that of Alton Court, was based in Ross until 1956 when it was sold to a concern in Stroud which itself later merged to beome part of West Country Breweries. In turn they were taken over by Whitbread in 1963 and this also explains, in part, the large number of Whitbread pubs.

Even if there hasn't been a strong tradition of brewing locally, there certainly has when it comes to the growing of hops. Even now hop production makes a visual impact on much of the countryside.

Originally the English drank ale rather than beer, ale being hopless and so sweeter and thicker than beer. The latter's relatively bitter taste found an unwilling public at first with several towns forbidding the use of hops as did Shrewsbury in 1519. But the preservative value of the hop soon came to be realised and the taste acceptable.

The first hops were imported into England from the Netherlands around 1400 through the Kent ports. Kent already possessed strong connections with Holland through the established wool and cloth trade and as from 1524, when the government encouraged the growth of hops, Kent was the obvious county for the establishment of the new hopyards. Dutch experts were brought over between 1549 and 1533 to teach Kentish farmers the necessary techniques, and this early Dutch influence is still recognised in words such as Kilderkin and Firkin.

As hop growing spread throughout the country, those parts of Worcestershire and Herefordshire particularly blessed with suitable sites, became especially noted for hop production. Site is especially important for this crop as a hop has a permanent rootstock which will be in production for ten to twenty years. The hop needs a well sheltered and well drained soil which can vary from a light loam to a heavy clay, but a soil which must retain plenty of water during the early part of the season so the plant can obtain the quantities of nutrients it requires. In summer the plant's roots can reach twelve feet down in order to reach the watertable. In Worcestershire and Herefordshire these requirements were and are met by the alluvial soils of, for example, the Teme and where shelter can be provided by high hedges.

In 1574 Reynolde Scot wrote the first book in English about hop growing entitled 'A Perfite Platforme of a Hoppe Garden'. This highly illustrated book was only 56 pages long but served as the basic manual for decades, and many facets of tillage haven't changed to any great degree. Scot recommended planting two or three roots in a hole about one foot square and one foot deep which was then filled with a fine manure or compost. This need for manure, and especially potash, often led to impoverishment of other parts of the farm as the hopyards tended to take all the farmyard manure.

A later writer commented 'It is very evident in the counties of Worcester and Hereford, where it is very common for a farmer who occupies 200 acres of land, to apply the greatest part of his muck to the nourishment and support of ten or a dozen acres of hops and to neglect every improvement upon 30 to 40 of pasture, merely for the sake of its producing alder poles for his plantation. ... In short, the business of cultivating hops and farming is incompatible, each requiring constant attention.'

Hop growing spread rapidly and by 1655 fourteen counties including Herefordshire and Worcestershire are recorded as growing hops, though a full third of the total output was grown in Kent. By the end of the 1600's bottled beer was on the increase and in 1710 an act restricted preservatives in beer to the hop, and imposed a duty of 1d. per lb. on English hops and 3d. per lb. on imported hops. In 1715 the act was renewed and the levy was gradually raised till the government made an about turn and abolished it in 1862. In 1768, a poor year for the hop harvest, the levy raised just under £26,000 in Worcestershire, whereas in a good year, 1779, it raised just over £160,000. Bets used to be taken from springtime onwards as to the likely value of the hop levy. Tithes were also levied on the hop normally at one eleventh or twelfth of the value of the harvest.

In 1724 Defoe recorded that hops were being extensively planted in Herefordshire. Kent was still the primary area though some loss of hop land was occuring there as the practice developed of planting fruit trees between the rows of hops, which were then grubbed up once the trees had reached a reasonable size. The Alton-Farnham area of Hampshire was also becoming an important hop-growing area. By 1750 paler beer was becoming popular which favoured the Farnham varieties which were subsequently grown more extensively.

The yield per acre varied enormously from year to year, between 2 cwt. and 15 cwt. depending upon the weather and extent of manuring and liming. During the 1800's various rock phosphates and nitrates were used. But yield was also affected by pests and diseases for which there were no known cures or preventatives, though stripping the bines of their lower leaves and spraying with the Dutch Squirt 'which casts its water twenty feet high and thereby washes off the breed of lice, ladybird, and slug or snail that are bred and nourished by the honey-dew' appeared to be of some assistance.

Though Goldings was one of the more important varieties nation-ally, in 1852 the most favoured local varieties were Cooper's White, Canterbury Whitebine, Jones's and Mathon. The latter takes its name from the parish of Mathon in Worcestershire, but botanically is very similar to the Canterbury Whitebine and Farnham Whitebine and they're probably all the same species. William Cobbett whilst visiting Worcestershire, wrote in his Rural Rides for 26 September 1826: 'The hop-picking and bagging is over here. The crop, as in the other hop-countries, has been very great, and the quality as good as ever was known. The average price appears to be about 75s. the hundred-weight. The reader (if he do not belong to a hop-country) should be told that hop-planters, and even all their neighbours, are, as hop-ward, mad, though the most sane and reasonable people as to all other matters. They are ten times more jealous upon this score than men ever are of their wives; aye, and than they are of their mistresses, which is going a great deal farther. I, who am a Farnham man, was well aware of this foible; and therefore, when a gentleman told me that he would not brew with Farnham hops, if he could have them as a gift, I took special care not to ask him how it came to pass that the

Farnham hops always sold at about double the price of the Worcester; but if he had said the same thing to any other Farnham man that I ever saw, I should have preferred being absent from the spot: the hops are bitter, but nothing is their bitterness compared to the language that my townsman would have put forth.'

Some hops are easier to pick by hand than others, the Fuggle especially so. This had been introduced commercially to Kent by Richard Fuggle, though the first plant is said to have grown from a seed that fell from a picker's pocket together with some crumbs from his lunch. It soon became a popular variety as a mid-season hop of good size and quality.

Before mechanisation, when hops were hand picked, pickers came to the farm from the neighbouring cities and were housed in huts and barns. Pickers were paid piece-work rates at an agreed price per bushel of hops. At first the record of bushels picked by each picker was kept by the tallyman, a name derived from the French word tailler to cut, for he would be equipped with a series of numbered sticks about twelve inches long and one inch wide which were sawn in half horizontally over three quarters of their length. The longer piece was retained by the tallyman and when a bushel had been picked, the picker would give the tallyman his piece of stick who would then lay it alongside the corresponding numbered stick and cut two grooves across the side of them. Thus only those two sticks would totally correspond and there was no way that anyone could cheat on how many bushels thay had picked. Over time, and with increasing education, tokens were given instead and later still records were kept in a book. Most pickers averaged around fifteen bushels a day. As the years progressed the pickers' accommodation had to comply with certain minimal standards, which encouraged growers to look to mechanical methods rather than investing money in buildings that were used only briefly during harvest time.

The United States was the first country to develop a hop picking machine whilst the first English machine was made in 1934 though it only came into wide use after the Second World War. The bines are cut about two feet above ground level and just under the top wire by a tractor mounted attachment. The bines then fall into a trailer behind the tractor and are taken to a covered picking plant where they are hung on an overhead track from where the machine plucks the hops.

The picked hops are then laid on a dry horse hair or equivalent cloth over slats above the furnace in the kiln. Kilns were orginally built 16 feet square, but then it was felt that round kilns would give a more even heat and became the order of the day, built with a diameter of the same 16 feet. In fact as the heat rose to where the hops lay the square kilns provided as even a heat as the round. The top of the kiln was fitted with a revolving cowl which encouraged the through draught and prevented a downward one. The wheelwright traditionally made the cowl which in the West Midlands tended to be pointed like a witch's hat, unlike the rest of the country where they were truncated at the top. Modern kilns are fitted with a fan to encourage the air flow and instead of a cowl have louvres built into the top of the walls. After drying they are raked to the press at the end of the first floor cooling room and a pocket is hung in a strap slung under the foot of the press. The hops are pressed into the pocket, which is then sewn up and dropped down to the ground floor for storage.

Whilst it is never easy in agriculture to adapt to changes in demand because of the lead time between planting and harvesting a crop, the problem is exacerbated with hops as the wirework is designed to last 20 to 30 years and the plant itself will produce for anything up to 20 years. Therefore in hard times each grower is faced with a decision

*Oast house at Brierley*

35

either to scrap the hopyard or to carry on in the hope for better times. Because of the wartime food shortage however, the decision was taken out of the growers' hands when the government intervened in the market in 1917, reducing the hop acreage to half its 1914 total. Soon afterwards though, a poor harvest in 1918 and a prohibition on imports except under licence led to an increase in acreage. That was followed by a rise in beer duty in 1920 which reduced consumption at a time when crop yields were good, and much of the crop went into store. Quotas were introduced for five years till 1925 when all control ended and growers formed the English Hop Growers Ltd, a co-operative which represented the growers of nine-tenths of the total hop acreage. Members delivered all their hops to the co-op and agreed not to increase their own acreage. However the co-op's marketing was hampered by the quantity of hops already in store and when good crops followed in 1925 and 1926, it asked members to reduce their acreage. However the growers outside the co-op expanded production, causing many to leave the co-op in frustration. It was wound up in 1928.

In 1929, 1930 and 1931 many hop growers left the business and profits for the rest increased. Better control of diseases meant however that production still rose, and in September 1932 the Hops Marketing Board was set up, quotas were reintroduced and all hops had to be sold through the Board. Producers were only paid for hops produced in excess of their quota if they could be sold. In 1972, with the entry of the United Kingdom into the EEC, whose intervention system differed from that of the British system of deficiency payments and marketing boards, the Hops Marketing Board became a limited company.

The renaissance of real ale stimulated by CAMRA has led to renewed demand for the Fuggle hop which is grown extensively in Worcestershire and Herefordshire. Seeded hops have been traditionally used in the production of English bitter, however as the seeds count for roughly 15 per cent of the weight of the hop, brewers and hop growers are now tending to plant seedless varieties with, as yet, unknown consequences for the taste of the great British pint.

# CUSTOMS, TALES AND FOLKLORE

Much of an area's folklore is not peculiar to it, being similar or even identical to that throughout England and Wales. For example there are many wells with healing properties; or sprigs of thorn taken from that at Glastonbury which flower at midnight on Twelfth Night; or tales of dragons; even tugs of war which are said to have their origins in historical events; not to overlook a general belief in ghosts, fairies and of course witches.

In Herefordshire, charms against witches included one whereby wittan and rowan (birch and mountain ash) were placed over doors on May eve, sometimes in the form of a cross, the dying and dead twigs being left till their replacement the following year. In his diaries, Kilvert relates: 'This evening being May eve I ought to have put some wittan over the door to keep out the 'old witch' but I was too lazy to go out and get it.'

Other charms against witches included horseshoes; a stick of elder with 9 notches on it; or a pattern of 9 crosses chalked on the doorstep. If you believed that attack was the best form of defence, then you could drive a knife or large nail into the witch's footprint to break her power; or induce the witch to remove her power by burning the heart of an animal stuck with pins; or burn a sprig of broom or a lock of hair of the person bewitched; all of which were supposed to cause the witch agony and force her to return and undo her spell.

Fairies were also commonly believed in, at least up to the 1870's, and in Monmouthshire up to 1900. The beliefs associated with fairies included a dread of being carried off by them, or of stepping inside their rings. Belief in fairies was widespread in Wales where they were thought of as small, often invisible beings who could fly, steal from homes, lead people astray in wild places, but reward those who treated them well, whilst retaining the ability to punish others with illness.

There was also a belief in brownies who were said to be helpful in homes and on farms, though they could be mischievous and troublesome. Roman coins and even a Roman pavement at Painscastle were felt to belong to fairies, and when found, coins were often hidden again, so as not to encourage their attention.

Ghosts or evil spirits often had to be 'read down' by either six or twelve parsons into a snuff box or other container which was then buried, often in running water, though the story of Thomas Vaughan at Kington tells of the burial taking place in Hergest Pool.

Many old customs relate to the quest for a husband. Girls used to walk backwards upstairs and into their bed whilst eating salt from half an egg shell. This was supposed to produce a dream which would foretell the status of their husband—if the man in the dream offered her a glass of water the husband would be poor, if the drink was ale then he would be a tradesman, and if wine, then he would be well off.

If a girl picked a rose on midsummer's eve and kept it till Christmas, it was supposed to be snatched from her bosom by her future husband. If a quicker way of winkling out the future husband was desired, then apple pips could be placed in a fire whilst a man's name was called out. If the pip shrivelled up then the man was deemed to be worthless, but if it exploded then his love would be unbounded!

Around the Malverns, especially, on the death of the master or mistress of the household, any hives of bees they had owned would be covered with a black cloth and the hive struck with the front door key, whilst the bees were told of the death. If this custom was omitted, it was feared that further disaster would follow.

Various national customs were common in the area, such as Halloween which has a long tradition, as does May Day and the less well known Oak Apple Day. Oak Apple Day, 29 May, celebrates both the anniversary of Charles II's birthday and of the Restoration. At Christmas the local bands would parade the neighbourhood leading up to the day itself, when they would play through the middle of the night as a reminder that Christ was born at midnight. At New Year it was believed that it was lucky for a dark haired man to be the first to cross the threshold, reflecting an equally strong belief nationally.

At Easter various games involving eggs occurred, whilst the two days afterwards were given over to the Hocktyde festivities. During these women were given special preference, and could draw a rope across a road and demand a toll from all men who wished to pass.

For the three days before the Feast of the Ascension, known as the rogation days, the boundaries of the parish were marked out or beaten. This was necessary for as the population grew, many parishes erected chapels in the parts furthest from the parish church. These chapels, meaning literally 'in place of', still formed part of the parish and beating the bounds was to clarify to which parish they belonged and to whom the congregation owed their allegiance. During this time prayers were proffered in church for the harvest and for the flocks and herds, and this practice gave the period its name of Rogation from the Latin rogare, to ask.

Until relatively recently the parish was the basis for local government, having developed from the Saxon Hundred and its moot, or meeting. The Parish Meeting tried most of the lesser offences, only major cases were passed on to the manorial courts and later the assizes. Stocks were used for the smallest crimes, and the pillory for the more serious. Those who had caused grave offence could often only reinstate themselves in parochial favour by remaining in the church porch for the Sunday service over a successive number of weeks. Sometimes the offender had also to be clad in a white sheet whilst completing this pennance. A whipping post was used for beating vagabonds, the legal definition of whom kept altering down the years. Initially it seems to have been confined to those begging without a licence, but was later extended to include idle people trying to obtain money by any type of crafty means: free-lance buskers, university students begging without a licence from their vice-chancellor and even to idle people generally.

Poor people often found work at harvest time, a time for celebration—for the labourer in having work, and for the farmer in bringing in the harvest. Two major agricultural celebrations were common, though they have now largely died out, partly due to mechanisation.

At harvest time the reapers used to leave a small patch of corn standing which was then tied up in four bunches to resemble the four legs of a mare. The four bunches were then all tied together at the top, after which the reapers had to try and cut off the ears of corn by throwing their sickles at the 'mare'. The reaper who eventually succeeded had pride of place at the harvest supper table opposite the landowner, this supper being washed down with ale or cider.

Wassailing used to take place at both harvest time and Twelfth Night. At six o'clock, one large and twelve small fires were lit in a field at the highest point where wheat was growing. All those present drank cider until the fires had died down, when everyone retired to the owner's home for a meal. At nine or ten o'clock the cowhouse was visited where a large plum pudding with a hole in the middle was placed, in turn, over the horn of each ox as cups were filled with ale and each ox was toasted with words such as:

'Here's to thee (name) and to thy white horn,
God send thy master a good crop of corn;  ⁓
Oh wheat, rye and barley, and all sorts of grain,
You eat your oats, I'll drink my beer,
May the Lord send us a happy new year.'

Tales of historical figures also abound. One tells of Earl Harold, who spent much of his life fighting the Welsh on the borders before he became king. It relates that Harold did not die at the Battle of Hastings, but instead was removed from the battlefield under cover of darkness, his weapons and insignia being placed on the body of one of his compatriots who was subsequently buried at Waltham Abbey. Harold was meanwhile carried to the borders, where he held many manors, and was gradually nursed back to health. When fully recuperated he lived the life of a hermit in the Golden Valley before becoming a monk in Chester.

Folklore of a more local nature relates to one Jack o'Kent or Jacky Kent who lived on the borders of Herefordshire and Monmouthshire. He was widely known by 1595 when his life formed the basis for a character in a play. The most likely real life character about whom the tales grew was either a Welsh Franciscan friar named Dr. John Gwent who died in 1348, or a learned astrologer called Dr. John Kent Caerleon who lived in the fifteenth century and who wrote a treatise on witchcraft. Jacky Kent is said to have sold his soul to the devil as a boy in exchange for the power to do whatever he set his hand to, and to be able to command the devil as his servant whilst he lived. At one time he ordered the devil to build a bridge across the Monnow at Grosmont in the course of a single night, but in return the devil demanded the soul of the first to cross the bridge. Jack threw a bone across for a dog to chase, so all the devil had was the soul of the unfortunate beast. When Jack died the devil was to take him body and soul, whether he be buried inside or outside of a church. But he had himself buried in the thickness of a wall of either Grosmont, Kentchurch or Skenfrith church—which is not clear—so that he was neither in nor out. As for his soul, he asked for his liver, which was often equated with the soul, to be left out so that it would be fought over by doves and ravens. Presumably the doves won for the stories told about him are kind to his memory.

# LITERATURE, ART AND MUSIC

When it comes to a consideration of the artistic and literary merits of the area, it is perhaps natural that Elgar's should be the first name to come to mind. What is more surprising is to learn that Hereford and Worcester has been the cradle for old and middle English.

English was essentially the language of the ordinary folk. As the Saxons had pushed west, so their culture fused with that of their British neighbours. When the Normans invaded, they did little to affect this—contenting themselves with superimposing a new ruling class on the existing system. The court used French, whilst the church and more educated used the language of the church—Latin. Latin, which had developed into a precise language, was also used for legal documents, treaties and charters. However as the local families provided the servants and wet nurses, so the sons and daughters of the new nobility grew up with a knowledge of the language of the people.

For many decades, though, English was very much the third language of the court, of clerks and of writers. **Walter Map**, a clerk at Henry II's court, used both Latin and French, not English. Map was of Welsh descent, though he was almost certainly born in Herefordshire, possibly at Wormsley, around 1140. His parents were in Henry's service and Walter was educated at Paris, before being employed at Henry's court. He travelled extensively over Europe on royal duties, but on Henry's death his connection with the court seems to have ended.

In the literary world, Map is known for his *De Nugis Curialium*, or courtiers' tales or trifles. The dispute over the translation of the title tells us something about Map and this work—to many modern eyes it is a series of tales, but one suspects that in contemporary eyes Map was seen as a wit.

The work is full of Herefordshire legends and court gossip, written as a series of notes and jottings and never ordered for publication. It was put together over a decade, starting in 1182. From references by other contemporary and slightly later writers, it also seems that the world should credit Map with the authorship of the first Lancelot romances. And if that is insufficient acclaim, it appears that much of the satirical Latin verse in circulation in the twelfth and thirteenth centuries can also be attributed to him.

Map was educated, but the poorer monks at the smaller and more dispersed settlements tended to use the language they knew best— English. Worcestershire lay on the edge of the main cultural area bounded by Winchester, Gloucester and Westminster, and so at the margins of the area influenced by French and Latin.

In the early thirteenth century a group of writings called *The Ancrene Wisse*, The Anchoresses' Rule, were written in Wigmore Abbey in Herefordshire. The author is believed to have been **Brian of Lingen**, and his work shows the introduction of some French words into the local English, but the resulting 'Wigmore English' doesn't appear to have had wide usuage. *The Ancrene Wisse* is a treatise on how female recluses should order their lives and became so popular that it was translated into Latin and French. The work includes some of the earliest English rhetoric: 'For what is it that makes us strong to suffer hardship in God's service and to wrestle valiantly in times of temptation against the Devil's assaults, but the hope of a high reward? Hope keeps the heart in health, whatever the flesh suffers; as they say, "If hope were not, heart would break." But Jesu, mercy! How stands it with those who are in the place of all grief and misery with no hope of escape, and yet heart cannot burst?'

Another monk, who signed himself 'The tremulous hand of Worcester' was responsible for translating and updating various earlier works, but the best known original early work in English also came from Worcestershire.

*Piers Plowman* was written by **William Langland** who is thought to have been a son of the de Rokayles, tenants of the Despensers at Hanley Castle near Ledbury. He might have been an illegitimate son, though the differing surname doesn't necessarily indicate that, as at that time it wasn't the automatic custom for offspring to take their parent's last name. He was educated, perhaps at Malvern Priory, and moved to London in 1335 or 1336 with his wife Kit and daughter Calote. There they lived in Cornhill where Langland earned a living from clerical work.

The poem exists in three texts, each one a worked over, amended and added to version of the earlier. The earliest, or A text as it is known, was written in the late 1360's, the much longer B text whilst he lived in London towards the end of the 1370's and the incomplete C revision around the 1380's or 90's, after Langland had returned to the Malvern area where he died around 1398.

The whole work is a vision or rather a series of visions sometimes one within another, with Long Will being the dreamer and providing the links in the tale, whilst the titular hero, Piers the Plowman, crops up sporadically often seeming to disrupt the flow of the poem which is concerned with a search, at first for money and then for truth which he decides is more important for the soul.

In this constant searching the dreamer comes into contact and enters into discussion with a whole range of people including other ploughmen, merchants, minstrels, friars, jugglers, a knight and members of the clergy. As his thoughts develop he feels everything in the world possesses order and harmony except its one rational occupant —man. For this the clergy bear the brunt of his ire, from the members of the papal and bishop's courts to ordinary parish priests, pardoners and especially the friars. After them in his distaste come lawyers, doctors, grocers, minstrels, jesters and shoddy workmen.

Gradually he becomes convinced that love is the panacea for all troubles and advocates that the clergy should preach and practice this, for he decides their current lack of charity nullifies all their work. Then through the clergy's love of man will come the love of God— rather than the other way around.

In its conclusions the poem largely accepts the existing structure of society as Langland knew it, though encouraging man to use his wealth and power to proper Christian effect. The poem is therefore essentially a piece of conservative writing. However it does consider ethical problems of wealth, inheritance and hierachy and also sets out an alternative ideal of community ownership with moderate provision for all, with the commons having power over the crown. It is this dream element, together with the attacks on the representatives of the church and the selection of the ploughman as the central character, a class of people together with labourers who were much exploited, which led *Piers Plowman* to be one of the rallying cries in the Peasants' Revolt.

Whilst in England British and Saxon culture had fused, in Wales that of the British remained largely intact, if somewhat affected by the Danes and Vikings who settled in the south-western part via Ireland. *The Mabinogion* is one of several books—that known as the White Book of Rydderch being the earliest—which recorded the tales which were

43

passed down the generations from father to son and were given a wider audience by travellers. Because these tales were recorded between the 1200's and 1400's they have become infiltrated with threads of Saxon and Norman myth and legend as well.

The tales include stories about King Arthur, Owein, Peredur and Geraint which approximate to the mythology of Cretiens de Troyes and Thomas Malory, but also delve further into the past with tales of British heroes in Roman and even pre-Roman days. Many of the Arthurian tales do not seem to have been used by Troyes and Mallory, for few of the characters re-appear in their works, even allowing for the French adaptation of names. However there are resemblances and the bowls, cauldrons and other assorted containers probably helped inspire the idea of the Holy Grail. As to the title of the Mabinogion, four of the tales end by stating 'so ends this Branch of the Mabinogi'. Early translators took this to mean that as mab means boy, they were tales for children and that Mabinogion was the plural. However no such word seems to have existed in Welsh and experts still debate over the meaning of mabinogi.

As Norman and English power and strength increased, so too did the range of their appointments. The lords marcher not only built their power base along the marches but extended it throughout south Wales. One of their knights, William de Barry, married a granddaughter of Rhys ap Tewdwr, whose famliy were rulers of the south-west Welsh princedom of Deheubarth.

By their marriage they had three sons, the youngest of whom was Gerald de Barry, better known later as Gerald Cambrensis or **Gerald of Wales**, born around 1145. Being a younger son he went into the church and was appointed by the archbishop of Canterbury as his personal legate. With this power he excommunicated the sheriff of Pembrokeshire and suspended the archdeacon of Brecon for living with his mistress. Gerald was made archdeacon in his place and was to be based at Brecon for many years.

When his uncle, the Bishop of St. David's died he was one of the four archdeacons of the diocese nominated as potential successors. He was then aged just under thirty and already had strong feelings as to how the church should conduct its affairs, desiring for St. David's to become an archbishopric in its own right and owe allegiance direct to the pope rather than through Canterbury. However Henry II had strong memories of the murder of Thomas à Beckett just 6 years previously and, wanting a 'quiet' bishop, looked elsewhere to exercise his preference.

*Piers Plowman*

His long term dream destroyed, Gerald devoted more time to learning and writing and over his next fifty years he wrote seventeen books which have survived, including *The Topography of Ireland* and *The Conquest of Ireland* written when he was Prince John's chaplain on his expedition to Ireland. He also esccorted Archbishop Baldwin on his crusade raising mission in 1188 through Wales and the borders, when he wrote *A Journey Through Wales* and the *Description of Wales*.

Another churchman, of different passions, was **Thomas Traherne**, born a few centuries later in 1637 in Hereford. He was the son of a poor shoemaker and seems to have been orphaned early on in life for he was cared for and brought up by a well to do relative, Philip Traherne, an innkeeper and one time mayor of Hereford. He seems to have given Thomas a good education for at the age of fifteen Thomas was at Brasenose College, Oxford from where he graduated in 1656. The Protectorate was still in existence and at the end of 1657, aged just twenty he was given a lay appointment at Credenhill. It was only after the Restoration that he seems to have been ordained by the Bishop of Oxford and re-presented to the living at Credenhill, where he remained the incumbent vicar till his death in 1674. In 1669 he moved to London as the chaplain to Sir Orlando Bridgeman, the Lord Keeper of the Great Seal till 1672. Whilst in his service he also acted as minister at Teddington Church, and it may be that a curate performed his duties at Credenhill.

Whilst living in Herefordshire he wrote some poetry, and in 1673 in London he completed an anti Roman Catholic work titled *Roman Forgeries*. He also wrote *Christian Ethics* which was published after his death, but is best known for his work later called *Centuries* which he wrote from London to Mrs. Hopton in Kington. When he had been in Herefordshire they had met at a group she had formed for the study and practice of religion, the group forming ideas which were akin to early methodism. The work itself, being private correspondence, was only later found by chance on a London bookstall.

Moving on in time and place, 1809 saw Edward Barrett Moulton-Barrett buying the Hope End estate and its 475 acres outside Ledbury with money made from sugar plantations in the West Indies. Edward and his wife Mary moved in with three children. Over the next six years they altered the sevententh century house to turn it into an oriental version of the original, complete with the addition of a metal dome and minarets.

Their eldest child, **Elizabeth Barrett Barrett**, was given a strict and religious upbringing. Her early years were however fairly blissful, until she had a prolonged illness from 1821. Then in 1828 her mother died and in 1831 the family fortune began to fall apart and the sale of Hope End had to be faced. It was at this time that she started her diary, with the first entry dated 25 June 1831. Years later the diary was to pass to her brother George who was then in his seventies, and he tore out 56 of the 144 pages and partly deleted a further 18, leaving a distorted view of her life at this time.

Elizabeth fully entered the literary world in the 1840's and 50's with her love poems and poems about the wrongs of the world which caught the sense of unease amongst many Victorians over the course of the Industrial Revolution. Robert Browning read these poems, wrote to her and eventually they arranged to meet. After their secret marriage in September 1846 he was for many years known only as Mrs. Browning's husband, indeed she was even proposed by the Atheaneum as Poet Laureate on Wordsworth's death. But apart from poetry she also translated the classics and wrote *Aurora Leigh*, a long novel in blank verse.

After the marriage, the Barrett Brownings lived mainly in Italy, where Elizabeth died in 1861, just six years after her success with *Aurora Leigh*. She never wished to return to Herefordshire due to the memories it held, and it wasn't long after her death that the oriental Hope End was demolished, the minarets being blown up with gunpowder. The owner, Mr. Hewitt, built a house in the Victorian Gothic style on a hill above the old site and he also altered the grounds. However the stable gateway was later reconstructed.

**Robert Francis Kilvert** was born in 1840 and lived at the time when the Empire was still growing, confidence reigned and before the intimations of decline associated with the Boer War. His family lived at Chippenham in Wiltshire and he was educated privately, before going to Oxford, becoming ordained and then acting as a curate for his father for a number of years. In 1865 he was appointed as curate to the parish of Clyro where he lived and worked for seven years. He and the Welsh Borders were made for each other—his diaries sparkle with the border vitality and wit, and there is no heavy Victorian empire builder moralising in the diary extracts. He was a practical rather than a political man, and rather than preach at those less able to cope, he did what he personally could for them.

In 1872 he returned to be a curate to his father, before moving as vicar to north Radnorshire for a year and then returning to his much missed borders as the vicar in Bredwardine, not far from Clyro, in 1877. In 1879 he married Elizabeth Rowland from Woodstock, but died suddenly from peritonitis just a month later, and was buried in the graveyard of his parish church.

The surviving diaries cover the period from the last couple of years at Clyro, but they suffer from great gaps because his wife is believed to have destroyed two volumes which dealt with his courtship of her. The remaining twenty-two volumes were passed to an elderly niece of Kilvert's who destroyed a further nineteen volumes. The extracts from the remaining three which cover his life on the Welsh border give a tremendous picture of the scenery, lives and tribulations of the area, some of which have little changed today.

**John Masefield** was born in 1878 at the Knapp, a large Victorian house in Ledbury and was to claim later that his life as a child was lived in paradise. On John's grandfather's death the family moved into his house, The Priory, in the centre of Ledbury.

It was during these early years that John Masefield first gained an interest in water and ships. He spent hours by the Gloucester to Hereford canal. At the age of ten he was sent away to a boarding school and at thirteen joined the school ship, H.M.S. Conway which was permanently moored in the Mersey. Here the education was partially based around gaining a grounding in sailing, even though sail was then giving way to steam. It was during his school years that he first started to write poetry, if with no great confidence. When aged sixteen he left and joined the Gilcruix, a four masted barge belonging to the White Star Line and which was bound from Cardiff to Chile. He was sea sick and the ship had a rough time passing through the Roaring Forties and round Cape Horn. After the ship had arrived at Iquique, the nitrate port, he sufferd first from sunstroke and then from a nervous breakdown. The captain was a kindly man and a passage home was arranged by steamship.

In the winter of 1894 he was back at Ledbury where one of his aunts derided him for not be able to stick the conditions on board ship. This provoked him to use his Conway contacts to sign on with a ship then at New York. However he had thought better of the enterprise even before he had set foot on board and instead, on arrival in New York, linked up with another man for a life of vagrancy during which he started to pen more poetry. It was this period which seems to have given him his concern for the underdog in life.

On his eventual return to England his sister found him work as a clerk in London, and over the next few years he was pulled between his love of the country and of the life of the capital, between the insecurity of writing and the security of a job. Eventually he chose the combination of freelance writing and London, and struck up a friendship with Yeats which soon led him into the literary world. In fact the writer's insecurity was not to last for long for his sea ballads soon found a ready market in The Outlook, Tatler, Speaker and Pall Mall Magazine. However the income that this produced was not enough to live on and he his friends helped by pushing work his way, including the preparation of the footnotes for a new edition of Keats and as the exhibition secretary of a gallery of English painting for a trade exhibition in Wolverhampton. Meanwhile his writing continued, branching out into narrative as well as book reviews, and the first edition of 500 copies of his salt-water ballads, including the famed *Sea Fever*, sold out within six months.

In 1903 he married Constance Crommelin, over eleven years his elder. His second book of verse was published in October 1903 and he then became a sub-editor on The Speaker, a Liberal paper, whilst also writing pieces for the Manchester Guardian largely based on his American experiences.

In 1906 he was called in to help advise on Shaw's play *Captain Brassbound's Conversion*. His own first play was a flop, but his second, a tale set by the Severn and based upon a story he heard when young, was a success. During 1908 amd 1909 he wrote two more novels but started to find it a struggle to write. Then in 1909 the Masefields rented a country cottage in Buckinghamshire and thoughts of his childhood life seemed to come flooding back. During 1911 his walks in the countryside gave birth to *The Everlasting Mercy*, a poem about a lecherous drunkard of Ledbury who then meets a Quaker lady, undergoes a moral and Christian conversion and becomes a ploughman. The poem started the revival of the narrative poem and others followed including *The Widow of Bye Street*, again set in Ledbury.

During the First World War the government used his talents for propaganda. In April 1930 he was offered and accepted the post of poet laureate on the death of Robert Bridges.

On 23 October 1930 he was made a freeman of the City of Hereford and in his acceptance speech he spoke of the England of St. George, Arthur, Chaucer, Langland and Shakespeare, rather than that of a commercial John Bull England. He wished, he said, for a revival of life lived close to the soil: 'I know no land more full of bounty and beauty than this red land, so good for corn and hops and roses. I am glad to have lived in a country where nearly every one lived on and by the land, singing as they carried the harvest home, and taking such pride in the horses, and in the great cattle, and in the cider trees. It will be a happy day for England when she realises that those things and the men who care for them are the real wealth of a land: the beauty and the bounty of earth being the shadow of Heaven.'

Masefield died in May 1967. He wanted his ashes scattered in the open air, but they were in fact laid to rest in Poets' Corner in Westminster Abbey.

Hereford lays claim to one actor and one actress, though rather tenuously through birth only. **David Garrick** was born at the Angel Inn where his mother was staying whilst accompanying her husband who was a recruiting officer for Colonel James Tyrell's regiment of dragoons. Garrick was baptised in All Saints Church on 28 February 1717, but always considered Lichfield his home town being the city where he spent his youth. The actress **Nell Gwyn** was born on 2 February 1650 in Pipe Lane, since renamed Gwyn Street, by the side of Hereford Cathedral. Little is known of her early life, but once on the London stage the diarist Samuel Pepys took an interest in her, as did Charles II by whom she had two illegitimate sons. One died young, but the eldest was created Duke of St. Albans. By coincidence his son was to become bishop of Hereford, and arranged for the old buildings in Pipe Lane to be pulled down and incorporated into the grounds of the bishop's palace.

These stage players may have slight connections, but the artist **Brian Hatton** was not only born in Hereford but he and his family spent many years in the county and many of his drawings and paintings are of the county, its people and horses. He was born in August 1887 at Carlton Villas in Whitecross Road, the eldest child with two younger sisters.

Brian was drawing with apparent ease and clarity by the age of two, and was soon drawing horses and livestock seen at Hereford Market. When aged just eleven he won the Gold Star at the Royal Drawing Society's exhibition, an exhibition open to all aged under 20.

In the 1899 Royal Drawing Society's exhibition, he won several awards, but not the Gold Star, solely because Princess Louise felt she could not award it to the same person twice. Instead he was presented to her at Kensington Palace, rode her horse, and started a friendship with Colonel Collins, her equerry, who was to often write and encourage him and whom he was later to visit on many occasions.

It was widely suggested, not least by Colonel Collins, that Brian should attend Trinity College, Oxford and an uncle offered to pay the fees. However there was the question of gaining admission and he visited a cramming school at Ewyas Harold on the Welsh border run by the Reverend Bannister, who was later to become a canon at Hereford Cathedral. He lodged near the vicarage and seems to have worked hard, for little drawing took place, though he spent much time walking over the surrounding hills. He passed his exams at the second attempt and was to enjoy his time at Oxford, meeting a range of people, attending lectures as he wished and finding the works of artists in the galleries.

He gained an introduction to the archaeologist Flinders Petrie and joined his expedition in Egypt in November 1908. At first he was based in Luxor then Memphis, but rather than draw and paint the antiquities, as he was supposed, he concentrated on the sunsets, goat herds and people. However, his health was still not over strong and after recuperating from a bout of whooping cough he returned to England, where his mother died in the summer of 1909.

The whole family was affected by this death for she had been the mainstay and organiser of the family, but at least for Brian his first commissions started coming the following spring. This led to a realisation that he now needed to make London rather than Hereford his base, and was so encouraged by Collins and others. In 1912 he moved into a studio in Kensington, just after Collins' death. Work was soon forthcoming and in 1913 he went to Windsor Castle to draw members of the royal family. In 1914 he had a picture accepted for the Royal Academy, and also painted a semi-impressionistic painting entitled *Sunday Morning in the Park*. It was also suggested that he illustrate an edition of Masefield's *Everlasting Mercy*, but this came to nothing. At the end of July he went to Belgium with his Uncle Charles, but they returned early on 4 August, the day that war was declared.

He returned to Herefordshire and in early September he joined the Worcestershire Yeomanry as a trooper, where he could make use of his riding skills. In 1915 he was sent to the Dardenelles, but arrived in time for the evacuation. In December he was posted to Egypt.

In early April 1916 he was involved in a skirmish with some Turks and Arabs and, from letters home, seemed to enjoy the episode. However later that same month he was in a group of 180 yeomanry guarding about 50 engineers at some wells to the east of the Suez Canal. Early one morning a column of between 2 and 3,000 Turks called at the oasis and a fight errupted in the morning mist. The outnumbered British were all killed or taken prisoner, and Brian Hatton's body was later discovered in the desert by the Australians. He had obviously tried to ride for reinforcements from the Gloucester Regiment which was nearby. He was twenty-eight years old.

His sister Marjorie helped found the Brian Hatton Gallery in Hereford. After the war many appreciations of his work were made, but perhaps that which encapsulates his style best stated: 'He was not, as some artists are, a spectator; he is part of the countryside and country life, people, horses, animals; you feel the wind.'

**Edward Elgar** was born on 2 June 1857 at The Firs at Broadheath, to the west of Worcester. He was writing music at the age of ten, but it was the Three Choirs Festival held in Worcester in 1869 which appears to have stimulated him. He was encouraged by his father and by family friends, to the extent that he wanted to go to Germany to study. But the family couldn't afford the costs and instead he entered the law. But this didn't suit, and after a year he left to work in his father's music shop.

By August 1877 he had saved enough money to visit London and take violin lessons with Adolphe Pollitzer, a friend of Mendelssohn. Pollitzer expressed interest in Elgar's compositions, but lack of money forced Elgar back to Worcester where he filled a vacancy for a violin in the Worcester Amateur Instrument Society. In 1878 he accepted the post of Director of Music for the County Lunatic Asylum at Powick.

In 1882 he had saved enough to travel to Germany for three weeks. This visit inspired him to write his first full orchestral piece, the Intermezzo Monesque, which was played in both Worcester and Birmingham. More pieces followed, but then, as would be the case throughout his life, he fell into a period of inactivity. He resigned his post at Powick, but persevered with the Amateur Instrument Society and teaching. At this time one of his Malvern pupils was Alice Roberts, a daughter of Major-General Sir Henry Roberts. The two seemed to enthuse each other and he set some of her poems to music. Despite the fact that she was nine years older than he, that the majority of her aunts, cousins and other relatives were horrified, and although she was a follower of the Church of England and he was catholic, they became engaged in September 1888. The marriage followed next spring.

Alice's encouragement led to him starting on his first major work, The Black Knight, and he was also commissioned for a piece, Froissart, for the 1890 Worcester Three Choirs Festival. But returns from composition were slight and Elgar had to devote more time to teaching. However The Black Knight was completed in 1893 and 1895 saw new commissions. One was for the Worcester, and one for the North Staffs Festival, where some of the committee had argued for a piece by Grieg. For the latter he chose the theme of King Olaf, and

*The Firs, Broadheath*

once written he sent it to Novellos who handed over the work to a young new editor, August Johannes Jaeger.

Jaeger liked Elgar's music, gave constant encouragement and the two soon struck up a close friendship, Jaeger later becoming Nimrod in The Enigma Variations. Elgar then turned to the Worcester piece, Lux Christi, retitled Light of Life in agreement with Novellos. In the summer he began the orchestration of the two pieces, setting a tent in the garden at Forli, his home in Malvern, and flying a Union Jack to denote when he was at work and not to be disturbed.

At this time Elgar wanted to write for the full orchestra, but his desire was fulfilled almost by accident. After a day of teaching in Malvern, he sat down at the piano, an instrument he tended to use for aimless ramblings, preferring the violin as a guide when composing. On this occasion, after he had been playing for a while, Alice spotted what she thought was a good tune. Elgar hadn't noticed it but kept playing till Alice recognised it once more, and so was born the Enigma.

53

Elgar was later to say that through the Variations 'another and larger theme "goes", but is not played' and he often referred to 'it', never a tune or theme. As he composed this work he altered it to see how it might be written by other people with their personalities, in one instance Dan, the bulldog belonging to Dr. Sinclair, Hereford Cathedral's organist. The Variations was first performed in June 1989. The Variations brought renewed acclaim: he received a commission for the principal piece in the Birmingham Festival of 1900, Worcester wanted a symphony for the Three Choirs Festival, whilst Norwich Festival wanted a short piece.

When the Black Knight had been performed in Birmingham in 1895, the Elgars had visited the oratory at Edgbaston founded by Cardinal Newman and where he had written his Dream of Gerontius. Since then Elgar had considered writing a choral piece based on the Dream, but subsequently thought of a Gordon Symphony. The Victorian hero Gordon of Khartoum was known to have liked Newman's work, and a popular copy with Gordon's appended notes and comments had been published.

It was Elgar's often proposed symphony which the Three Choirs hoped for, but his thoughts now returned to the Dream as a choral work to fulfill the Birmingham commission.

The Dream of Gerontius only highlighted the difficulties of composing for a living as its relative intricacy resulted in few performances and lack of royalties. So Elgar wrote a couple of more profitable short pieces—the first Pomp and Circumstance marches for Henry Wood's promenade concerts, and a Coronation Ode for the new king. March number 1 was received so enthusiastically that Wood had to play it three times before the rest of the concert could proceed.

A commission followed for the 1903 Birmingham Festival for which Elgar wrote The Apostles. This was received with even greater enthusiasm than Gerontius, and Edward VII now patronised Elgar's work. As a result honours started to flow and in June 1904 he was knighted. The same year the Elgars moved to Plas Gwyn, one mile to the east of Hereford. The flatter land made life easier for Elgar's summer cycling, and the house was more private, though perhaps less inspiring than his house in the Malverns.

The three year cycle of the Birmingham Festival coincided neatly with Elgar's own composing cycle. Gerontius had been followed by a gap to The Apostles and now there was no new major work again, just another Pomp and Circumstance march. But Jaeger's encouragement led to the appearance of the Introduction and Allegro.

Then his father's old sea faring chest was given to him as a birthday present by his brother Frank, and this appeared to stimulate a return to his old themes and music and he wrote a flurry of short peices. Alice and he went to Italy where the flurry continued, and after a short bout of influenza, he once more turned to his symphony. After many years of incubation his first symphony received its premiere at Manchester. Not only was it Elgar's first, it was also England's, and it was rapturously received.

Success provided further stimulation and a violin concerto followed in November 1910. Though the critics may have given varied reports, it was perhaps the pinnacle of Elgar's achievement as far as popularity was concerned and the enthusiasm for his music boosted his morale. Riding the crest of this particular wave he completed the second symphony in just two months. But at its premiere in May 1911 the house was half empty, and repeat performances were even less well attended. He became filled with self doubt, and for a while concentrated on conducting. Soon everyone's attention was switching to world events. In 1914 he added his signature to those of Lord Milner, Field Marshall Lord Roberts and Rudyard Kipling as one of twenty 'distinguished men' to a pledge to oppose the Home Rule Bill if it was passed. Elgar had always had an interest in politics—at one time he was offered the mayoralty of Hereford, but turned it down, though later, in one of his musical depressions, he considered offering himself as a Unionist candidate at a by-election in Worcester.

With the outbreak of the First World War, festivals were suspended and Elgar became a special constable in Hampstead, to where he had moved, though he had to resign in February 1915 due to ill health. Composition turned to war themes, composing Carillon to symbolise Belgium's plight and Polonia for Poland. Music and politics were now as one and he added his signature to the Manifesto for National Service which appeared in the Times, whilst expressing his rural concern for the horses involved in the war.

Later, as hopes grew for the end of the war music began to flow again and in the spring of 1918 the Elgars rented a house in Sussex where they could hear the rumble of guns as the last major German offensive was reversed. He completed a Romance, and after the Armistice Falstaff was revived to great acclaim. In a mood of relief and happiness he completed a piano quintet, a violin sonata and 'cello concerto. After the completion of Gerontius he had stated that he wanted to write no more, that he had reached his peak. Now after completing the 'cello concerto he penned 'Finis R.I.P.' below its entry in his personal list of works. Whereas he returned to music after Gerontius, his few works after the concerto were all items that returned to earlier sketches and ideas, for he was about to lose his manager, organiser and wife. Alice had been ill with cancer for some time and in the summer of 1920 she died in Elgar's arms. Her life of support, encouragement and advice was gone and no-one could replace it. He did not care for the world of the 1920's and pined for the Worcestershire of the pre-war world with its memories and people.

He spent many of his last years in and around Worcester. He made new friendships with George Bernard Shaw, who worked behind the scenes to try and encourage a third symphony, and with Yehudi Menuhin whom he conducted in many performances of the violin concerto, including the classic gramophone recording. But illness was catching up with him in the form of bronchitis, lumbago and sciatica, and he died in February 1934. He was buried by Alice's side in Malvern.

# A WELSH GLOSSARY

Many Welsh words are found in place names, and the more locally common of these and their meanings are set out below.

Afon—river
Allt—wooded slope, side of a hill
Bach—small, little
Bedd (Beddau)—grave(s)
Betws—church, secluded spot
Blaen—end, top, head of, vale
Blaenau—borders, mountain region
Bron—slope, brow of hill, bank
Bryn—hill
Bwlch—pass
Caer—castle, fort, camp
Capel—chapel, place of worship
Careg—stone
Castell—castle, fortress
Cefn—back, ridge
Celli—grave, copse
Clawdd—dyke, embankment
Coed—wood
Craig (Creigau)—rock(s)
Croes—cross
Cwm—dingle, vale, brook
Dol (Dolau)—meadow (s)
Epynt—ascent, slope
Efin—boundary
Ffrid—lower part of a hill
Garth—enclosure
Gwern—alder grove or swamp
Hafod—summer dwelling or upland farm
Hen—old

Hendre or Hendref—winter dwelling or lowland farm
Heol—road, street, paved way
Llan—church, (anciently) a level space
Llanerch—glade, clear space
Llwybr—path
Llyn—pool
Llys—hall, court, palace
Maen—stone
Maes—field
Mawn—peat, turf
Mawr—great
Meifod—summer farm
Moel—bare hill
Mynydd—mountain
Nant—brook
Newydd—new
Pandy—fulling mill
Pant—hollow, low place
Pen—head, top, end
Pistyll—cataract, waterfall
Plas—place, mansion
Pentre—village
Pant—bridge
Pwll—pool
Rhiw—slope, slanted track
Rhos—moorland
Tomen—mound
Sarn—causeway
Ystrad—vale, valley floor

# A HEREFORDSHIRE GLOSSARY

Ackern, Ackum—acorn
Arl, Orl, Orle—alder
Bannut—walnut
Blackhole—burial place
Boosey Pasture—field next to
  cowhouse
Borrow—the sheltered side
Brock—badger
Burr Oak—a pollarded oak
Chark—charcoal, coal
Close—field
Cockshut—glade where
  woodcock were netted
Coney—rabbit
Conigree—rabbit warren
Cootchy Place—nook, retreat
Cossey, causey—causeway
Dumble-hole—derelict claypit
  or quarry
Gore—triangular piece of land,
  or small field between two
  larger ones

Gorsty—full of gorse bushes
Gospel oak—tree under which
  the gospel was read during
  beating of the parish bounds
Hom, Homme, Holme—low flat
  land near a river
Hope—small valley branching
  out into a larger one
Knap—steep ascent of road
Leasow—pasture land
Lepping-stone—mounting block
  on the roadside
Low—mound or tump
Mathon—wild camomile
Mere—grass division between
  field strips
Piece—field, enclosure
Pleck, Plock—small field
Prill—small stream
Quick—thorn hedge
Quob—boggy ground
Rack—a narrow track

# FROM ABBERLEY TO YARPOLE

**Abberley.** The most striking feature is a 161 foot high clock tower in the style of Big Ben, built by the landowner supposedly to annoy his adjoining owner. The village also contains two churches. The oldest is the Norman St. Michael's, built on the site of an earlier Saxon church in the village centre. It fell into decay in the nineteenth century, but the chancel was restored in 1963 and is now in the care of English Heritage. It has a pleasant warm atmosphere, there is a Saxon tomb cover and some carved corbels. St. Mary's church, to the north-west of the old village, was built to replace St. Michael's in the mid nineteenth century in the English Decorated style.

**Abbey Dore.** The village is on the line of the old Roman road which served the fort at Clyro and parts of the road were discovered in the old station yard in 1901 and 1909.

The abbey was founded by the Cistercians around 1147 by Robert Fitz Harold of Ewyas, grandson of William I. It had 17 granges or farms at its height, 9 of which were in the Golden Valley, the others forming a large sheep holding in Breconshire; Abbey Dore wool commanding amongst the highest prices in England. The present church consists of the transepts and chancel of the old abbey and contains the remains of medieval wall paintings, including one of a skeleton, as well as vaulted roofs and columns.

Grace Dieu was a daughter abbey founded by John of Monmouth in 1216, and was founded near the Hendre on Offa's Dyke path, although not a stone is now left.

Gerald of Wales spent much time attacking the monastic orders for not strictly following their rules, but even he had kind words for the early Cistercians: 'They avoid all superfluity in dress, shunned coloured garments, and wore nothing but woollen. In cold weather they put on them no furs or skins of any kind, and made no use of fires or hot water. As was their clothing so was their food, plain and simple in the extreme, and they never ate meat either in public or private, except under pressure of serious illness. They were conspicuous in charity and given to hospitality; their gate was shut against no one, but stood open at morning, noon, and evening, so that in almsgiving they surpassed all other religious sects.' But for later Cistercians he wrote: 'An excellent priest, vicar of a neighbouring parish, who had again and again been of service to the abbey of Dore, once went to pass the night there. After being received without honour and entertained on the scantiest fare, he wandered through the rooms and offices, and came at last on an inner chamber, where he found the abbot and eight or ten monks feasting royally on fatted capons, geese and flesh of all kinds, and drinking the choicest wines and mead out of silver cups.'

On the road from the village to Withington lie Abbey Dore gardens which are open to the public. There is a tea room, local bookshop, gallery and much besides the gardens themselves.

*Aberedw.* The small village lies in a wooded valley below the limestone crags of Aberedw rocks. Among these rocks is a cave in which Llewelyn ap Gruffyd is reputed to have hidden before being captured and killed in 1282. Kilvert writing in his diary notes: 'About a hundred yards from the road amongst the rocks and bushes was Llewelyn's cave with a door. We went in. There was a step down into it and the cave was a square dark small chamber just high enough to stand upright in, and at the further end a hole or shaft, probably a chink in the rocks, up which we could thrust our arms and sticks without feeling the end. Names were carved on the walls.'

Of the castle not much is known, except that most was destroyed to make room for the station. Fragments of two towers and intervening walls remain and can be reached through a gate from the left of the minor road through the village, just before it meets the B4567.

*Abergavenny.* The town may be on the site of the Roman town of Gobannium, but the castle was founded by Hamelin de Baladun in the eleventh century, and was later given to William de Braose. The Welsh drove him out for a while until Henry II helped him regain it as well as prevailing on the Welsh to recognize his suzerainty at Gloucester. To celebrate this and as an act of goodwill, de Braose invited the local Welsh clans to a banquet at which the guests laid down their arms at the entrance door, as was traditional. During the meal de Braose asked his guests to renounce their practice of bearing arms in the land of Gwent. They refused and de Braose had them all murdered, earning for himself the title of the 'Ogre of Abergavenny.' The Welsh had their revenge later, storming the castle and killing the garrison. The castle was also sacked in 1404 by Glyndwr and by General Fairfax in 1646. Its remains are open to the public, and consist largely of part of the keep and entrance gateway.

The church of St. Mary's contains a series of stone, alabaster and wooden monuments from the thirteenth to seventeenth centuries in the Lewis and Herbert chapels. They include the crusader George de Cantelupe in wood, and Jesse and the tree of life. The town also has a museum.

In the eighteenth century the town had a brief period as a health resort; and is surrounded by hills, one of which, the Skirrid, has a cleft in the south side which local tradition says was formed by an earthquake at the time of the Crucifixion.

**Aconbury.** The name means an old fort inhabited by squirrels. A priory of Augustinian nuns was established here by Margaret de Lacy, of which the remnants are built into the courthouse and church. The latter is now redundant and locked, though some remains can be seen in the outside of the south wall.

The first water taken from St. Anne's Well after twelve o'clock on twelfth night is supposed to be of great medicinal value, especially for eye troubles. The well lies in a field about a quarter of a mile west of the church, and cannot be reached by a public footpath.

For a walk starting from the priory remains, see walk 72.

**Acton Scott.** Here, off the A49 about five miles north of Craven Arms, there is a working farm museum open to the public and which shows a farm as it was before the petrol engine altered work practices. It has a variety of the rarer breeds of cattle, sheep, pigs and poultry as well as heavy horses. Traditional farm activity can be seen, and there are exhibits of the tools and equipment of past years.

**Adforton.** On the road from Ludlow lie the remains of Adforton Abbey, about a mile from the junction with the Leintwardine to Kingsland road, at Grange Farm. The Elizabethan gateway can be seen clearly from the road.

Hugh Mortimer founded an Augustinian priory here in 1179. The priory was destroyed by the Welsh in King John's reign, and was reconstructed by Edmund Mortimer around 1379.

*Almeley.* The village contains two castle mounds called Twts after the Anglo-Saxon word toot, meaning a lookout.

There are faint indications of there having been a Roman camp in the area, but the twenty foot high mound near the church is the site of a castle built, probably, during the reign of King John, perhaps on the site of an earlier wooden structure. Henry III visited it in September 1231 whilst en route from Painscastle to Hereford, and is said to have received homage here from Simon de Montfort, when Simon was seeking restoration of Leicester lands to his family. The remains of fishponds can be seen by the stream to the south-west.

Batch Twt, or Oldcastle Twt, lies to the west of the village. It is reputed to be the birthplace around 1360 of Sir John Oldcastle the Lollard, though it is more likely that he took his name from the castle and was born elsewhere in the village. Sir John served as sheriff of Herefordshire until the seventh year of Henry IV's reign and helped contain Owain Glyndwr's revolt. He gradually accepted Lollard thought, questioning the supremacy of the pope, rejecting the doctrine of transubstantiation—the belief that the bread and wine taken at Holy Communion become the body and blood of Christ—and arguing for the bible to be translated into English—a very radical programme for the time. He was declared a heretic despite the interventions his friend of youth, Prince Hal, who tried to make him tone down his views. He was arrested in 1413 but escaped from the Tower of London with the help of London Lollards. He then became involved in an abortive coup attempt whilst his former protégé, Henry, was at war in France, was hunted down and eventually recaptured at Broniarth. He was burnt alive on Christmas Day 1417. Much of his character was used as the basis for Shakespeare's Falstaff.

For a walk around Almeley and its twts see walk 41.

*Astley.* The first church was a priory built in the early 1100's, and part of this original Norman nave and chancel still remain. The priory was attached to Abbey of St. Taurinus near Rouen, and with the suppression of alien priories in 1414 was then attached to the college of Westbury in Gloucestershire. When this in turn was suppressed by Henry VIII, the manor and its living passed into private hands. Apart from the Norman doorway and other remains, there is part of a Jacobean pulpit, the sixteenth century Blount tombs and the tomb of Frances Havergill. She was the sixth daughter of Canon Havergill, the rector from 1816 to 1841, and became well known for the many hymns she wrote.

Astley Hall, the home of the former conservative prime minister, Stanley Baldwin can be seen across the fields from the church. It is now a nursing home.

**Aston.** Here, to the east of Burrington, is found a magnificent tiny Norman church dedicated to St. Giles, an abbot from southern Gaul and the patron saint of beggars, cripples and lepers. The entrance has a well preserved and finely carved tympanum above the doorway. The nave has several Norman windows, and on its walls are painted red flowers. These probably date from the Norman period, though they were only rediscovered during the restoration of the church in 1879. There is a twelfth century font of carved stone. Both the church and the churchyard are well cared for.

About 120 yards north-east of the church lies the castle tump, probably the site of a motte and bailey castle.

For a walk starting from this church, see walk 17.

**Aston Munslow.** The White House, open to the public, dates from Norman times, but most of the remains are of the fourteenth century medieval hall with its sixteenth and eighteenth century additions. In the grounds are the remains of a dovecote and a range of barns and buildings, including a seventeenth century coach house, granary and cider house (with press) and sixteenth century stable block, which house a farm museum. A memorial rose garden commemorates Hilda Murell, the rose grower and anti-nuclear campaigner who some still feel died in mysterious circumstances.

**Aymestrey.** The name means Aepelmund's tree. The church has a sixteenth century carved rood screen and sixteenth century floorstones. The stone corbels supporting the roof timbers have finely carved human heads. The church may well have acted as the stables for Edward, Duke of York's troops before the Battle of Mortimer's Cross in 1472.

**Berrington Hall.** The house was started in 1778 by the Harley family, passed to the Rodneys by marriage, the Crawleys by sale and, in part payment of estate duties, to the National Trust who now have the care of the building. It lies to the north of Leominster just off the A49 and is open to the public.

The main portion is a four storey building designed by Henry Holland. There is a courtyard to the rear formed by a laundry, bake-

*Figure at Bosbury*

house and other service buildings. The outside is quite austere with the exception of a large portico.

Inside the house there is a marble hall, library, drawing room with an elaborate ceiling and French furniture, a boudoir also with French furniture and a Van Goyen coastal landscape, various more personal rooms, an interesting staircase hall, bedrooms and a dining room with four large naval pictures depicting Admiral Rodney's successes. Three of these are by Thomas Luny.

**Birtsmorton.** From the grounds of the church you can glimpse the impressive building of Birtsmorton Court. This was once the home of the Nanfan family who hired Thomas Wolsey as a clerk, so starting him on his career to become Henry VIII's chancellor. The village has a waterfowl sanctuary open to the public.

**Bockleton.** A Saxon church probably predated that of 1160, which forms the core of the existing building. There are south and north Norman doorways with arcades of arches above. The chancel dates from the thirteenth century and the Barneby side chapel, with the Elizabethan tomb of its founders, was built in 1560. The church is spacious, with an avenue of trees along its approach.

**Bosbury.** This is one of the oldest possessions of the bishopric of Hereford, being the site of a settlement since King Offa's time. Bishop Aethelstan, who rebuilt the cathedral, died at his palace in Bosbury in 1056. The old palace stood to the north of the church where Old Court Farm now stands. The entrance to the gatehouse remains, together with part of the curtain wall, but the rest was dismantled in the seventeenth century.

The existing church was largely built between 1186 and 1200, and comprises the present nave and chancel. The north and south aisles were added later, and the Morton chapel, a locally rare example of perpendicular architecture, was added around 1530. There is also a fifteenth century screen, a massive separate belltower originally used as a refuge, and a fourteenth century preaching cross. The latter was spared by the puritans when the words 'Honour not the +, but honour God for Christ' were engraved on its arms.

For a walk just to the north of Bosbury, see walk 53.

***Brampton Bryan.*** The castle stands on private land though a glimpse of the main remains can be had through the trees after leaf fall. It was founded in the latter years of Henry I. In 1293 the de Brampton's heiress married Robert de Harley, at a time when the castle was described as a tower with curtilage, garden and vivary and was held from the Mortimers through the combination of performance of castle guard at Wigmore for 40 days in wartime, and a small annual rent.

The Harleys were one of the few Herefordshire families who took the

*Figure at Bosbury*

65

side of parliament in the Civil War. Sir Robert Harley was an M.P. in London at the time of the outbreak of the war, and defence of the castle was left with his wife Lady Brilliana. Due to royalist indecision the castle was not besieged immediately, allowing it to be strengthened. A siege eventually commenced on 26 July 1643, but was fairly shortlived as it was lifted on 6 September after the royalist defeat outside Gloucester.

Lady Brilliana died on 10 October, and in the following spring a force under Sir Michael Woodhouse, who had just taken the small nearby castle at Hopton, invested Brampton Bryan with artillery. After the outworks had fallen under the battery, the castle surrendered.

At Oliver Cromwell's death there was a great storm, which was said to be caused by the devil dragging his body across the park— Cromwell and Harley had quarrelled over the king's execution.

The earliest remains are the entrance gateway which was probably built in the reign of Edward III. The bay windows and ornamental additions were made to the interior when it was converted into a domestic residence in the middle of the sixteenth century. It was rebuilt in 1661 and some of the rooms were inhabited till around 1850 when it was damaged by a storm.

The church was rebuilt in the 1650's as it had been burnt during the siege of the castle. The roof is of triple hammerbeam construction, and the pulpit and flooring around the altar have much inlaid woodwork.

*Bredwardine.* The site of the castle, which lies to the south of the church, overlooked the ferry which preceeded the bridge, and was moated on the landward side. The manor was granted to John de Bradwardine after the Norman Conquest, but had become the property of the Baskerville family by 1227. (The Baskervilles were a local family who gave Conan Doyle permission to use their name for *The Hound of the Baskervilles* so long as the story was set elsewhere.) In the 1300's the castle was held by Hugh Lacy for the service of one knight's fee to the castle of Brecon.

The castle might have been one of the many strengthened without royal licence during the wars of Stephen and Matilda, and being condemned as Castra Adulterina, was largely dismantled during the reign of Henry II or III. Certainly in 1374 it was described as a 'toft with appurtenances called the castel place', and 70 years later was in ruins.

The church is early Norman, though it was partially re-erected in the fifteenth century having been damaged by Owain Glyndwr.

Norman doorways remain in the north and south walls, and inside the church are two monuments, one to either Walter Baskerville or Walter de Bradwardine; and the other to Sir Roger Vaughan who died at Agincourt defending Henry V. The huge bowl shaped Norman font is carved from a stone not naturally found in the area.

Outside, to the north of the church, is the tomb of Francis Kilvert the Victorian clergyman and diarist who was vicar of Bredwardine from 1876 till his death in September 1879.

Some of Kilvert's diaries for this period have survived and his entry for 5 December 1878 includes: 'Today was the tithe audit and tithe dinner to the farmers, both held at the vicarage. About 50 tithe payers came, most of them very small holders, some paying as little as 9d. As soon as they had paid their tithe to Mr. Heywood in the front hall they retired into the back hall and regaled themselves with bread, cheese and beer, some of them eating and drinking the value of the tithe they had paid.'

**Brilley.** The name is derived from the Anglo-Saxon for 'burnt clearing', though the area probably remained wooded for some tme as there is a record of the sheriff of Hereford ordering a road to be cleared through Brilley Forest to Huntington in the mid thirteenth century.

There used to be a stone called the funeral stone outside the churchyard, and coffins were carried around it three times before entering the churchyard. But this custom can no longer take place as the stone has been broken up.

**Brinsop.** Brinsop Court has retained many of its original features, but is not open to the public. The court used to be moated with a drawbridge and contained a chapel, crypt, dungeon and blacksmith's forge together with the living quarters. Now only the moat is left, together with the early fourteenth century hall and two large fishponds. To its north-west, between the court and the minor road from which the court can be seen, lies a field called the 'old town pasture' which contains various earthworks and hollows. These almost certainly mark the outlines of an old medieval settlement centred on the court.

The church, to the south of the court, contains a tympanum of St. George slaying the dragon, and one tradition has it that St. George killed the dragon nearby. There are also twelfth century carvings of animals and men over the north door in the church. One window commemorates William Wordsworth who used to stay in Brinsop Court when it was owned by his brother-in-law. He wrote several sonnets whilst in the area, including *Wait, Prithee, Wait.*

*Broadheath.* Elgar was born here at The Firs which now houses an Elgar birthplace museum.

*Broadwas.* This twelfth century church is signposted from the A44 to the west of Worcester, but when we've tried visiting, the door was annoyingly locked and there was no sign of where to obtain a key. There is a preaching cross near the church, and inside there is supposedly some Norman work, a fine trussed roof and two old piscinae.

*Brockhampton.* (Near Bromyard). The chapel, of which only the walls remain, dates from the twelfth century and lies outside the moat which surrounds the house. The Tudor gatehouse over the moat dates from the end of the fifteenth century and is open to the public together with part of the house, as it is in the hands of the National Trust.

*Brockhampton.* (Near How Caple). This unusual thatched church was built in 1901 by Alice Foster of Brockhampton Court in memory of her parents. Inside the church has a more intimate feeling than many, but still manages to give that feeling of aspiring to the heavens as its pillars rise up from low walls.

For a walk starting from the church and including Capler Camp and the Wye, see walk 74.

*Bromfield.* The Benedictine priory was dissolved by Henry VIII, but the massive Tudor gateway still stands on a corner of the churchyard. The church contains an oak nave roof from the sixteenth century and a painted chancel ceiling. This is all that remains of a once completely painted chancel, dating from 1672, and has been described as the 'Best example of the worst period of ecclesiastical art.'

John Giffard of Bromfield was a self seeker of the latter 1200's. Attaching himself to de Montfort's cause when the marcher lords were under pressure from de Montfort's ally the Welsh, he ensured he was quickly taken prisoner by the royalist forces at Lewes anticipating, wrongly, de Montfort's defeat. However by the time of Evesham he had re-allied himself with the royalists and so avoided any subsequent fines for the restoration of his lands. He had no real love for Edward I

*Brockhampton Church, near How Caple*

though or the law, for during Edward's absence on crusade at the start of his reign, we hear of Giffard forcibly capturing and marrying a rich widow so as to add to his lands. Despite her pleas the marriage was upheld, though he had to pay Edward 300 marks for not having obtained his consent.

**Bromyard.** The minster or missionary church was founded by 840 and over the next century the resultant settlement grew to become the third most important town in Herefordshire. The existing church largely dates from the twelfth century, though some of the earlier stone was re-used, including the two carvings above the south doorway, one of St. Peter and one of a consecration cross. After the Conquest the bishop of Hereford built a small palace near the church, from the gateway to which developed the town's market. Prior to the Black Death the town's population grew to some 1,200 people, but this plague appears to have affected Bromyard more than many places. By 1801, the year of the first national census, the population had only recovered to 983. Continuing stagnation and the low rents led to the town becoming a dumping ground for paupers from the surrounding area. The census of 1851 shows that only 45 per cent of the then population were born in Bromyard, with 31 per cent born elsewhere in Herefordshire and 22 per cent outside the county. (The missing 2 per cent were visitors.) The level of poverty and lack of investment in buildings and infrastructure led to a poor level of health; in the mid 1850's the mortality rate was only exceeded by 11 other towns in the country.

Still, in the 1900's, Bromyard underwent something of a revival, partly due to the coming of the railways. Stock from the neighbouring farms could now be finished and loaded on to trains for the major towns. A large annual autumn horse fair was also held, until the tractor replaced the horse. Now Bromyard, as with many small towns and large villages in the neighbourhood, is seeing new housing built. This is of brick, reflecting the Georgian and Victorian fashion of building a brick veneer on the front of many of the buildings in the centre of the town, behind which the old medieval original still lurks.

**Bronllys.** The castle lies on the road between Bronllys and Talgarth and was founded by de Pons of Clifford. It was fortified against Glyndwr and in the mid fifteeenth century the Welsh bard Bedo Brwynllys lived here. It is now in the care of the Welsh Office, and the round keep is open to the public.

***Brngwyn.*** The church contains one of the oldest bells in Wales, dated 1200, although the church dates largely from the seventeenth century. The tall pre-Christian pillar stone in the chancel dates from between the seventh and ninth centuries; the cross was carved on it at a later date. On the south-east external corner of the chancel are two horizontal carved figures on a quoin stone, one male and one female, though the date of carving is unknown.

Kilvert, writing in his diary on 16 March 1870 tells a story about Llanship on Brngwyn hill: 'Morgan went out with some hot milk (for the lambs) and showed me the remains of the moat, where the Scotch pedlar was hidden after being murdered for the sake of his pack while lodging in the house, and his skeleton was found when the moat was cleaned out. The moat that is left is a broad deep formidable ditch and a rather long pond at one end of the house and full of water. It extended all round the house and had to be crossed by a bridge. Llanship is a fearfully wet swampy place, almost under water and I should think very unhealthy. One of the twin yews was lately blown down and cut up into gate posts which will last as long as oak. The wood was so hard that Morgan said it turned many of the axes as if they were made of lead.'

***Builth Wells.*** This town has always been essentially a market town for the surrounding valleys and hills. It had a short life as a spa town when the local gentry tried to popularise it and built a promenade from the bridge to the Park Wells. But when Lady Hester Stanhope settled at Glan Irfon, she favoured and promoted the Glana Wells, to the detriment of Builth. Now it serves as centre for pony trekkers and anglers, and is the home for the Royal Welsh Show each July.

***Burghill.*** The church has a carved rood screen, and of the several monuments, one is to a nephew of Edward V. Another is to a traveller who circled the world prior to 1619 and whose tablet includes a globe. The churchyard is full of ancient and new yews, the ones on either side of the path to the entrance being known as the twelve apostles.

***Burton Court, Eardisland.*** This house is open to the public, advertising itself as a typical squire's house rather than a stately home. It consists of a Great Hall which dates from the fourteenth century whilst the rest of the rooms on display date from the Regency period. These include a billiard room and library. On display in the rooms are costumes and miniature fairground toys.

**Bury Ditches.** A hillfort on Tangley Hill above Clun, it has up to three high and oval shaped banks encompassing an area of over seven acres. On the north side the ditches are 30 feet deep and 68 feet wide. It was probably a British camp, but might be the site of a fort of a sixth century Saxon chieftain. There is a tale that fairies have hidden a pot of gold on the hill, and have a left a slender gold wire visible to guide the seeker.

**Canon Pyon.** This was one of the manors given to Hereford Cathedral by Wulviva and Godiva, sisters of Leofric, Earl of Mercia.

Nearby are two small hills called Robin Hood's Butts, though also known singularly as Pyon Hill and Butthouse Knapp. Several tales relate to how these hills were formed. One is that Robin Hood and Little John were each carrying a spadeful of earth with the intention of burying the monks at Wormsley, but were told they were looking in the wrong direction and dropped their earth, thus forming the hills. Another version has it that there was a wager between the two men about who could jump over Wormsley Hill to Canon Pyon. They each tried, but each clipped the summit, in the process knocking out the earth to form the two smaller hills.

**Capel-y-ffin.** The name means chapel on the boundary, and lies on the boundaries of Gwent, Herefordshire and Powys. The monastery on the site was built in 1870 by the Reverend Joseph Leycester Lyne for his unorthodox foundation of Anglican Benedictines for both monks and nuns. He called himself Father Ignatius and when he died on 16 October 1908, the foundation lost its inspiration, the church became ruinous and dangerous and part had collapsed by 1920. The remains are now incorporated into a private house.

Kilvert mentions a visit to the monastery site on 5 April 1870: 'Father Phillip was digging. Brother Serene or Cyrene was wheeling earth to him from a heap thrown out by the excavation dug for the foundations of the monastery. He seemed very much oppressed by his heavy black dress, for the sun was hot and he stopped when he had wheeled his empty barrow back to the heap and stood to rest and wipe his streaming brow. They both seemed studiously unconscious of our presence, but I saw brother Serene glancing furtively at us from his cowl when he thought he was under cover of the heap of earth ... It does seem very odd at this age of the world in the latter part of the nineteenth century to see monks gravely wearing such dress and at work in them in broad day ... The masons had raised the foundation

*The pulpit, Clodock*

73

walls to the level of the ground and believed the house would be built by the end of May, which I doubt ... The monks have bought 32 acres.'

**Castle Frome.** This settlement boasts a mainly Norman church which was sympathetically restored by the Victorians. Its masterpiece is a fine, some say the best, late twelfth century Romanesque font. Formed from one piece of stone the carvings show that English work was beginning to be influenced by that from Italy. The story told on the bowl is, appropriately, the Baptism of Christ. The church also has a seventeenth century tomb and effigies.

**Clifford.** The castle was one of five in Herefordshire mentioned in the Domesday Survey and was in the possession of Ralph de Todeni, William the Conqueror's standard bearer at the Battle of Hastings. It has no great military history, but was the home of Fair Rosamund, Henry II's favourite. Oaks are supposed to have been growing in the courtyard around 1500, at a time when the castle probably fell into disuse. The existing remains include a fragment of the northern wall and part of a round tower in the north-west corner. The remains are on private ground, but a good view can be had from the B road between Hay and Whitney at Clifford.

Clifford was also the site of a small cell of Cluniac monks founded by Simon Fitzwalter in Henry II's reign. Its site is now occupied by a modern house called The Priory.

**Clodock.** The story of St. Clodock, or Clydawg, is told in the note on Ewyas Harold. The church itself stands on the place where the cart carrying his body stopped and the oxen refused to cross the Monnow. A pillar of fire subsequently rose from the ground and was taken to mean that God was showing his pleasure at the building of the church.

The church has the only dedication to St. Clodock. It has a Norman nave with many seventeenth century family box pews, a three decker pulpit and some medieval and eighteenth century murals. A minstrel's gallery built around 1715 still stands, and behind the pulpit is a ninth century inscription on a slab to the wife of Guinndas.

**Clun.** *Clunton and Clunbury*
*Clungunford and Clun,*
*Are the quietest places*
*Under the sun.* A.E. Housman

Its present quietness belies its history as before the Norman Conquest Clun was the centre of a large manor worth 25lbs of silver a year to the Saxon earl, Edric, an earl the Normans eventually overthrew around 1074, when Picot de Say built the castle. The last of the Says was one William Butterall under whom the castle was stormed by Prince Rhys in 1195. Llewelyn burnt the town in 1213, then a revolt in 1216 by John Fitzalan who held the castle, led to King John besieging and burning it. Records of 1272 note that the castle was 'decayed', but that nevertheless the town had a Saturday market and fairs at Martinmas and Whitsun.

The castle remains, including part of the keep, lie on the west of the town in a dominant position on a bend of the river. On the north-east of the town lies a small hospital, orginally built in 1614 for twelve poor men. Between the two lies the town hall which was built in 1780 and now contains the local museum.

Parliamentary soldiers occupied the church in the Civil War, when it was partly burnt in a royalist attack. However the Norman tower with its double roof survived, and the north aisle's roof has carvings of angels and shields.

*Clyro.* Robert Francis Kilvert served as curate for seven years here from 1865, and kept a diary which gives a colourful feel for the area.

On 12 April 1870 he mentions his local: 'Last night the Swan was very quiet, marvellously quiet and peaceful. No noise, rowing or fighting whatever and no men as there sometimes are lying by the roadside all night, drunk, cursing, muttering, maundering and vomiting.'

Again, for 7 October 1870 'There was a murderous affray with poachers at the moor last night—two keepers fearfully beaten about the head with bludgeons and one poacher, Cartwright, a hay sawyer, stabbed and his life despaired of.' Later still: 'Clyro people demolished the stock and whipping post after seeing the stocks broken by two people who then went and rejoined the Hereford militia.'

The vicarage now houses a gallery which concentrates on the work of local artists.

*Cotheridge.* This is a quite different church, both inside and out. The latter is whitewashed and has a timber belltower, whilst the inside is entered through a side chapel. There are box pews and much panelling in the chancel, for which there is a Norman arch.

***Craswall.*** The name means cress stream, and this is the site of an alien priory founded by Walter de Lacy in 1222, and which was subordinate to the abbey at Grandmont in Normandy. It was confiscated by the crown in the reign of Edward IV, along with many other such priories.

The remains are hard to find, in fact the vicar of Clodock and Longtown wrote in 1919: 'To describe the exact location of the priory so that others may have the rare and enjoyable experience of visiting it, is almost beyond the wit of man.' Matters have since been improved, and walk 63 goes close by.

Of the buildings only part of the priory church and chapter remain and are very overgrown. Much of the stone was incorporated into the building of Abbey Farm above the site. To the south, along the stream, lie two fishponds one of which has recently been cleared, together with the remains of a medieval earth and masonry revetted dam of a larger fishpool which is now drained.

***Credenhill.*** The hillfort on a wooded hill to the north of the village is twice as large as any other in Herefordshire, enclosing 49 acres. It dates from the Iron Age and excavations indicate it might have been the pre-Roman capital of the area, with a population of some 8,000. (For more on hillforts see Croft Ambrey.) It has been partly damaged by quarrying and is now obscured by forestry plantations, but two ramparts with three entrances remain. It can be reached by a public footpath signposted off the minor road that leads from Credenhill to Tillington.

The best known vicar of Credenhill has been Thomas Traherne, a note about whom is included in the chapter on literature.

***Croft.*** The site of the present house belonged to Earl Edwin, though probably during Edward the Confessor's reign it was granted to Bernard de Croft who certainly held it at the time of the Domesday Survey.

One of his descendents, Jasper de Croft, fought in the crusades and was knighted on the capture of Jerusalem in 1100; a later descendent married one of Glyndwr's daughters, and Richard Croft supported the Yorkist and Mortimer cause in the Wars of the Roses. He aided the future Edward IV at the nearby Battle of Mortimer's Cross, and at the later Battle of Tewkesbury captured Prince Edward, the son of Henry VI. However he managed to survive the arrival of Henry VII who made him a knight baronet after the Battle of Stoke where he helped defeat the pretender Lambert Simnel.

*Croft Church*

Sir James Croft, a supporter of Lady Jane Grey, was condemned to death by Queen Mary, a sentence which was later changed to one year's imprisonment and a £500 fine. Queen Elizabeth I later appointed him Governor of Berwick, though he was relieved of the command when the English were beaten back at the Battle of Leith. He later returned to favour and was sent as a commissioner in 1588 to treat with the Spaniards in Flanders. Subsequent evidence however suggests that he was in Philip of Spain's pay all the time.

The Crofts supported the royalists in the Civil War, Sir William being killed in a skirmish at Stokesay in 1645. He was succeeded by one brother who died not long after, then by another who became bishop of Hereford. The latter won renown when Cromwell's soldiers turned their muskets on him as he was preaching in the cathedral, so he turned his sermon into a denouncement of sacrilege.

Crofts represented the area in parliament for several centuries, until debts mounted and the property was sold in 1746, to be re-acquired by later descendents in 1925.

The house is now in the care of the National Trust and is open to the public. Its atmosphere is very English, with oak panelling, old clocks and exhibits from Croft Ambrey. The church contains the tomb of the Yorkist Richard Croft and his wife.

The chestnut avenue to the west of the castle is supposed to have been planted from seeds found on an Armada ship wrecked on the Welsh coast. Trees near the castle itself include the wild cherry, Californian redwood and incense cedar.

*Croft Ambrey.* Excavations carried out between 1960 and 1966 by the Woolhope Club show that the earliest rampart, enclosing just over five acres, was built around 550 B.C. Much of the area contained within this rampart was levelled, the soil helping form the rampart, and on this flatter plateau a settlement was built of square and rectangular huts arranged alongside tracks. The settlement was extended at around 390 B.C. when the rampart which can be seen today was constructed, enclosing an area of just under nine acres. Gateways were flanked with stone walls, and a timber walk built on top of the rampart. Later a second ditch and bank was built, probably to help enable the fort to be defended by a small group if many of the inhabitants were themselves away on a raiding party.

The houses within the walls were simple timber-framed affairs, but the whole area appears to have been covered in them—some 274 in number. Even if half, the smaller ones, are assumed to be stores and granaries, and an average household size of four is taken, the population of the inner area would have been 548. Outside there are traces of other buildings and it is reasonable to assume a population of some 800 or 900 people at the time of the Roman Invasion. As with other such sites, the Romans stormed and burnt it to the ground, the survivors being forcibly resettled in the valleys. However some returned and created a site adjacent to the walls for continuing their pagan worship, a site which was used for a couple of centuries.

For a walk around Croft Ambrey, see walk 27.

*Cusop.* Under the large yew tree beyond the entrance porch to the church lies the grave of William Seward, a follower of Wesley and Whitfield, who was injured in 1740 by a mob when preaching in Hay and who died a week after the incident.

To the north-east of the village, on a wooded hill stands Mouse Castle, which was probably a Pele tower, a tower house built solely to withstand bands of marauders. It is mentioned during the reigns of Edward II, Edward III and Richard II when it was held by the de Clavenoghs, one of whom took part in the execution of Edward II's favourite Piers Gaveston. The stonework has long since been used for parish roads and farm house repairs, and the castle is now just a tree covered earthwork on the edge of the wood. The mound to the southwest of Cusop Church may well be the site of another castle.

For a walk which starts from the church, see walk 61.

*Dilwyn.* The name derives from Dilewe which means a secret or shady place, and certainly the village sits in a little fold in the ground. The manor was held by the crown until Henry III granted it to his son Prince Edmund on the fall of its previous lord, Simon de Montfort. In turn Edmund granted part of the lands to the priory of Wormsley.

In the chancel of the church there is a tomb dating from Edward II's reign, and is probably that of a Tirrell. Around the font are fragments of tiles dating from the thirteenth and fourteenth centuries, and some of the gravestones are now also retained within the church.

*Dinmore.* The settlement was founded in the royal forest of Marden when land was granted by Henry I to the Knights Hospitallers who established a commandery. These grants were confirmed and extended by kings Richard I and John, so that the commandery soon had cells at Garway, Harewood, Rowlstone, Sutton, Upleadon and Wormbridge. With these many dependent settlements and the surge of interest in the order with the Third Crusade, Dinmore became the Hospitaller's third or fourth most important commandery out of about fifty scattered throughout England and Wales.

Each commandery was in the charge of a knight who had given services to the order in the Holy Land or at its later headquarters on Rhodes and then Malta. The order had been established to provide charitable provision for pilgrims (that of the Templars was for the pilgrims' protection), and Dinmore provided training for the order, and a quiet resting place for the injured and invalided. It would also care for local travellers, the sick and the needy. Of all Dinmore's commanders, Sir Thomas Docwra was probably the most eminent. Having survived the siege of Rhodes in 1480 he was appointed to Dinmore in 1486, before becoming Grand Prior of the English order at Clerkenwell in 1501. He was one of Henry VIII's favourites and was present in 1513 at the Field of the Cloth of Gold where he was 'appointed to ride with the King of England at the embracing of the two kings.'

Anyone could seek sanctuary at the order's churches, of which two documented cases are recorded at Dinmore, one for 1485 concerning an alleged theft and one an alleged murder in 1491. The church was rebuilt in 1370, though some of the twelfth century tower, walling and doorway were incorporated.

The Hospitallers received many Templar possessions on the latter order's disbandment in 1310, and when the English Hospitallers were themselves disbanded by Henry VIII, the manor house was granted to Sir Thomas Palmer, who was later beheaded for supporting Lady Jane Grey's attempt to gain the throne. The present manor house dates from the sixteenth century, but most of the structure is of later date, and the cloisters were not built till the 1930's. These, with their stained glass windows, together with the music room are open to the public.

*Dorstone.* In the thirteenth and fourteenth centuries the castle was held by the Solers family from the Mortimers. In 1403 it was entrusted to Sir Walter Fitzwalter who strengthened it against Glyndwr. It was still in existence in the mid-seventeenth century, for on Wednesday 17 September 1645 a diarist with the royalist army noted: 'The whole army met at a rendezvous on Arthurstone Heath near Dorston Castle, and from there his majestie marched to Hom Lacy, the seat of the Lord Viscount Scudamore.' There are no remains of the castle now.

The church was rebuilt in the nineteenth century, but the original chapel on or near the site is believed to have been dedicated by Richard de Britto, one of the four knights who killed Thomas à Becket in 1170, after he had served fifteen years pennance in the Holy Land.

On the summit of Dorstone Hill lies Arthur's Stone which can be reached by car. The visible remains are the entrance to a collective neolithic burial chamber built around 3000 B.C. Much of the stone was removed in the 1800's for building purposes, and half of the cap-stone to the entrance has subsequently broken away. Numerous neolithic and bronze age flints have been found nearby.

*Eardisley.* In the Domesday Survey 'Herdeslege', meaning a clearing in the wood, is noted as owned by Roger de Laci. The castle is described as a 'defensible mansion' and was probably only turned into a castle proper in the twelfth century, for a castle is recorded here during Henry III's reign.

In 1262 Llewelyn advanced on Hereford, plundering Eardisley and Weobley and besieging Roger Mortimer in his castle at Wigmore. Bishop Aquablanca of Hereford appealed to Henry for support. But many of the local marchers rebelled under Roger Clifford of Eardisley and, calling on de Montfort to lead them, advanced on Hereford and took the bishop prisoner. The bishop was widely hated as he had obtained papal letters which were left blank except for the pope's seal. The pope then empowered him to sell these letters, filling in the pages with fictitious reports of work done on behalf of the purchaser at the papal court, and ending with a complete veto on any form of legal or other action to contradict the contents of the letter. The money so raised was then used by the pope in a war with his christian neighbour, the emperor Frederick. The constant demand of the pope for revenue for this most temporal of causes was one of the reasons for de Montfort's clash with the king. Aquablanca was imprisoned at Eardisley Castle, but released soon after as Henry temporarily came to terms. However the bishop had had enough, and presently returned to his native Savoy where he died.

Over the next hundred years the castle passed from the Cliffords to the de Bohun earls of Hereford, till the earldom was extinguished in 1372.

The castle was burnt in the Civil War when it was in the ownership of a branch of the Baskerville family, and all that now remains are a mound and ditches hidden by woodland on a piece of private land behind the church. Spear heads and armour have been found in the moat.

The church contains a fine Romanesque font with carvings of Christ despoiling hell, battling knights and a lion. The aisle contains a mixture of English and Norman arches.

Tram Square at the northern end of the village is the old market area, the original grant of a right to hold a market being given in 1225. This market continued till quite recent times.

***Eastnor.*** This house, open to the public on selected days, was designed by Sir Robert Smirke for the first Earl Somers in 1812. There is a large medieval style hall, two libraries, a drawing room designed and furnished by Pugin in 1850 and a first floor chapel. At the entrance gate lies an estate village with a church largely dating from 1851 and designed by Sir Gilbert Scott.

***Ewyas Harold.*** One of the early kings of the small kingdom of Ewyas, a name which means sheep district, was Clodock. He led a saintly life, but was considered somewhat abnormal by his subjects. One day he was waiting for a hunting party who found him in meditation by the river, and set upon him. Clodock was canonised and a shrine was built near his place of murder.

In Edward the Confessor's time the castle was held by Osborn Pentecost, one of Ralph the Timid, Earl of Hereford's mercenaries, and was damaged in the wars between the English and the Welsh from 1050 to 1060. At the Conquest it was held by the Saxon earl, Edric, and later, at the time of the Domesday Survey, by Alured de Merleberge. Alured surrendered the castle to the Harold of the village's name, though history leaves little record of him. His son founded Abbey Dore at the beginning of Stephen's reign.

The castle passed through many hands, and was last fortified by Sir William Beauchamp against Glyndwr. The church has a strong tower which was probably used as a refuge by the inhabitants of the old borough. Both, along with Abbey Dore, can be seen on walk 66.

*Four Stones.* On a minor road leading south from Kinnerton (to the east of New Radnor) lie the Four Stones in a field just south of a crossroads and opposite a farm building. There are several legends attached to them. One is that four kings are buried between them, and if you stamp on the ground you can supposedly sense the hollow sound of their burial chamber. Another is that when the Four Stones hear the sound of Old Radnor Church's bells, they go down to the Hindwell brook to drink.

The stones also lie on ley lines. These are curious things, and owe their existence to a Herefordian called Alfred Watkins. A well known and respected man, when out riding one day in the hills near Bredwardine, he noticed that many ancient sites and buildings lay in straight lines. This set him off on years of research with maps and on the ground before he presented his theory that many such buildings and sites owed their position to ancient straight trackways which traversed the countryside. He called them ley lines due to the presence of many places ending in -ley or its derivative which were on their route. Track markers included not just hillforts, tumuli, standing stones and church towers (themselves often built on pre-christian sites), but also notches on hills, avenues of trees, and flashes or ponds which caught the early morning or late evening light. Since Watkins' initial work, others have coupled ley lines with some mystical earth force.

*Fownhope.* 'Fown' may relate to the colour of a notable building in the past, whilst there is some discrepancy about the derivation of 'hope'.

82

*Stocks and whipping post, Fownhope*

Some feel it may come from the hop, others from hope, the name of a small valley which feeds into a larger one, of which there are several in the locality.

The village has one of the largest churches in Herefordshire, and it contains a twelfth century Norman stone tympanum depicting the Virgin Mary holding Jesus. Other items of interest include a nine foot long fourteenth century chest carved from one piece of oak. This was found in the belfry in 1975 and contained vestments and silver, possibly put there for safekeeping during the Civil War. The stocks and whipping post are preserved outside the church on the main road.

**Garway.** The name derives either from the hill encampment overlooking the Monnow—the Gearwy or water camp—or from Gouroue's church.

The church was a preceptory of the Knights Templar being one of six such churches in England. The Knights Templar were founded by nine French knights in 1131 to protect pilgrims in the Holy Land, Garway being granted to them in 1199. At the dissolution of the order in 1310 the church passed to the Knights Hospitaller.

The church has a massive square bell tower, used as a refuge in times of trouble and possibly as a prison, which is connected to the nave by a short passage. The nave is separated from the chancel by a saracenic style Norman arch with zig zag patterns. To the south lies the Templars chapel built around 1210.

In the farm buildings below the church lies a fourteenth century columbarium or dovecote; built in 1236 it contains 666 pigeon holes. It may be visited with the prior permission of the farm.

**Glascwm.** According to Gerald of Wales: 'In the church there is a handbell which has most miraculous powers. It is supposed to have belonged to Saint David and in an attempt to liberate him, a certain woman took this handbell to her husband, who was chained up in the castle of Rhaiadr Gwy in Gwrthrynian, which castle Rhys ap Gruffyd had built in our time. The keepers of the castle not only refused to set the man free, but they seized the bell. That night God took vengeance on them, for the whole town was burned down, except the wall on which the handbell hung.'

Kilvert writes of the countryside round about: 'Round the great dark heather-clothed shoulder of the mountain swept the green ride descending steeply to the Fuallt farm and fold and the valley opened still more wide and fair. The beautiful Glasnant came leaping and

84

*Garway Church*

rushing down its lovely dingle, a flood of molten silver and crystal fringed by groups of silver birches and alders, and here and there a solitary tree rising from the bright green sward along the banks of the brook and drooping over the stream which seemed to come out of a fairy land of blue valley depths and distances and tufted woods and green and gold and crimson and russet brown.'

**Golden Valley.** The valley's name probably comes from a corruption of the River Dore, pronounced as the French d'or meaning golden.

Large irrigation works were carried out by Rowland Vaughan who was the author of a book published in the sixteenth century called *The most approved and long experienced water works*. In it he writes: 'The Golden Vale, the Lombardy of Herefordshire, the Garden of the old Gallants, is the paradise of all parts beyond the Severn. I propose to raise a Golden Valley, being the pride of all that countie bordering on Wales, joyning on Ewyas Lacy; the richest, yet for want of employment, the plentyfullest place of poore in the Kingdome. There be, within a mile and a half from my house, every way, five hundred poore habitations, whose greatest means consist in spinning flax, hemps and hurdes.' He had a belief in a new system of organizing society which

85

included well irrigated and prosperous land, and parsons to teach the children. Part of his early utopia is seen in the remains of channels and ducts near the River Dore.

**Goodrich.** So called after Godric's castle which was built in pre-Norman times, though it is not mentioned in the Domesday Survey because Archenfield, the area round about, had been ravaged and laid waste by the Welsh. The impressive remains of the castle, now in the care of English Heritage, lie above a ford which it guarded.

With the end of Godric Mappestone's line the castle reverted to the crown and in 1204 was granted by King John to the Earl of Pembroke. The crown again resumed control in 1245, when it was passed to the Munchesney family who later sided with Simon de Montfort. It eventually passed to Richard Talbot of Eccleswall who improved the castle with the ransom money of French prisoners he had taken in the Hundred Years War. He also founded the nearby priory of Flanesford to the south, which has recently been converted into holiday cottages. The Talbots were created earls of Shrewsbury in the fifteenth century.

In 1616 the castle passed to the Earl of Kent by marriage. In 1643 it was garrisoned by the Earl of Stamford for parliament, but on his withdrawal to Gloucester the castle passed to the royalists and was garrisoned by a force under Sir Henry Lingen. An attempt at a surprise attack by Colonel Birch only resulted in the burning of the stables. After the surrender of the king in 1646, a more regular investment and the cutting off of supplies eventually forced the castle to surrender. The parliamentary forces then slighted the castle walls.

**Great Witley.** There was a manor at Great Witley since Norman times, but its time of opulence did not start until it was acquired in 1655 by the Foleys. Over the next 183 years the Foleys gradually extended the mansion, created parkland, and built the current renaissance church, much of the internal decoration coming from an auction at Edgware Palace. It became the finest baroque church in England. The village was also resited to its present position. In 1837 gambling losses forced the family to sell, and the estate was acquired by the Dudleys. Their wealth, made in the Industrial Revolution, continued the transformation of the house into a place renowned for its elegance. In turn they were forced to sell in 1920, then the house was gutted by fire in 1937. Now the property is in the care of English Heritage—the church has been restored, the rest of the buildings are being made safe, and with the parkland they still give an impression of the former grandeur.

***Grosmont.*** The name derives from the French for a big hill. The castle was started in Henry II's time as part of a triangle of defences with White and Skenfrith castles, and later became one of Henry, Duke of Lancaster's favourite residences, when they came under his control.

In 1233 Henry III was embroiled in a civil war with Richard Marshall, Earl of Pembroke, and the Welsh. Henry was an appalling general, if brave soldier, and made a tentative push into Wales from his base at Hereford. Having reached Grosmont he stayed in the castle, whilst most of his followers encamped outside. With little or no watch kept, the Welsh seized the advantage and swept those outside the castle walls aside, forcing Henry to retreat back into England at the earliest opportunity.

English revenge only came some 150 years later. In 1405 Glyndwr's lieutenant, Rhys the Terrible, ransacked the town but left the castle. Prince Henry counterattacked the Welsh in the town, defeating them and killing 1,000 before pursuing them to Brecon. The castle is now in the care of the Welsh Office and is open to the public.

***Hanley William.*** Here there is a small church with a Norman chancel and a thirteenth century nave. There is a timber tower, a Norman font and a pulpit carved from a single timber. The church is approached from the side away from the road, and has a quiet rustic feel.

***Hay on Wye.*** The walled town and castle were built in 1150 by Roger, Earl of Hereford and Lord of Brecon, to try to block the 'Royal Progress' of Henry II to Clifford and his Fair Rosamund. The core of the castle was probably built earlier by Philip Walwyn, one of Bernard de Newmarch's knights in his conquest of the area, though he may have built his castle on the earlier site near the church.

It later passed to Earl Milo Fitzwalter of Hereford and Constable of Gloucester who was a supporter of the Empress Maud in her wars with King Stephen. By marriage it later passed to the de Braose family and thus to the Ogre of Abergavenny and his wife Maud. They supported the barons cause in a most ruthless way, and seeking revenge King John attacked and burnt Hay in his last campaign in 1216. Maud, who was credited with superhuman powers, was alone among the Norman aristocracy in accusing King John to his face of murdering his nephew, Prince Arthur. For this she was captured in Ireland where she had fled and starved to death in Corfe Castle.

The castle was destroyed by Llewelyn in 1231, was rebuilt and then besieged by him again in 1263, and in 1265 in the civil war when he was supporting Simon de Montfort. It was once more sacked around 1400, this time by Glyndwr, and the walls were raised. The square tower and gateway of the castle are incorporated in the later Jacobean house in the centre of the town, and is not open to the public.

To the north of the Wye, and just to the north of Offa's Dyke path where it bends away from the river, lie the earthworks which mark the site of a twenty-five acre first century Roman fort. (Offa's Dyke path provides a walk along the north bank of the Wye and is signposted from the bridge.)

When the Brecknock and Abergavenny canal had been built, the canal company called a meeting on 11 June 1793 at which it was proposed a canal should be built from the River Usk to the Wye at Whitney, thus joining the navigable sections of each river. The canal would be used to supply coal to the area, especially to Hay.

The scheme proved too ambitious and instead a plan for a tramroad was proposed in 1810 and largely supported by the original canal company. In 1812 a route was planned which had a rise of 154 feet from Brecon to Hay, whence it went on to Eardisley. The Hay to Brecon portion opened on 7 May 1816 and the Eardisley section on 1 December 1818 crossing by the old toll bridge at Whitney. The guage was 3'6" and the trams carried up to 2 tons. The tramway was sold in 1860 to the Hereford, Hay and Brecon Railway Company.

A couple of miles outside Hay, on the minor road to Hay Bluff, lies Twyn-y-beddau, the mound of the graves. When excavated a vast number of bones were found, and tradition says a great battle was fought here during Edward I's reign—though some say the battle was fought earlier—and the Dulas Brook ran red with blood for three days afterwards.

The town is now noted for its range of second hand bookshops.

**Heath Chapel.** Near Upper Heath to the west of the Brown Clee hill, the chapel stands in a field and is a perfect early Norman building consisting of a nave and chancel without a tower or belfry. The only door has rich Norman carvings on the exterior. It is a chapel of ease and hence has no churchyard.

**Hereford.** There is evidence of a brief period of Roman occupation from around 70 to 100 A.D. before Kenchester was founded a few miles to the west. But by the eighth century there was a town established at Hereford which was fortified by King Offa against the Welsh after the Battle of Hereford in 760.

Hereford was the centre of a bishopric under Offa, suggesting that there might have been an earlier British settlement. Originally the cathedral was of timber and the first stone would have been used after Offa had King Ethelbert's body reburied here. Ethelbert was King of the East Angles and had been murdered by Offa who feared that by marrying his daughter he would gradually acquire his kingdom. To redeem himself Offa built a shrine for Ethelbert and lavished gifts on the cathedral.

In 930 King Athelstan summoned the Welsh princes to a conference at Hereford where the Wye was made the boundary between the English and the Welsh. Hereford became a shire town and the home of one of the royal mints. The shrine of St. Guthlac joined that of St. Ethelbert and the two attracted so many pilgrims that it enabled the cathedral to be rebuilt by Bishop Aethelstan between 1012 and 1056.

Edward the Confessor appointed his nephew Ralph, Count of Vexin, as Earl of Hereford who built the first castle and installed a Norman garrison, but was defeated by the Welsh only two miles outside the city which was then burnt. Harold Godwinson, later King Harold, was sent to restore order which he duly did. He also started the rebuilding of Hereford which he had enclosed by a stone wall containing six gates—Wye Bridge, Eign, Widemarsh, Bye Street, St. Owen's and St. Nicholas.

After the Conquest, Hereford became the centre for an earldom and a base for royal operations aginst the Welsh. In 1067 an attack on the city by a combined Saxon and Welsh army was beaten off; in 1098 it was taken by rebellious marcher lords in a revolt against William II who retook it. During the reign of Stephen, Milo Fitzwalter held the city for Matilda for three years until it was taken by Stephen and the city to the west of the Wye Bridge was destroyed.

Bishop Reinhelm (1107-1115) built the new cathedral; a stone bridge was built around 1100 to replace the wooden one. In 1121 an annual three day fair began, extended to seven days in 1161; tanning, milling, weaving and the wine trade grew in importance. By the end of the eleventh century the cloth industry had grown, the city had a wealthy Jewish community and pressure on land wihin the city walls had become intense—there were already three religious houses founded outside the walls—St. Guthlac's in 1143, the Hospitallers on Widemarsh Street and the Templars in St. Owen's Street.

Roger Fitzwalter, son of Milo, was restored to his possessions by Henry II, but he rebelled and Henry took the castle, from when it remained in royal hands till Charles I disposed of it. King John was a regular visitor using the city as a base in his wars with the barons, as did Henry III, where one of his favourite foreigners, Peter Aquablanca from Savoy, was made bishop. He was particularly hated by the English as a puppet of the pope who used him unscrupulously to raise money for papal needs. Matthew Paris, one of the chroniclers of the times was to record in 1258 that 'The bishop of Hereford, who had by his treachery injured the whole kingdom of England, was, by a visitation of the Lord, deservedly disfigured by a most foul disease, namely morphew.' In 1261 Roger Clifford led many of the local barons in support of de Montfort and captured Hereford and its bishop. After the Battle of Lewes and during the unfolding events which led to Evesham, both Henry and his son Prince Edward were imprisoned in the city. Edward managed to escape whilst out exercising his horse on Widemarsh Common and met up with Roger Mortimer at Wigmore.

The castle, meantime, had been considerably strengthened, as were the city walls. ·Work on the latter had probably continued sometime after the charter of 1189 which required the burgesses to assist with the construction of fortifications. When finally completed the wall was 2,350 yards long, had 17 semi-circular bastions about twenty feet high and remained intact till the end of the eighteenth century.

The market stretched from St. Peters Church to All Saints in the west. To the north of it lay the Jewish quarter with its synagogue. The cathedral churchyard was walled, but evidently had easy access, for in 1389 a licence to enclose it and lock it at night was granted since pigs were digging up the bodies of the dead, unbaptized infants were being secretly buried at night and it was being used as a cattle market.

In 1265 the castle consisted of a Great Tower and numerous halls, chambers, kitchens, courts and stables. The whole was surrounded by a wall and towers and had a vineyard attached. All that remains now is the castle cliff building which was the medieval water gate of the castle and later the governor's lodge. After Edward I's conquest of Wales the castle lost its importance.

The cathedral gained the shrine of Thomas de Cantilupe who died in 1282 and the flow of pligrims to the three shrines continued the prosperity of the city. Thomas de Cantilupe was bishop of Hereford from 1275 till his death in 1282. In 1300 a commission investigated his alleged miracles, which included the curing of bouts of frenzy, the curing of cripples and the raising to life of a drowned child. 17 such miracles were approved, the remaining 204 were not able to be fully looked into in the time commission was allowed. But it was sufficient to recommend canonization.

The town was ravaged by the bubonic plague in 1348 and again in 1361, but the wool trade gradually restored its prosperity, and the city served as a base in the campaign against Glyndwr.

During the Wars of the Roses Hereford saw several of the rival armies pass through and the chief Lancastrian prisoners from the Battle of Mortimer's Cross were executed in the city.

Hereford declared for the royalist faction in the Civil War, but was occupied by a parliamentary force under the Earl of Stamford in October 1642. In December the force moved on to Gloucester; a second parliamentary force occupied the city in April 1643, but only remained a month. From then till 1645 the city was in royalist hands, but the king's Irish troops angered the residents who demanded and partly obtained justice before Prince Rupert attacked one of their meetings and hanged three of its leaders. In 1645 the Scots under Lord Leven besieged Hereford but withdrew in September. In early December Colonel Birch took the city by a ruse. After a forced march from Ledbury in heavy snow, he smuggled an advance force up to the gates in some hay carts, and then rushed the captured gateway with forces hidden behind Aylestone Hill. Soon after the war was over, the castle was sold and was turned into a park.

The city gradually declined despite its orchards, cider and cattle, due to the difficulty of navigating the Wye and the appalling state of the roads. The Wye was partially blocked by weirs which were owned by the king, and the position was improved under the Commonwealth when the Wye was made navigable to Monmouth, and after a local act of parliament was passed in 1727, to Hereford. This saw the start of the city's revival. In 1777 the down traffic included 9,000 tons of corn and meal and 2,000 tons of cider. Coal was brought up. With the coming of the railway the use of the Wye declined and many stretches silted up. The railways brought an increase in population and attendant industrialization. The cattle market was begun in 1856 and together with cider production and light industry is presently one of the main employers in the city.

The interior of the cathedral largely dates from the Norman era with Norman arches in the lower part of the nave and the work in the south transept. Later English work is seen in the choir, the Lady Chapel and chantry chapels and more recent architecture in the upper part of the nave in the rebuilding of the 1790's. The cathedral contains many tombs of bishops, knights and nobles, the shrine of St. Thomas Cantilupe, various painted and carved screens as well as the Mappa Mundi which shows the world as it was perceived in the Middle Ages. There is also a treasury and chained library open to the public.

The city contains several other places of interest. The city museum is housed above the library and contains displays of excavations of some old sites in Herefordshire and on local history. It shares premises with the art gallery which contains work by local artists as well as housing many exhibitions.

There are also the Churchill Gardens Museum at 3 Venns Lane, just off the Worcester road at the top of Aylestone Hill. It contains displays of costumes, glass, porcelain and furniture, as well as work of the Hereford artist Brian Hatton.

The Waterworks Museum is located on Broomy Hill Road a mile to the west of the cathedral and is located in a Victorian pumping station which forms part of the display.

The Bulmer Railway centre lies on the A438 to the west of the city centre and contains the GWR steam locomotive, the King George V. Almost opposite is the Museum of Cider which shows traditional methods of cider making, an additional section showing the history of Bulmers. Much of the museum is in fact to be found in Bulmers' original buildings.

The Old House in High Town, the pedestrianised centre, was built around 1621 and though altered over time has been restored to its seventeenth century condition and contains a hall, kitchen, parlour or sitting room and bedrooms furnished largely with seventeenth century furniture.

All Saints Church at the other end of Broad Street from the cathedral contains a smaller chained library than the cathedral's and which can be seen by appointment. It also contains carved screens, a chest and choir stalls dating from between the fourteenth and eighteenth centuries.

St. Peters Church to the east of High Town has fifteenth century choir stalls and a chancel in the early English style.

St. John's Hospice, Chapel amd Museum lie in Widemarsh Street and can be reached after a short walk from the centre of the city over the ring road. The remains of the former Blackfriars Monastery and the fourteenth century preaching cross can be seen in the gardens outside.

A mile out from the centre of the city, on a roundabout on the road to Brecon, stands the White Cross. It might have been erected in 1349 as a thanksgiving for the ending of the plague, but more likely it marked the temporary position of a market to reduce the chance of infection by the plague. On market days the traders would deposit their goods and withdraw. The town dwellers would then advance and take what goods they wanted and leave money in their stead. The cross is also said to have been erected by Bishop Cantilupe on the spot where he heard a miraculous ringing of the cathedral bells.

*Hoarwithy.* The village's name is derived from the whitebeam which was a tree often used in marking boundaries.

The church was restored in the Italianate style in 1860. It is reached up a flight of steps which leads into an open cloister on two sides of the church and which has mosaic flooring. Inside is more gilt mosaic above the altar and several windows of Italianate stained glass. The restoration was designed by the architect J.P. Seddon, on the commission of the then vicar, William Poole.

*Holt.* The site of the old village lies on the banks of the Severn, and here is the castle, now part of a large house, and the church. The church dates from a few years after the Conquest, the nave containing fine Norman carvings in the doors, windows and chancel arch. A side chapel was added around 1360 and contains a re-sited tomb of a lady, dating from 1280. There is some medieval stained glass, and above the altar some Italian mosaics, purchased and brought to Holt.

*Hope under Dinmore.* Rowland Leinthall led eight lancers and thirty-three archers at Agincourt, where he won a knighthood and much ransom money from French knights captured on the field. With the money he began the building of Hampton Court, which he completed in 1435 when he was granted licence by Henry VI to crenellate the mansion and impark 1,000 acres. It was sold to Sir Humphrey Coningsby around 1510. His descendent Sir Thomas Coningsby founded Hereford Hospital after fighting under the earl of Essex with the protestant Henry IV of France, in his resistance to the Catholic League and the Spanish army in 1591. Sir Thomas Coningsby provided the model for Puntarvolo in *Every Man out of his Humour* by Ben Johnson.

The house is not open to the public, though much of the exterior can be seen to the south of the Gloucester road. Of the original building the fifteenth century gatehouse, chapel and north walling remain.

*Hopton Castle.* The castle was given to Walter Clifford around 1165 by Henry II, and it had an insignificant history until 1644, when it was besieged by the royalists in the Civil War. At the time there was a rule of war that if an indefensible position was held, the garrison were liable to be killed on surrender. The parliamentarian garrison held out for between two and five weeks, and when it succumbed, out of its garrison of 33, 29 were executed. According to some sources it was only the governor who survived to be sent to Ludlow as a prisoner.

There is no direct access to the castle, but it lies close to the junction of minor roads from Bedstone and Hoptonheath from where the square tower and earthworks can be clearly seen. For a walk which includes views of the castle, see walk 4.

*How Caple Gardens.* The village gains its name from the Capel family who gained the manor in the early thirteenth century. It remained with them for many centuries before passing to Sir William Gregory. He won a by-election in Weobley in 1678, was re-elected the following

*Hopton Castle*

year and after the king had refused three times to accept parliament's nomination for speaker, became the compromise candidate. The gardens at How Caple Court were laid out in Edwardian times and are currently undergoing repair and replanting and are now open to the public.

**Huntington.** The castle was built in 1230 during the reign of Henry III by William de Braose, Lord of Brecknock. It was passed down to the de Bohuns who supported the baronial cause and who, together with Llewelyn, took Mortimer's castle of New Radnor. Prince Edward marched to Mortimer's aid and together they took Huntington, Hay and Brecon Castles. It is believed that the eldest son of the then de Bohun earl retook Huntington later that year, before being captured at the Battle of Evesham, where his father fought on the royalist side.

The de Bohuns were foremost in banishing the Despensers, favourites and advisers of Edward II, and the then earl was slain at the Battle of Boroughbridge on 16 March 1321, when Edward temporarily regained control of his kingdom.

The de Bohun line ceased in the 1300's and Richard II used the opportunity to create his eventual usurper Henry Bolingbroke as earl of Hereford. Huntington Castle became his possession until he ascended the throne as Henry IV, when he granted the castle to

Edmund de Stafford, Duke of Buckingham. Buckingham was slain at the Battle of Shrewsbury in 1403 fighting Harry Percy, but the castle was strengthened against Owain Glyndwr. Still, by 1460 the castle was worth nothing, though was probably still habitable as a later Duke of Buckingham sought refuge there when pursued by Richard III. The last duke became a victim of Cardinal Wolsey in 1521.

In 1670 the keep was still standing, but now only part of the keep and one tower remain of an enclosure about 75 yards long by 46 wide. The outer court was probably fenced by a palisade or hawthorn hedge. The remains are slightly overgrown, but can be reached from behind the houses at the crossroads.

In the field to the south of the castle the mounds and hollows, which are the traces of the abandoned medieval borough site, can still be seen.

**Kempley.** The old church lies almost due west of Dymock on a minor road, and contains eleventh or twelfth century frescoes of a Byzantine character in mainly red and blue colours. The chancel ceiling depicts 'Our Lord in majesty' as described in Revelations, whilst on the walls are the twelve apostles together with the figures of Walter and Hugh de Lacy and two bishops. The paintings were rediscovered in 1872 when the then vicar noted colour under the whitewash which had presumably been applied by the puritans. Apart from the paintings the church is plain and simple, with the exception of the Norman archway with its dog tooth pattern between the nave and chancel.

The village moved to a new site where a church was built in 1903. St. Mary's was declared redundant in 1976 and has since passed to the care of English Heritage.

For a walk in the surrounding countryside, see walk 77.

**Kilpeck.** At the time of the Conquest, Kilpeck was given to William Fitz Norman and the castle was probably started soon after. The church though is of Saxon origin and the name Kilpeck derives from the British for St. Pedic's cell. The long and short Saxon building work can be seen in the outside buttress to the north-east corner of the chancel, whilst the present church is largely the work of William's grandson Hugh de Kilpeck. Hugh was succeeded by co-heiresses, the eldest of whom married Robert Waleran, a former sheriff of Gloucestershire and supporter of Henry III against de Montfort. He had no heirs and the castle passed to his nephew, whose son granted much of the associated estates to Dore Abbey.

Not surprisingly the castle was ruinous by the fifteenth century, and it is the church that is the attraction, its carvings having a uniqueness of style. The portal over the south doorway depicts Eden with the temptation of man; a carving of a lion and dragon in a fight; a serpent and hosts of birds and fishes, some with human heads. Thre is a frieze around the outside of the church, and the clarity of the carvings owes much to the quality of the local sandstone.

A path leads off from west of the church over a stile to the castle site which still contains fragments of the keep stonework, and another stile to the north of the church leads to a footpath which crosses a field of rises and hollows covering the old medieval village.

For a walk to the south-west, see walk 71.

**Kingsland.** The village is so called because King Merewald, son of Penda of Mercia, who founded the first church at Leominster around 660, is said to have had his residence here on the castle mound between the church and the rectory. Leland, on his travels in the fifteenth century says: 'There was a castle at Kingsland, the ditches whereof and part of the Keepe be yet seen by the west part of Kingsland Church. Constant fayme sayeth that King Merewald some-times lay at this place.'

The mound and ditch can be seen from the footpath that connects the west of the churchyard to the minor road.

The fourteenth century church was founded by Edmund Mortimer, who died in 1304 as the result of a wound suffered in a skirmish at Builth. In the north porch there is an unusual chamber called the Volka chapel. It has a raised floor at the east end as though for an altar, and in the wall of the church is a recess under which lies a stone hollowed out into the shape of a human figure—possibly for a tomb. The chapel's origin may have been as the cell of a recluse. The chancel has a painted ceiling.

**Kington.** Harold Godwinson took the land and town for himself after quashing a rising by the local inhabitants who had joined in a Welsh raid on Hereford. Thus at the time of the Domesday Survey in 1086 the manor was in royal hands, though still classified as waste due to the warfare.

Henry I granted the manor and honour of Kington to Adam de Port in 1108, a grant which included 23 knights fees scattered as far afield as Dorset, implying an intention to establish a major castle at Kington and probably a borough settlement.

In 1173 Roger de Port rebelled against Henry II and some of his lands were granted to William de Braose, perhaps as compensation for the Welsh occupation of Radnor. The only known reference to the castle is in 1186 when repairs to the palisade are mentioned, so it might just have been a watch tower on the mound near the church. The castle was in any event abandoned around 1230 when Huntington had a new Borough marked out, though the plan was never fulfilled.

Through marriage Humphrey de Bohun controlled both Huntington and Kington in 1246, and by 1267 the settlement seems to have spread down the hill to where the centre of the town now lies.

Kington is one of the few places in this area where the Rebecca toll gate riots of the 1830's occurred. These protests were directed at the tolls payable to use the roads for such commonplace journeys as going to market. The protesters, who had widespread public support, were often men who disguised themselves as women and blackened their faces before attacking, dismantling and sometimes burning the toll gates. The name Rebecca may have been taken from Genesis chapter 24 verse 60: 'The descendent of Rebecca will possess the gates of them that hate them.' It was during this time that the drovers' roads, which bypassed toll gates, came into existence. The small houses of the toll gate keepers can be seen right on the roadside at many places in the area.

The tramroad mentioned in the note on Hay on Wye was extended in 1820 from Eardisley to Kington to serve the quarry at Burlingjobb and an iron foundry in Kington. However the opening of the Leominster to Kington railway in 1857 took most of the traffic.

The church was probably founded in the 1100's, though the earliest surviving part is the tower which was originally detached from the rest of the church, providing a point of refuge for the town's citizens. There is a fine early thirteenth century chancel, and the church contains the tomb of Thomas Vaughan and his wife Ellen. He fought on the Yorkist side in the Wars of the Roses and was killed at the Battle of Banbury in 1469. Ellen was given the name of 'Gethin', meaning the terrible, for when in her teens she attended an archery tournament at which she shot her brother's murderer. Their home was Hergest Court which is reputed to be haunted by a black bloodhound, a tale which formed the basis for Conan Doyle's *Hound of the Baskervilles*.

One of Herefordshire's more notorious folklore tales relates to Thomas Vaughan. Apparently his spirit tormented animals and people alike to such an extent that the trade at Kington Market was affected. The townsfolk arranged for twelve parsons with twelve candles to wait in the church, together with a woman with a new born baby, so as to try to read the spirit down into a silver snuff box. When Vaughan's spirit appeared it overcame all the parsons save one who managed the deed; the snuff box was then buried in the bottom of Hergest Pool and a large stone placed on top.

The three yew trees on Offa's Dyke on Rushock Hill are called the Three Sisters. They were planted in the eighteenth century for three sisters of Knill Court; but they are also known as the three shepherds from a local legend that has them as a memorial to three men who died in a sudden winter snowstorm whilst attending their flocks.

To the west of Kington lies Hergest Ridge across which runs Offa's Dyke path. Near the summit of the ridge is a boulder called the Whetstone which is reputed to go down to drink in the stream below the hill, every morning that it hears a cock crow. One tale tells that a weekly market was on the ridge to avoid an outbreak of disease in the town in the reign of Edward III, during which wheat was sold on the stone, and hence the name 'whet'.

On the lower slopes of Hergest Ridge, lie Hergest Croft gardens, which contain a rhododendron collection that is large in both height and numbers, and an old style kitchen garden. The gardens, open to the public, include the national collection of maples and birches, and are laid out in a mixture of formal, park and woodland settings.

**Kinnersley.** The church tower was erected in the reign of Henry I and it is likely that the first castle was built at the same time. Some of the Duke of Buckingham's children were hidden here during his abortive rebellion against Richard III. The Elizabethan house encompasses the medieval castle which, though until recently an old peoples' home, is now open to the public on selected days.

The church has Victorian decorative paintings in the nave and chancel, a reredos with Jacobean carvings, a pulpit which has some Flemish carvings dating from 1530, and a fine alabaster monument.

**Knighton.** The 'town of the horseman' lies on Offa's Dyke. It was used as a base from which the Saxons could patrol Offa's border.

The area lay deserted for 30 years after the warfare with the Welsh in 1052-1055, after which the Normans might have established a castle on the Bryn-y-Castell site in the east of the present town. The Welsh wars of the twelfth century led to the establishment of further defences, and a castle was established in the town in 1182. The manor was held in succession by Llewelyn, de Erdinton and the Mortimers. The town was burnt in the wars of the 1260's, and Glyndwr attacked and burnt the castle in 1401.

In the north-west corner of the town, adjacent to the Youth Hostel, is the Offa's Dyke Heritage Centre which contains local information.

***Knucklas.*** Knucklas may have been the Caer Godyrfan from whence came Guinevere, the wife of King Arthur.

The Mortimers tried to resettle a borough from Knighton at Knucklas, but nothing of the attempt remains. The castle was built in 1242 by the Mortimers, to be taken by Llewelyn in 1262 and in 1402 by Glyndwr. At the foot of the castle hill is a piece of land called the 'bloody field', where the Battle of Beguildy was fought between the Mortimers and the Welsh in 1146.

A path leads up to the castle mound from the metalled lane which follows the railway line on its north-west side. The path leaves the lane where the latter makes a turn to the right away from the railway, and if you can fight your way through the first forty yards, you should be able to make it to the top.

The village also contains a Victorian railway viaduct with crenellations and gothic towers at each end.

*Ledbury.* The earliest known settlement was above where the town now stands at Wall Hills camp, a site covering thirty-six acres. Ledbury itself was built around the church founded in 720 as a mission centre for the area. This early church was rebuilt in the 1100's, a building itself largely rebuilt between 1230 and 1350. The wedge shaped market area was added at right angles to the old market in Church Lane by Richard de Capella, bishop of Hereford, in the 1120's. The town gained its first charter in 1138 which unusually granted a Sunday market, much to the annoyance of many of the clergy. Then in 1232 Bishop Hugh Foliot decided to match the generosity of his canons who had founded a hospital in Hereford, and founded St. Katherines in Ledbury. This hospital was built to provide for the spiritual and material needs of the poor, aged, sick and distressed, as well as for the needs of travellers and pilgrims. Hospitals, often staffed by monks, tended to follow the monastic-corporate way of life, and the layout at St. Katherines reflected this, with a great hall containing beds along the north and south walls and a chapel at one end. The farm and service buildings adjoined the site. The almshouses were rebuilt in the nineteenth century by the architect of Eastnor Castle, Samuel Smirke.

Controversy rages over which St. Katherine is commemorated. From the dates given in the town's charter it is likely that it is St. Katherine of Alexandria, rather than her namesake, the local St. Katherine of Audley. Katherine of Audley, who in fact was never canonised, was a cousin of Edward II who had been told she would only find a resting place where the church bells would ring of their own accord. When she arrived in Ledbury she found the bells ringing, but the belfry locked, and settled in the town in 1313. In the church, what is now referred to as St. Katherine's Chapel was designed as a chapter house as part of a larger plan to make Ledbury a collegiate church, a plan which was never fully realised. Nevertheless the chapel windows include some of the best examples of ballflower work, a form of ornamentation in which Herefordshire is particularly rich.

The market house, begun in 1617, is supported on sixteen chestnut supports taken from Malvern Chase, and was modelled on that in Hereford. Around it occurred a skirmish in 1644 between roundheads under the command of Colonel Massey who were billeted in the town, and forces under Prince Rupert. As soon as Rupert heard that Massey was in the town, he sent troops to cut off any retreat to his home base of Gloucester, and forces to break down the barricades erected across the Homend. As soon as these were cleared Rupert led his cavalry against the parliamentarian horse gathered at the market hall. During this encounter both Rupert and Massey are said to have had horses killed under them, but the eventual result was in Rupert's favour. Displayed in the church are some bullets taken from the west door, together with a sword which belonged to the parliamentarian Major Backhouse who was mortally wounded in the fight.

Ledbury saw some of the worst Toll gate riots in the area during the agricultural depression in the mid 1730's and early 40's.

Ledbury is also the birthplace of John Masefield, Poet Laureate from 1930 till his death in 1967, who based many of his rural works on remembrances on the Ledbury and its countryside of his youth.

The well known Church Lane, which runs from the market hall to the church, also includes a Heritage Centre in the Old Grammar School (itself previously a guildhall for local wool merchants) and a museum in the restored and re-sited Butcher Row House.

*Leintwardine.* Watling Street passes to the east of the town, and the Romans built two camps here, one around Watling Street and one where the town now stands. The banks of the latter camp still stand at various points around the village.

The church has a medieval defensive tower and contains a memorial to General Sir Banastre Tarleton off the Lady Chapel. He was a cavalry officer in the American Wars of Independence, who returned to live in Leintwardine.

*Leominster.* The town derives its name from Leofric's Minster, a nunnery founded by the Saxon earl, Leofric of Mercia who died in 1033 and who was married to the famous Lady Godiva. It was the earlier Merewald, son of Penda of Mercia, who founded the original church and who is also reputed to have built a castle one mile to the east.

In 760 the Welsh ravaged the town and two centuries later the Danes massacred all its inhabitants. The town was also caught in the rivalry of earls Leofric and Sweyn Godwin, and later still in 1210 it was burnt by the marcher lord, William de Braose.

King John visited the town on his journeys along the marches, and on one visit permitted the monks not to have their dogs expeditated —whereby the ball of the front foot was cut out so that the dogs could not then hunt the royal deer.

Henry I attached the priory to the Benedictine abbey at Reading and at this time the priory was supposedly a holder of many christian relics. The chancellor of the diocese of Hereford drew up a list of bones and fragments which the priory contained, including:

'Twoo peces off the Holye Crosse.
A bone off Marye Magdalene, with other more.
A bone off Saynt Davyde's arme.
A bone off Saynt Edward the Martyr's arme.
A bone off Saynt Stephen, with other more.
A chawbone of Saynt Ethelmond.
Bones of Saynt Margarett.
Bones of Saynt Arval.
A bone of Saynt Andrewe and twoo peces off his crosse.

There be a multitude of small bonys, etc, wyche wolde occupie iiii schetes of paper to make particularly an inventorye of any part thereof.'

There was also a 'Holy Maid' at the priory who was said to live on Angels' food and who was kept in a room within the choir of the priory. When the prior said mass, a portion of the host detached itself, as if by a miracle, and flew to her mouth from the altar. However some influential sceptics opened up the room and the 'maid' then confessed and explained the 'miracle' —the host in fact flying to her room by being attached to a long hair which she pulled in. The room was also found to contain a secret door whereby, as the resulting report stated: 'the Prior might resort to her and she to him at their pleasure.'

Owain Glyndwr met a royalist army outside the town after the latter's victory at Shrewsbury over the Percies, and retreated without a fight.

After the death of Edward VI the local protestants supporting Lady Jane Grey's claim to the throne camped on Cursneh Hill overlooking the town. However the town's catholics slew them earning many grants and favours from Queen Mary, but also giving the town the epithet of 'Bloody Lemster.'

*Almshouse figure, West Street,*
*Leominster*

103

Leominster's trade was based on its wool market, and the merchants of both Hereford and Worcester clubbed together to have the market days so re-arranged that the trade flowed their way. The town's later prosperity has depended upon short lived industries and more recently the industrial estates.

The large church which was gutted by fire in 1699 and largely rebuilt, contains a ducking stool, the last recorded use of which was in 1809 when one Jenny Pipes was taken round the town in it and then ducked in the river by an order of the magistrates. A similar event was ordered in 1817, but the ducking didn't take place as the water level was too low. The punishment was usually given to all shopkeepers and traders who gave short measure or sold adulterated food. Records show it was frequently used in the fifteenth and sixteenth centuries.

The most notable building in the town after the church is that of the Butter Market, built by Charles I's carpenter, John Abel, in 1634. In 1853 the local corporation decided that it stood in the way of redevelopment and put it up for auction, selling it for £95. A Mr. Arkwright bought it for the same sum from the purchaser and offered it back to the corporation if they could find a site for it—but they refused the offer. Mr. Arkwright then rebuilt it just outside the town, and it still stands on that site, which is now in the town, near the playing fields by the church and is used a council office. The town also contains a local museum in Etnam Street.

The Leominster canal was planned to link Leominster with the Severn via a coal quarry at Marlbrook. The Marlbrook to Woofferton section was completed in 1796 after the route had been altered due to a tunnel collapsing. It was never joined to the Severn as proposed as the railways superseded the canals at this time. Part of the Leominster to Mamble canal can still be seen to the west of Berrington Hall, near Orleton, where there is the end of a tunnel, and at Little Hereford where there is an aqueduct which carried the canal over the Teme.

**Lingen.** The name derives from the Celtic for a brook with clear water. After the Norman Conquest the town was held by Turstin from the Mortimers, from whom it eventually passed to the Lingen family, one of whom was a royalist commander in the Civil War.

The castle itself is a motte and bailey which lies behind the church and is reached by a stile from the rear of the churchyard. The motte is 22 feet high and 63 feet in diameter.

One mile south-east of the church on the western edge of Limebrook Wood, and approached by a minor road that turns to the east about a mile to the south of Lingen, are the remains of Limebrook Priory, a nunnery founded around the time of Richard I's reign. An ivy clad section of wall lies adjacent to the road, behind which lie some grass covered mounds. Some of the priory's old wooden beams have been used in the construction of the nearby houses and cottages.

**Little Malvern.** Around 1171 two brothers Joceline and Edred became hermits and founded a small Benedictine priory here for themselves and a few other monks who had separated from the priory at Worcester, but to which it became subordinate. The priory was dedicated to St. Giles, owned some land in Ireland and seems to have had a history of slack monastic rule. In the 1400's Bishop Alcock of Worcester referred to the priory as being under the 'myslyvyng and dissolute governance of the bretheryn ... byn vagabonde and lyved lyck laymen, to the pernicious example of all Cristen men.' In 1480 the monks were sent to Gloucester for reinstruction, the priory was rebuilt and a new prior greeted the returning monks. It continued in existence till the dissolution of the small monasteries in 1538 when it had a prior and six monks.

During the life of this priory, a young monk who had taken a vow of chastity, fell deeply in love. As a punishment he had to crawl on his hands and knees once a day from the bottom to the top of Ragged Stone Hill behind the priory. He managed it for a while, but his willpower cracked late one day and he cursed the hill and all those on whom its shadow should fall. Occasionally a cloud collects over the hill which, it is said, can take on the black towering shape of a monk in his habit, and which casts a far longer shadow than the hill itself.

The remains of the priory, consisting of the area under the tower and the choir of the original building, is open to the public. Because of the building's abbreviated proportions, it has a lofty aspiring atmosphere, encouraged by the tall east window and its glass. The court to the west of the priory was originally a medieval house forming part of the monastic buildings. Part is open to the public on selected days.

**Llanbadarn-y-Garreg.** The church is of a primitive style, being built in the thirteenth or fourteenth centuries. It has an old font and a rood beam and fifteenth century screen with a faded painting.

**Llandeilo Graban.** There are wide views towards the Brecon Beacons from the south-west corner of the churchyard.

There is a tale told that the last dragon slaying in Radnorshire took place here. The dragon was in the habit of sleeping on the top of the church tower by night. A ploughboy made a dummy out of a log of oak, armed it with numerous sharp and barbed hooks, dressed it in eye catching red and fixed it on top of the tower. The dragon duly saw it and moved in to attack, hitting it with his tail. Infuriated by the resulting pain he savaged the dummy with his teeth, claws and wings as well, eventually winding himself around it and bleeding to death.

*Llandrindod Wells.* Use of the spa waters was made by the Romans, who called the settlement Balnae Silures. Perhaps it was due to the healthy waters that they founded a practice camp on Llandrindod Common.

It was a well known spa in the seventeenth century, but was then neglected to 1736 when a Mrs. Jenkins is supposed to have 'rediscovered' the saline spring and sulphur well. In 1746 *A Journey to Llandrindod Wells in Radnorshire* was published which eulogised the spa, and this was followed by an article in the Gentleman's Magazine in 1748. Its popularity revived, a large new hotel was built and a racecourse laid out. Dr. Linden from Germany published work in 1754 which further boosted the town's fortunes, but then the gamblers and malcontents moved in. The spa fell into disfavour, and one hotelier even knocked down his hotel to discouarge people from visiting.

Then in 1817 Dr. Williams from Aberystwyth published another favourable article, and the town was once more on the up. It was still a very small town: the population in 1801 was just 192; by 1858 it had risen to around 250, of whom 34 were visitors, and to 350 in 1871. But the coming of the railways in 1866 allowed it to blossom. By the end of the century the spa had 90,000 visitors annually and the necessary accommodation, ballrooms and other amenities required to provide for this great influx, explain the very English Victorian look of this town in central Wales. Unlike other spa towns, it managed to cater for many tastes and has held on to this in the twentieth century, providing a base for those wanting quiet or time to explore central Wales.

*Llanelieu.* Outside the chuch porch are two incised stones, one dating from the sixth century and the other from the fifteenth. Inside the church are a double rood screen of primitive style, a painted rood loft and a wall painting of a lion.

*Llanfilo.* The church has a pre-Norman font, and an intricately carved rood screen which has vine leaves and grapes over six quadrilateral pillars with decorative heads and bosses, with five seated figures of apostles between them and the Virgin Mary in the centre. The figures above are more recent, being carved in 1925.

*Llangorse Lake (or Savaddan).* The lake lies between the Black Mountains and the Brecon Beacons, and there's a tradition that the Roman city of Laventium lies submerged beneath it—its houses being seen beneath the waters well into the thirteenth century. In his record of his tour with Archbishop Baldwin in 1188, Gerald of Wales relates: 'The local inhabitants will assure you that the lake has many miraculous properties ... it sometimes turns bright green, and in our days has been known to become scarlet, not all over, but as if blood were flowing along certain currents and eddies. What is more (it can be) completely covered with buildings, or rich pasture lands, or adorned with gardens and orchards.'

Gerald also tells the following tale: 'In the reign of Henry I, Gruffyth, son of Rhys ap Tudor, on his return from the King's court passed the lake. Earl Milo wishing to draw forth from Gruffyth some discourse concerning his innate nobility, addressed him: "It is an ancient saying in Wales that if the natural prince of the country, coming to this lake, shall order the birds to sing they will immediately obey him." Earl Milo needless to say failed in his attempt, then Gruffyth falling on his knees towards the east, as if he had been about to engage in battle, with his hands uplifted to heaven he thus openly spake: "Almighty God, who knowest all things, declare here this day Thy Power. If you have caused me to descend lineally from the natural Prince of Wales, I command these birds in thy name to do it," and immediately the birds, beating the waters with their wings, began to cry and proclaim him. When Earl Milo reported this to Henry, the latter said: "It is not a matter of so much wonder, for although by our authority we commit acts of violence and wrong against these people, yet they are known to be the rightful inheritors of this land."'

*Llanthony.* On a raid against the Welsh, William de Lacy of Longtown Castle was struck by the splendour of the valley containing the remains of a chapel dedicated to Saint David at Llandewi nant Honddu, and decided to settle as a hermit in the valley. He was joined in 1103 by the chaplain to Henry I and they rebuilt the chapel.

Hugh de Lacy provided the funds for the two to found a monastery for 40 Augustinian canons under the patronage of the Empress Matilda. During the Welsh rising of 1135 the monks fled to Hereford whose bishop, Robert de Bethune, was a past prior of the foundation. He obtained the grant of new lands at Gloucester, where Llanthony Secunda was established. Gradually the monks neglected Llanthony Prima, until restoration of Norman control brought new grants of land between 1180 and 1200, after which a rebuilding took place. The present remains date largely from this time. After 1399 the monastery declined and it soon became subordinate to Llanthony Secunda.

Gerald of Wales writes in 1188 about the setting of the priory, its founders and its priors: 'As (they) sit in their cloisters in this monastery, breathing the fresh air the monks gaze up at distant prospects which rise above their lofty roof-tops, and they see, as far as any eye can reach, mountain peaks which rise to meet the sky and often enough, herds of wild deer which are grazing on their summits. This was formerly a happy, a delightful spot, most suited to the life of contemplation, a place from its first founding fruitful and to itself sufficient. Once it was free, but it has since been reduced to servitude ... uncontrolled ambition, the ever growing vice of ingratitude, the negligence of its prelates and its patrons and, far worse than all of these, the fact that the daughter house, become a step-daughter, has odiously and enviously supplanted its own mother.'

Later: 'In my opinion it is a fact worthy of remark that all priors who did harm to the establishment were punished by God when their moment came to die. Clement ... made no attempt to reprove the brothers or to restrain them whem they plundered the house and committed other outrages. In the end he died from a paralytic stroke. Prior Roger did even more damage than his predecessors. He stripped the church of all its books, ornaments and charters. Long before his death he became paralysed. ... All the things and creatures ... are there in great abundance, and yet we are so insatiable in our wicked desires that each in turn seems insufficient for our needs. We occupy each other's territory, we move boundary fences, we invade each others plots of land.'

The priory ruins were bought in 1807 by Walter Savage Landor, the poet and author, together with the surrounding estate, and he planted the bare slopes with trees and planned to build a mansion. Only a ruined stable block on the hill overlooking the site remains.

Apart from the central portion of priory ruins, in part of which there is an inn open in the summer months, there are the remains of the gatehouse which lie to the west on the road that leads north through the valley.

For a walk from the priory up onto the hills see walk 68.

*Llanveynoe.* The name is a corruption of Llan Beino or Church of Beuno, a Celtic saint who, amongst other miracles, is credited with the raising of six people to life.

The small church is situated on a hilltop immediately opposite the eastern face of the Black Mountains, and has two early sculptures inserted in the south wall. One is a panel of a crucifix over four feet high and is believed to be Hiberno-Saxon, with tenth century lettering. The other may be a pagan stone christianized, or vice versa. Both were found outside the present churchyard, in which there is a monolithic standing cross which dates from between the tenth and twelfth centuries.

*Llanwarne.* The name means church by the swamp or alders, and the old church dates from the thirteenth century and fell into disuse and eventual ruin when the new church was built. The churchyard cross is probably fourteenth century and the lychgate fifteenth. The walls are virtually intact but roofless, giving the whole church, not surprisingly, a different atmosphere from most.

*Llowes.* The church was founded in the sixth century by St. Meilig, who is believed to be buried on the site. The church itself was rebuilt in 1853, and an unusual stone cross which once stood in the churchyard was later moved into the church. The stone is called the Moll Waulbee Stone, after a giantess called Moll who supposedly built Hay Castle in a single night. Either, so the story relates, the stone fell from her apron as she passed en route to Hay, or else she felt it in her shoe and angrily hurled it across the border whilst building the castle. The character of Moll is believed to be

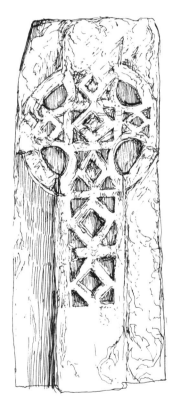

*Cross, Llowes*

109

based on Maud de St. Valery, the formidable wife of William de Braose. The carvings on the stone date from the sixth or seventh century on one face and from the eleventh century on the other.

For a walk which starts from the church, see walk 60.

**Longtown.** After the Norman Conquest it was granted to the de Lacys. Gilbert de Lacy took King Stephen's side in the wars with the Empress Maud, but grew tired of the fighting and joined the Knights Templar. His brother Hugh de Lacy accompanied Henry II to Ireland and for his services received the lands of Meath and the custody of Dublin. When he married a daughter of the Prince of Connaught Henry became suspicious that he was founding an independent kingdom. His estates were confiscated, so his son rebelled in Ireland, a rebellion that was later put down by King John. Subsequent payment of a large fine by the family reconciled them to John, whom they later supported against the majority of the barons.

The de Lacy's castle appears to have had only one major military encounter, when it was surrendered to Prince Howell of North Wales in 1146 after a siege by the joint forces of Cadell, Meredydd and Rhys who built a great battering engine. However it was fortified against Owain Glyndwr some two and a half centuries later.

The remains are now in the care of English Heritage and include what is perhaps the earliest round keep in England, raised on an artificial mound, together with an inner and outer bailey, some of the stonework of which still remains.

For a walk onto the Black Mountains which starts from the castle, see walk 67.

**Ludlow.** Roger de Lacy bought the lordship of Ludlow and built a castle between 1086 and 1096, before joining in the rebellion of Robert, Duke of Normandy, against William Rufus. On Robert's defeat he was exiled and William Rufus passed on the estates to his brother Hugh. Hugh died childless and the castle passed back to the crown to be granted to one Fitz John who was later slain in a skirmish with the Welsh.

King Stephen then placed one of his favourites, Joyce de Dinan in the castle. He strengthened it but only to lose control to a baronial rebel Gervase Pagonel. Stephen unsuccessfully besieged the castle in 1139, though later he managed to regain it and handed it back to de Dinan. Distant heirs of the de Lacys then claimed the castle and the fortunes of the two parties alternated, the de Lacy faction were at one time routed outside the castle gates, whilst at another they captured the castle by a ruse only to have it taken back by the king. After several changes of hands between the de Lacys and Dinans the castle eventually passed by marriage to the Mortimers, and hence to the Duke of York prior to the Wars of the Roses.

During the early stages of these wars, in 1459, an army led by the Duke of York, with the earls of Shrewsbury and Warwick, retreated to Ludford Bridge in the face of a superior force led by Henry VI. Their only hope of victory lay in a surprise attack at dawn, but their ablest troops, the battle hardened garrison of Calais, defected overnight to the royalist cause under their adventurer commander Andrew Trollope. The Yorkist nobles then fled, some to Dublin with the Duke of York, and some to Calais with the Earl of Warwick from where and under whom they continued the Yorkist cause. The morning after the flight Henry took the town and castle and many of the town's leading citizens were killed.

Henry VII established the Council of the Marches of Wales at Ludlow and this remained in existence till 1669, with the exception of the period of the Commonwealth. The castle became the official residence of the Lord President of the Marches, and the castle was improved with the addition of lodgings, halls, chambers, record room and courthouse.

The castle's last siege occurred in June 1646 when parliamentarian cannon from Whitecliff Common over the Teme battered the castle into surrender. Due to the state of the castle in 1772 demolition was considered, but it was leased and later bought by the Earl of Powis who carried out some essential repairs. It is now open to the public.

The town itself was planned on a rectalinear layout by the Normans. Town walls were built in 1233, leaving much of the built up area outside them. Ludlow's early wealth was dependent upon the wool trade—dealing in wool itself and also in cloth made by local spinners and weavers. The wool trade declined in the early 1600's and with the ending of the Council of Wales and the removal of government officials, the town's prosperity declined. Glove manufacture in the late 1700's and early 1800's brought some respite; now tourism, the local industrial estates and the market provide local employment and wealth.

The parish church of St. Lawrence resembles a small cathedral, having been constantly enlarged and restored throughout its life. The church is well known for its carvings in the choir—especially the misericords, the stained glass and the various monuments.

The town is full of old and interesting buildings, from Broad Gate in the town walls, to the range of timber framed buildings of which the Feathers Hotel in the Bull Ring is one of the finest to be found anywhere. There is also a local museum and the Readers House.

**Luntley.** Near the junction of roads from Pembridge, Dilwyn and Broxwood stands a recently restored timber framed dovecote built in 1673, a date cut into the moulded frame above the door lintel. On the other side of the road stands the private residence of Luntley Court, also undergoing restoration.

**Lydbury North.** The church has a mainly Norman nave and tower, wall paintings dating from 1616 of the Creed, Lords Prayer and Ten Commandments; and Jacobean pews from around the same time.

Off to one side is the Plowden Chapel, which was founded by Roger Plowden who was taken prisoner at Acre in 1191 when serving as a crusader under Richard I. He vowed that should he ever escape he would build the chapel as a thanksgiving. Above the chapel on the other side of the church is a room which was used as the local school till the mid-nineteenth century.

**Lyonshall.** Originally called Lenehalle, the Hall of the Hundred of Lene, it belonged to Earl Harold prior to the Norman Conquest, after which it was granted to Roger de Lacy. It was later passed to Sir Simon Burley, tutor to Richard II. Burley was appointed tutor by Richard's father, Edward The Black Prince, and gave the young prince a thorough education spiced with the firm belief in royal, but benevolent central rule. This brought him into conflict with the selfish group of barons called the Appellants who later sought and obtained Burley's execution. The castle passed to the Devereux family who were ordered to put it into a state of defence against Owain Glyndwr, but by the end of the fifteenth century the castle was in disuse. The ruins lie behind the parish church.

The village once lay around the church and castle, but over time and with more peaceful conditions, its centre has shifted to the valley floor to the south.

**Madley.** Meaning good place, the village has a large village church which was built of local sandstone in the thirteenth and fourteenth centuries, since when it has remained largely unaltered. The crypt is believed to be the last constructed in medieval England, and made use of the natural dip in the ground so as to avoid unecessary excavation. Its roof is supported by a single octagonal column.

Additionally there is one of the largest Norman fonts in Britain; the remains of some thirteenth century stained glass; various monuments; a piece of Portuguese or Spanish carving behind the altar in the Chilstone Chapel, and a fifteenth century box pew made from the old rood loft.

Madley is supposed to have been the birthplace of St. Dubricius or Dyfrig who is said to have crowned King Arthur. In his own right Dyfrig founded a religious school at Hentland near Ross as well as a chapel at Moccas.

***Maesyronen Chapel.*** Signposted left off the Glasbury to Clyro main road, the chapel lies about half a mile up the lane at the end of a short track on the right. It is an early example of a nonconformist chapel and retains much of its original oak furniture.

***Malvern.*** The earliest settlers were the British tribes of the midlands who built the hillforts on the Malverns. These were commenced between 500 and 400 B.C. and would each have been home to several hundred people at the time of the Roman Invasion. As with other forts, they were attacked and burnt by the Romans, survivors being forcibly resettled in the valleys. The Anglo-Romans would then have held the area until the Saxons overwhelmed them around 500 A.D.

By 1016 the land was held by Alfgar and his son Brithric. Brithric was sent by Edward the Confessor as ambassador to the court of Baldwin V, Count of Flanders, where he attracted the attentions of Baldwin's daughter, Matilda. However Brithric ignored her advances and returned to England unmarried at the end of his term of duty. Duke William of Normandy then sought Matilda's love, and eventually the two were married. On William's invasion of England, Matilda determined to have what she saw as her revenge on Brithric, and had him seized at Hanley and imprisoned in Worcester, where he died.

Hanley was then the main settlement of the area, and King John's reign saw the construction of a castle at Hanley, from where the royal hunting grounds on the chase were managed.

Malvern Priory was founded by two monks called Aldwin and Guy who had requested permission to go on a pilgrimage to the Holy Land, but St. Wulstan, their mentor and bishop of Hereford, persuaded them that they would serve christianity to better effect by founding a Benedictine settlement at Malvern. It had a complement of some 30 monks and come the Dissolution, Bishop Latimer tried to save it due to its reputation as a centre of teaching and hospitality. But in the end it was sold to the townspeople for £30 to become their place of worship.

Malvern was not to really expand until it was adopted by the Victorians as a spa town. The initial impetus came from Dr. John Wall, a man involved in many local activities including the Worcester porcelain factory, who claimed curative powers for the water in the 1750's. However it was nearly a hundred years later when doctors James Wilson and James Gully moved to Malvern and started to really promote the town, its water and surroundings as a spa. Events then moved quickly and baths, treatments and boarding houses clustered around the hillside. But quacks were to follow hard on their heels and soon the Lancet and other reputable magazines were scorning the treatments offered at Malvern and the other spas. The hotels became schools; quarriers moved in on the hills.

In 1884 the Malvern Hills Conservators were formed to protect the hills, and by judicious use of compulsory purchase powers they soon restricted the quarrying. In addition they created paths and provided refreshment places. Two wells are still open to the public—St. Anne's Well a short walk above the town where the water emerges via a marble dolphin's head in the pump room; and the Holy Well in Malvern Wells.

**Marden.** Anciently the settlement was called Maurdin and was home to a palace of the Mercian king. When Ethelbert, King of the East Angles, was murdered by Offa of Mercia, his body was entombed here before being moved to a specially constructed shrine at Hereford Cathedral. The well in the church is known as St. Ethelbert's well.

To the north-west of the village is a four arch bridge over the River Lugg built in the sixteenth or seventeenth century.

**Martley.** The church contains wall paintings, some of red flowers as in other churches in the area. There is aslo an alabaster tomb of Hugh Mortimer, who was killed fighting for the Mortimer and Yorkist cause at the Battle of Wakefield in 1459.

**Moccas.** The Domesday Survey describes the land in the parish of Moccas as divided between St. Guthlac's Priory in Hereford and Nigel the Physician. But by the end of of the thirteenth century it had passed via the crown to the de Frene family. In 1294 Hugh de Frene obtained a licence from Edward I to fortify his manor house and 'to strengthen it with a stone wall without tower or turret and not exceeding 10 feet in height below the battlements.' However he did exceed these limits and had to pay a fine.

The castle site lies in a meadow to the east of the park, and the present house was designed by the Adams brothers. The chapel, which lies off the minor road to Preston-on-Wye, is open to the public.

Much of the land is a deer park with old oak trees. Kilvert tells of a visit on 22 April 1876: 'I fear those old grey men of Moccas, those grey, gnarled, low-browed, knock-kneed, bowed, bent, huge, strange, long-armed, deformed, hunchbacked misshapen oak men that stand waiting and watching century after century biding God's time with both feet in the grave and yet tiring down and seeing out generation after generation, with such tales to tell, as when they whisper them to each other in the midsummer nights, make the silver birches weep and the poplars and aspens shiver and the long ears of the hares and rabbits stand on end. ...They look as if they had been at the beginning and making of the world, and they will probably see its end.'

**Monkland.** Monk's Llan formed the endowment of a Benedictine cell of the Abbey of Conches in Normandy. It was suppressed along with other alien priories in 1415 by Henry V, and was granted to Sir Rowland Leinthall, one of Henry's band at Agincourt.

**Mordiford.** The village is best known for its dragon. Until 1811 the church had a large green dragon painted on its west end. Though this probably represented the Wyvern on the arms of the priory of St. Guthlac which held the living of Mordiford, it served as a reminder of the tale of the dragon which used to devour animals and humans in the neighbourhood. Nobody was willing to attempt to kill it, until a condemned criminal hid in a barrel at the dragon's favourite drinking spot. The barrel, as with many such stories, was barbed with knives and pike blades so that when the dragon realised there was a meal inside and attacked the barrel, it severely wounded itself. In the ensuing struggle both man and beast were killed.

The bridge dates from 1352, of which the main western arch is probably a remnant, but the bridge was much repaired in the fifteenth and sixteenth centuries.

**Mortimer's Cross.** The Battle of Mortimer's Cross was fought on Candlemas Eve in 1461, when the Yorkists under Edward Duke of

York, heir to the Mortimers, faced a Lancastrian army of Irish, Welsh and perhaps Breton levies under Jasper Tudor. On the morning of the battle, the severe cold weather gave rise to the appearance of a parhelion or three suns. Edward quickly turned this to his advantage and cited it as a good omen. The Lancastrian forces who had advanced up the Lugg valley from the south were showered with arrows from the woods on the ridge to their left and were routed, with fugitives being pursued to Kingsland, Eardisland and Shobdon. Edward then marched to Hereford where all his prisoners of rank were executed, and then on to London to claim the throne as Edward IV.

A monument commemorates the battle about a mile to the south in front of the Monument inn. It was probably here that the Lancastrians made their last stand, but the inscription gives the wrong date by one year, due to a later re-alignment of calendars.

Just off the Ludlow road at the crossroads lies an early watermill open to the public.

***Much Marcle.*** The church dates mainly from the thirteenth century and contains several carved effigies, of which two are of greatest interest. One is called the Grandison Tomb and is to Blanche Mortimer, wife of Sir Peter Grandison, and who died in 1347. The tomb has a canopy and contains panels with the arms of Mortimer and an effigy of Blanche. In the nave is a wooden effigy, a rarity in itself, of a man in civilian costume of the mid-fourteenth century and which represents Walter de Heylon, a landowner who probably lived at the nearby Hellens. There is also a late fourteenth century tomb, and the mid-seventeenth century tomb in black and white marble of Sir John Kyrle and his wife. The churchyard contains a yew with a girth of 30 feet and which is probably 1,000 years old. Its trunk is split open and contains a seat for seven people.

About fifty yards north-east of the church lies the motte and bailey known as Mortimers Castle, which was granted to Edmund de Mortimer by Edward I. The ruins of the castle were used to build the church tower, but the 20 foot high motte and some of the outer enclosure can still be seen.

Hellens is a Jacobean house dating from 1292, which was reconstructed in the seventeenth century. It contains fine paintings, panelling and an oak spiral stairway. The octagonal dovecote dates from 1641. In private hands, the house is open to the public and is reached down a drive on the other side of the B road from the church.

Walk 76 includes both Hellens and the church.

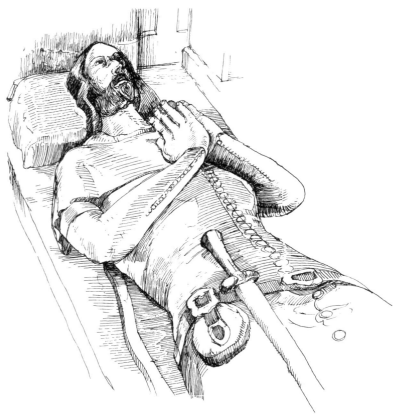

*Wooden effigy, Much Marcle Church*

**New Radnor.** Harold Godwinson is often reputed to have founded the town and castle in 1064 as a stronghold to defend the route from central Wales into England. He certainly advanced as far as this in his pursuit of the Welsh after their sacking of Hereford, but it is not definitely known that he founded the town.

After the Conquest the territory was in the possession of Philip de Breos, who almost certainly built a castle, laid out the gridiron street pattern for the borough and constructed the earthen town bank around the settlement.

The castle remained with the de Breos family until around 1240 when it passed by marriage to the Mortimers, but before then it had been captured five times—in 1163 and 1195 by Rhys ap Gruffyd, when

117

he also defeated a relieving army led by Mortimer and de Saye; in 1213 by Llewelyn; in 1216 by King John and in 1231 by Llewelyn again. It is also quite possible that Henry III recaptured it during his stay at Painscastle. Certainly Henry's brother, Richard Earl of Cornwall and King of the Romans, repaired it in 1231 and the Mortimers subsequently rebuilt it. However in 1264 it was once again taken by the Welsh when allied to Simon de Montfort. These Welsh advances were lost when Edward I invaded Wales.

In 1401 it once more passed into Welsh hands, this time those of Glyndwr who beheaded the garrison of sixty. By 1405 Henry IV had retaken possession and he installed a force of thirty men at arms and 150 archers under Richard, Lord de Grey. Almost 250 years later the town was held for Charles I, but was captured after a short siege.

A part of the curtain wall was still standing around 1850, and various excavations have unearthed cannon balls, cannon, floors, foundations and a well, but now only the substantial earthworks can be seen, dominating the town. They can be reached through a gate leading off the churchyard. The remains of the earthen town walls may be seen to the west and south of the town.

At the southern end of the main street stands a white marble profile, in Victorian Gothic, of Sir George Cornewall Lewis, New Radnor's M.P. from 1855 to 1863 who was Chancellor of the Exchequer, Home Secretary and War Minister in different administrations under Palmerston.

**Old Radnor.** A church has probably existed on or near the site from Saxon times, but the present church dates from the fifteenth and sixteenth centuries. The roof is of heavily carved timber and contains bosses and shields that used to bear the arms of the local lords.

The font is one of the oldest in the country, probably being hollowed out from an erratic, a boulder transported down the valley below by a glacier. It could have been used as a sacred stone in prechristian times and converted for use in the new religion as needs demanded.

There's a sixteenth century rood screen and what is probably the oldest Tudor organ case in existence, whilst in the north chapel are eighteenth century pictures of Moses and Aaron.

**Painscastle.** The old name was Caer yn Elfael and the settlement had a castle from at least the post Roman era. The present name derives from Pain Fitz John who built a castle in the reign of Henry I. Walter

Map records that Pain was Henry's chamberlain. Every night Henry took a goblet of wine to bed with him in case he was thirsty during the night. Pain came to see that Henry in fact never touched this, and took to drinking it himself. Then the inevitable happened, one night Henry awoke thirsty and discovered the goblet empty. Pain was forced to confess what had happened, to which Henry replied that one measure was certainly not sufficient for the two of them, and in future it should be doubled.

The castle later passed to William de Braose, the Ogre of Abergavenny. De Braose nursed a grudge against Trehearn Vaughan and invited him to an amicable settlement of their differences on the road outside Brecon. Vaughan agreed, but was seized, tied to a horse and dragged about the town before being beheaded. In 1198 Vaughan's relative Gwenwynwyn, Prince of Powys, invested Painscastle in retaliation. De Braose's allies released Gwenwynwyn's rival, Gruffyth ap Rhys, the claimant to the south Welsh throne, who raised a small force in aid of his ex-jailors. A battle was fought outside Painscastle and 3,000 of Gwenwynwyn's force were killed and almost twice as many taken prisoner.

In 1231 Henry III, whilst embarked on a fairly fruitless expedition against the Welsh, rebuilt the castle and held his court there for three months. Not much now remains, some ditches and ramparts lie on private ground but can be clearly seen from the road.

***Partrishow.*** Built in the eleventh century, though considerably altered since then, the church is dedicated to St. Issui who supposedly had a cell and a Holy well nearby in the dingle. The church now remains much as it was towards the end of the Middle Ages, with its anchorite's cell contained in the west end. The church contains a late fifteenth century rood loft and screen with rich carvings, including one of St. John, and one of a dragon eating a vine—the traditional image of the struggle between evil and good. Painted on the west wall of the nave is a figure of Father Time with scythe, hourglass and spade. Later texts have been painted over the other wall paintings. It also has a pre-Norman font, whilst outside there is a preaching cross of which only the lower part is original.

The church is included in walk 69.

***Pembridge.*** The houses along the main street of the village are nearly all of timber framed construction. Behind the New Inn lies the Butter Market which dates from the 1500's. One of the stones on which the market is built is the base of an old preaching cross, whilst the slots in the pillars are those in which the market tables rested. The building is now only a single storey high, but originally was two.

Duppa's almshouses, on the corner of Bridge Street, were built by Geoffrey Duppa and his son Brian, sometime bishop of Winchester. Four of the original six remain.

The parish church was built between 1320 to 1360 and has a separate belltower, the inside of which is built of massive timbers and contains the tower clock workings. The tower with its slit windows, served as a stronghold in the border skirmishes.

The west door of the church is bullet scarred from an occasion in the Civil War in 1645 when: 'Colonel Gradye's and General Gerard's regiments lying at Pembridge at 3 o'clock in the morning were beat up, one or two killed, most lost their horses and armes.'

The Rowe ditch to the west of the town is of unknown origin, but was probably built by the Saxons as a defence across the valley against Welsh raids.

For a walk in and around Pembridge, see walk 30.

***Pembridge Castle.*** One mile to the north-west of Welsh Newton, on the minor road to Garway, lies Pembridge Castle, so called as it was built by a family originally hailing from that village.

It is quadrangular and sheltered from the Welsh by the trilateral castles of Grosmont, Skenfrith and White, and is really a fortified manor house surrounded by a deep ditch. It has circular towers and a round keep at the north-west. Fragments of this thirteenth century keep and western curtain wall remain, but much of the remainder was built in the seventeenth century after it was severely damaged in the Civil War when a siege by Colonel Kyrle starved the royalist garrison into submission. It is not open to the public.

***Pendock.*** The keys to this redundant Norman church perched above the M50, can be obtained from the bungalow nearby. Walking from this bungalow to the church, you cross the mounds hiding the remains of the small priory. This was under that of Little Malvern, and would have supported a mere handful of monks. The church has some examples of Norman carvings and sixteenth century pews.

***Peterchurch.*** The church contains two main points of interest. The first is a plaster cast above the south door of a fish with a golden chain around its neck. There are several explanations for this. Some say that a fisherman caught it nearby in the Golden Well; others that monks kept it chained in the baptismal well half a mile away; yet others that St. Peter baptized converts in the Golden Well, blessed it and then threw in a trout around which a golden hair was tied and which was to live there forever. The second interesting item is the altar which consists of a piece of stone from Arthur's Stone at Dorstone and which is believed to have been used as an altar for some 5,000 years.

*Presteigne.* The church is a very old foundation, indeed the town's name is derived from Prestehemede, meaning priest-household. It probably formed the mother church for the area, and today there are still traces of Saxon walling in the north wall. However the present building dates mainly from the fourteenth century, with a chancel, Lady Chapel and south aisle of the late fifteenth century. There is a sixteenth century Flemish tapestry in the Lady Chapel.

The town used to have a castle, but it was destroyed in 1262 after a period of Mortimer control. However the old bridge across the Lugg remains, and in the High Street is the Radnorshire Arms which used to belong to Sir Charles Halton, Queen Elizabeth I's secretary. It opened as an inn in 1792.

*Rhos-Goch.* Here there is a national wetland nature reserve owned by the Nature Conservancy Council. A lake was formed here in glacial times, and over the centuries following it gradually filled with peat forming plants. In places these plants have formed drier hummocks which support other species. The reserve's national importance lies in the varied range of habitats and their inter-relationship. It is also a haven for birds and dragonflies. There is no public right of access across the reserve, but permission to visit it can be sought from the reserve's warden. To obtain this, initially contact the NCC at Plas Gogerddan, Aberystwyth.

*Rhulen.* The church is built in the early Norman style; it probably originated with a small monastery based in Glascwm, with Rhulen and Cregrina acting as small outposts. The large porch was used for parish meetings. There is a noticeable lean to the west wall which appears to have been that way for many years, whilst inside the church is dimly lit by just two windows.

*Richards Castle.* The settlement owes its name to Richard Fitz Scrob, one of the many Norman nobles with whom Edward the Confessor surrounded himself, and who built one of the three stone castles in existence at the time of the Conquest. Afterwards he retained possession, presumably on account of his Norman origin, and unusally the castle remained in the family until 1364 when the estate was split between two co-heiresses. By 1540 it had become uninhabited.

In 1645 2,000 royalists under the command of Sir Thomas Linsford were defeated by Colonel Birch on the wooded slopes nearby, and it is probable that the castle was still defensible then. However now only the motte, part of the keep and moat remain. Excavations carried out in 1962-4 showed that the motte had a twelfth century octagonal tower constructed on its summit, of which part remains, covered with its own debris. A curtain wall was added in the thirteenth century, which was subsequently thickened and altered.

The existing church was largely built in the fourteenth century, though the belltower dates from the second half of the thirteenth. It probably also formed part of the castle defences—all the openings face away from the castle except the door, which could therefore be covered from the keep itself. The south arcade of the church contains two large wooden screws which prevent the wall from falling southwards.

**Rock.** The church, which sits on top of an open hillside, can be seen for miles around. Much of the nave, especially the north wall, is Norman with carvings around the doorway and windows, and also on the chancel arch.

**Ross-on-Wye.** At the Domesday Survey the site formed part of the possession of the see of Hereford, with fishing rights on the Wye and free chase in the Forest of Penyard. In Edward I's reign an exchange was effected by which the crown gained the manor and its rights. However, the bishop had a small palace between the west end of the church and the north of the Prospect, for remains were discovered when the present Royal Hotel was built.

Ross is in part remembered because of John Kyrle—'The Man of Ross'. He was born in 1637, went to Oxford University and became a magistrate. He returned to Ross and became a benefactor of the town and its inhabitants. He arranged the baking of bread for the poor and needy, organised the rebuilding of St. Mary's church spire, laid out the Prospect Gardens which overlook the Wye and lie behind and to the west of the church and planted many elm trees around the town. He died in 1724 aged 87.

Rudhall's Almshouses, named after a royalist commander defeated in a skirmish in Ross during the Civil War, lie on the east side of Church Street, about 60 yards north-east of the church. They were built in 1575. The oldest part of the plague cross in the churchyard dates from the fourteenth century.

The seventeenth century market hall was built betwen 1660 and 1674. Five stone columns support an open timber ceiling with moulded beams on the ground floor. Incorporated into no.47 New Street are the remains of an early nineteenth century prison house.

Ross only gained its full name of Ross-on-Wye in 1930. The river is in fact inching its way towards the town, and the oak tree now standing in the middle of the meadow on the far side, is supposed to have been planted as a sapling on the banks of the Wye in the reign of Henry VIII.

For a walk from Ross, see walk 79.

***Rotherwas.*** The name means a cattle swamp and farm, and to the south of Hereford and in an industrial estate off the B4399 lies Rotherwas Chapel, a sixteenth century chapel for a private house which no longer exists. It has a hammerbeam roof, and the priest's confessional with an attached room to one side. The tower has a single arm clock on the side which faced the house. The chapel is now in the care of English Heritage and is open to the public.

***Rowlstone.*** The church is almost entirely Norman and contains carvings by the Herefordshire school of carvers who also left their mark at Kilpeck and Shobdon. They are concentrated in the doorway and the chancel arch, and seem to have been the work of one man, who was perhaps obsessed with birds and their rhythms. The south capital to the chancel arch contains two upside down figures. These may represent St. Peter being crucified head downwards, or it may be that the carver was less than happy with the end result and so upended the stone. Above the doorway is a tympanum representing Christ in Glory, held by four lively angels flying head downwards. The church also contains bracket candelabra of the fifteenth century.

***Saint Margarets.*** The tiny church has a rare pre-Reformation rood screen, presumably overlooked in the destruction of church ornaments during the Commonwealth. The upper and lower rails of the loft are carved with running vine and oak ornaments, and the bosses above have a variety of themes. The belltower has a dovecote; the walls have eighteenth century texts painted on them, and the small east window has a modern representation of St. Margaret as a sheperdess. One of the bells is inscribed 'Peace and good neighbourhood', a saying which is often used at the distribution of pax cakes in various churches in Herefordshire on Palm Sunday.

The outside of the church used to be used as a fives court, as were the outsides of several churches in the area.

Walk 65 starts from the church.

**Saint Weonards.** Near the church lies a tumulus which was excavated in 1855, when a cutting was made through it. Two internments were found, both alike. In each case it appeared that all of the ashes of the funeral pile had been placed on the ground at one spot, then a small mound of earth had been placed over them, upon which was built a vault of large rough stones. A circular embankment was then formed around the whole, and the workmen filled up the interior working towards the middle.

The mound is thought to have contained the body of St. Weonard, originally St. Gwainerth, a British saint said to have been executed by the Anglo-Saxons.

Several tales relate to the burial place, though none of them were substantiated by the excavation. According to one, St. Weonard was buried in a golden coffin; to another that he was buried on top of a golden coffer filled with gold, and on the coffer there was supposedly written 'Where this stood is another twice as good, but where that is, no man knows.'

About 800 yards south-west of the church, just off the minor road to Garway Common, is Treago Manor, a private residence which dates from the late fifteenth or early sixteenth century. It has four towers, the north-east one having square headed windows of the thirteenth century, the original building having been built in the late 1200's.

**Sarnesfield.** The manor was granted to Roger de Lacy by William I, and in Henry I's reign the family took its name from the village, which means field by the road. Sir Nicholas de Sarnesfield, who had been in the retinue of the Black Prince and a witness to his will, was appointed in 1382 as chief negotiator for an alliance with Wenceslaus, King of the Romans and of Bohemia, against Charles of France, John of Castille and Robert of Scotland.

John Abel is buried in a tomb near the church porch. He was one of Charles I's master carpenters and built the market houses at

*Sarnesfield Church*

Kington, Leominster and Brecon, and mills to grind corn during the siege of Hereford. The parson's dovecote is in the church tower.

**Shelsley Walsh.** The church lies off a private drive leading to the Court House, and you should park at the foot of this drive. The church is built from travertine, a local rock, which looks highly porous. The nave dates from the twelfth century, and the chancel largely from the thirteenth. There is a fifteenth century carved chancel screen and rood beam. The church also contains a wooden panelled tomb of Sir Francis Walsh, whilst the ceiling of the chancel is painted with stars. It has a very welcoming atmosphere.

**Shobdon.** The church was originally a chapel dedicated to St. Julyan, then in 1140 it became a full church after which it was granted to a priory of canons which Hugh Mortimer founded. However they moved on to Aymestrey due to lack of good water, before moving further north to found the abbey at Wigmore. Shobdon Church remained a daughter church of the new establishment.

When the new Italiante Church was built in 1756, the remains of the old were removed and re-erected in Shobdon Park. The carvings can be seen on the rise above the drive to the church, though they are now badly weathered.

125

The church lies at the end of a drive off the B4362 in the centre of the village, the outside of the church giving only a slight hint of the stunningly un-English Strawberry Hill Gothic interior. The financiers of the new building were the Bateman family, descended from John Bateman, a Fleming who had been naturalised under Charles II. He was a financier by profession and the family made a fortune in the East India Company and South Sea Company. Descendents of John Bateman were in turn created Viscount Bateman and Baron Bateman, but both strands eventually died childless, and the title finally ended in 1931. The Court was sold and much was demolished.

The mound at the eastern edge of the village is called the Cobbler's Mound, for the story goes that a cobbler met the devil coming to bury Shobdon which had boasted of having the finest church then known. The devil asked him the way, and the cobbler, guessing the devil's intentions, pointed to all the shoes he was carrying and replied that he had worn all of them out trying to find it too. The devil gave up his quest and dropped his earth.

Walk 28 includes the two Shobdon churches.

**Skenfrith.** Earth and timber defences for the castle were probably thrown up around 1071, and by the reign of Henry II the castles of the Trilateral—Skenfrith, Grosmont and White—were in the hands of the crown and administered by the sheriff of Hereford.

In 1201 the three castles were granted to Herbert de Burgh, and it was during the period of his tenureship that most of the existing masonry castle was built. The round tower was the last part to be built and was probably completed in 1244 by Waleran the German. In 1254 the castles were granted to Prince Edward, later Edward I, and in 1267 to his younger brother Edmund Crouchback, the first earl of Lancaster. In the 1260's the castles were fortified against Llewelyn, but were not attacked. The Treaty of Montgomery in 1267 recognized the Welsh conquests, but once Edward finally took the war to Wales, the castles ceased to be of major importance. It is now in the care of the Welsh Office and is open to the public. Behind the castle and on the Monnow lies the old watermill.

In the church is the tomb of John Morgan who died in 1557 and who was the last Governor of the three castles.

**Snodhill.** The remains of the castle, being mainly part of the keep and its gate towers, lie on a rise just off the road to Snodhill from the west, and can be reached across a stile. The castle was the abode of the

*Skenfrith Castle*

Chandos family, one of whom fought at Poitiers, and the last of whom fortified the castle against Glyndwr.

Snodhill Court below the castle is in part built from the castle ruins. The castle was described as ruinous by Leland in 1560, but even so it was bombarded by parliamentarian forces in the Civil War.

In Snodhill Park there is believed to be buried treasure, lying 'no deeper than a hen could scratch.'

*Stapleton.* An urban community was started in the twelfth century, though there is now little sign of it. A castle was built in the thirteenth

127

century and was pulled down in 1643 by the royalist governor of Ludlow in case it was used by parliamentarian forces.

The present ruins are of the seventeenth century house built on the mutilated castle earthworks, and are reached after a scramble up a path which starts at the stile at the corner of the road junctions.

There is a tale told that the lady of the castle was murdered by her husband who had accused her of infidelity. She foretold in proof of her innocence that white violets would ever more bloom around the castle at Christmas time, which they still supposedly do.

***Stockton-on-Teme.*** This fairly simple Norman church contains some Norman carvings, and the chancel, rebuilt in brick in the early 1700's, contains the tomb of Thomas Walsh, son of one of Henry VIII's chancellors of the exchequer. His family must have been penny pinching at the time, for they re-used the tombstone of Redulphus, the first rector at Stockton.

***Stoke Edith.*** There are six St. Edythas in Saxon mythology, and it is not known which gives her name to this parish, though it is most likely to be the daughter of King Egbert and would thus be the Abbess of Polesworth in Warwickshire who died around 870 A.D.

Stoke Edith House was commenced by Speaker Foley of the House of Commons (1694-8), and was planned by him and Sir Christopher Wren. The church dates from the same period and is classical in style with some stuccoed bricks of circa 1740. A gallery at the rear of the church has some raised pews.

***Stokesay Castle.*** This was once called Stokes, but was renamed after the Says, tenants of the Lacys. The hall and tower were built in 1284, when Lawrence of Ludlow, a wool merchant, gained a licence to crenellate his residence. His descendents held the house for ten generations.

It was held for Charles I in the Civil War but it was surrendered by its governor. The royalist governor of Ludlow then gathered a force of 200 mounted men and a large number of infantry and advanced to within a mile of Stokesay, only to be defeated. Sir William Croft and 100 soldiers were killed and 400 soldiers and 60 officers and gentlemen were taken prisoner.

The castle, which is in good order and is a fine example of the transition from castle to manor house, is open to the public. The church which stands nearby was rebuilt by the Puritans after its destruction when royalist cavalry entered it. It therefore dates from a period of rare church building and contains much of interest, notably the pews and wall paintings.

Local folklore records that two giants used to live on either side of the valley—one on Norton Camp and the other on Yeo Edge. A treasure chest lay in between, buried beneath Stokes. When one giant wanted to look at the treasure he had to have the key, which was tossed backwards and forwards between the hills. One of the giants went down with rheumatism, so when he tossed the key, it fell short, into the moat of the house where the giants couldn't find it. Supposedly when the key is found, so will the treasure.

***Stretton Sugwas.*** The name is derived from a bird known to the earlier inhabitants as a succa, combined with the old English for a swamp. The church was rebuilt in 1878 and has a black and white tower. Inside is a tympanum, almost Egyptian in character, showing Samson astride a lion, forcing open its jaws.

***Sutton St. Nicholas.*** The village is famous as the site of the palace of King Offa at which King Ethelbert of the East Angles was murdered. King Ethelbert was subsequently buried in Hereford Cathedral, upon which for atonement Offa lavished gifts of land, money and a shrine.

Excavations have established that an Iron Age village, inhabited during the Roman period, existed here. In the ditches outside the west gate were found skeletons bearing wounds indicative of a massacre, probably at the time the Romans stormed the camp.

Walk 55 includes the site.

***Tenbury Wells.*** The church dates mainly from the 1860's, but contains some interesting pieces, including a small canopied tomb of a crusader within the altar rails; a larger crusader tomb; a well preserved alabaster tomb of Sir Thomas Acton Adams (who prosecuted William Shakespeare for deer stealing and who formed the basis of his 'Justice Shallow'); fragments of a Saxon preaching cross and a chained book.

The town developed very late in life as a spa, already being an established market town. The saline wells were not discovered till 1839 during the search for a new water supply, and a pump room was designed in sheet metal to resemble an oriental pagoda. Those who used the spa tended to be people already stopping in the town en route between London and North Wales. Few new visitors were attracted, and most of those who stayed used the existing inns, accounting for the absence of large hotels as were built in many spas.

Walk 21 starts at the church and includes the banks above the Teme.

*Tretower.* This fortified manor house is in the Ystrad Yw, the vale of yew trees. Bernard de Newmarch, conqueror of Brecon, handed over Tretower to his squire Picard, whose family built the motte and bailey castle and circular keep. In the fourteenth century Tretower passed to the Bluets under whom the castle was sacked and burnt by Owain Glyndwr. By marriage the castle passed to the Vaughans who built and altered the house between the early fourteenth and mid-seventeenth centuries. The court is built around a quadrangle of two curtain walls with upper walkways. In the mid-fifteenth century Sir Roger Vaughan added an eastern range with a hall and solar, a stone barn on the east side and mouldings on the gatehouse. Chimneys and timber windows were added around 1630. The property is in the care of the National Trust and is open to the public.

*Tyberton.* The church is built of brick, with white walls and monuments inside. Around the chancel is a modern style carving with angels' heads and artefacts, which was supposedly executed in the eighteenth century by an itinerant Italian carver who called at the manor house nearby. There is a preaching cross outside.

*Upton Bishop.* In the outside of the south wall of the church are the head and shoulders of a man with his right arm raised, being fragments of a Roman tombstone.

*Upton-upon-Severn.* There appears to have been a settlement from Saxon days, the town catering for the needs of those plying the Severn. But it grew in importance once a bridge was built across the river, which then funnelled more trade through the town. The church was rebuilt in the fourteenth century, but now only the tower remains, its shape and copper cupola making a well known landmark.

The church provided shelter for Cromwell's troops in an attack on the royalist garrison in the town in the days leading up to the Battle of Worcester in 1651. The garrison had destroyed the central span of the bridge, but left a plank across it. An advance party of the parliamentarian forces crawled their way over this whilst the royalists were enjoying the town's inns. Once across they bolted themselves inside the church and fired on the garrison, holding out till they received support from cavalry which had forded the river lower down.

In the fifteenth century, one of the rectors was John Dee. He was a dabbler in alchemy and astrology, and cast a horoscope for Queen Mary and Philip of Spain. Mary imprisoned him for treason, making him a natural ally of Elizabeth. He won more widespread respect for his work on mathematics.

**Urishay.** On the road from Peterchurch to Urishay Common lies the remains of a fortified farmhouse built in Elizabethan times. It was defensive only, and its remains include a part filled moat and a chapel, now being restored.

**Vowchurch.** The church has a black and white tower, but its main interest is that it is built on twelve oak pillars, clearly seen from the inside, the stone walls not being structural. The roof timbers over the chancel date from 1348 and were repaired in 1618 by Charles I's carpenter, John Abel. On the rood screen are carvings of Adam and Eve.

Vowchurch stands opposite Turnastone, where there's another church. The tale goes that two sisters each wanted to build a church, the one living in Vowchurch saying: 'I vow I will build my church before you turn a stone of yours', and hence the name of each village. In fact the 'Vow' in Vowchurch means multicoloured, and Turnastone may derive from the old English for a thorn thicket.

For a walk from Vowchurch Common, see walk 64.

**The Weir.** This is a garden in the care of the National Trust which is open to the public. It lies off the A438 Hereford to Brecon road, within a few miles of Hereford. In spring the gardens are full of bulbs, blossom and buds, and in autumn the acacia garden and trees are in their seasonal colours. The garden is right on a bend in the Wye, and part of the river bank is walled up to make a grass walkway.

**Welsh Newton.** The church is the burial place of the martyr John Kemble who, aged 80, was caught in the accusations concerning Titus Oates' papist plots. He was committed to Hereford gaol, sent on to London, then recommitted to Hereford for trial. He was hanged on Widemarsh Common on 22 August 1679, and his grave later became a shrine to which pilgrims ascribed miraculous powers. He was canonized in 1970, and his grave lies to the west of the preaching cross in the churhyard.

Inside the church is a stone rood screen, probably built by the Hospitallers.

*Weobley.* The castle was probably founded in the late eleventh century by either Roger de Lacy or his brother and heir Hugh. However the Talbots were some of the earliest occupants, holding the castle for the Empress Matilda. King Stephen personally commanded the troops that captured it in 1140.

Later it was held by de Braose who used Weobley as his base when fighting King John with his ally Matthew de Gamage, Lord of Dilwyn. In 1208 or 9 they sacked Leominster.

The castle descended to the Devereux family who were later created earls of Essex. Leland described the castle in the fifteenth century as being 'a goodly castle but somewhat in decay'. The grassy moat and mounds are all that now remain.

The black and white village, which used to have a nail factory on its central green until it burnt down at the end of the Second World War,

*Memorial to Colonel John Birch, Weobley Church*

132

became the home of one of the best known parliamentary commanders of the Civil War—Colonel John Birch. He had been a puritan
trader in Bristol, but when the war interrupted and then ruined his
business he joined the local parliamentarian force, but had to flee
from Bristol when it fell to the initially successful royalists. He played
an important role in holding the south-east for parliament, and later
joined the relieving army sent by sea to Plymouth. From this city he
was part of the force led by Fairfax which broke out and drove the royalists before them.

He successively became governor of Bridgewater, Bath and then
Bristol. From this last city he mounted an audacious surprise attack in
the dead of winter on Hereford, capturing the city which a Scottish
army had recently failed to take. With the end of warfare he entered
parliament, but fell out with hard line puritans, favouring a government in which the head of state and parliament worked in co-
operation. Upon the Restoration he served Charles II in the excise
department, but eased himself out of office and public view in the
reign of his successor until the arrival of William of Orange. Upon
this news, though then past his prime, he went straight to the prince
who had landed in Dorset and helped direct his route to London,
avoiding bloodshed with troops who might have felt bound to support
James II. He helped shape the Declartion of Right and the curtail-
ment of the royal prerogative, before he finally left parliament to the
up and coming generation.

In his latter years he lived at Garnstone on the edge of Weobley. His
tomb is in the church, as is that of Sir Walter Devereux who was killed
at the Battle of Pilleth.

Walk 42 has Weobley as its base.

**Weston under Penyard.** Penyard Castle was built upon a wooded hillside
above the village. It was of no great extent, and dates from the first
half of the fourteenth century, probably being used as a royal hunting
lodge as it was situated in the Forest of Dean hunting area. Some of
the stone has been used for the rectory, but some of the walls still
stand on the hillside.

The church has a Norman doorway with two twelfth century heads,
one being that of a ram. The tower served as a lookout, and internally
the church has three narrow lights above the altar and is dark and
atmospheric.

To the north, on the minor road that runs from the west of the village from the A40 towards Bromsash, lies Bollitree Castle barns, built

as a mock castle. One of William Cobbett's closest friends lived in the house, and he stayed here on his rural rides.

*Wergin Stone.* Near Sutton St. Nicholas, on the left-hand side of the Hereford road stands the Wergin Stone, fenced off in a field across a drainage ditch. It stands about five feet high and the base contains a hollowed out cavity which slopes inwards, into which an annual payment or offering is supposed to have been placed. In about 1652 the stone appeared to move supernaturally, for it took nine yoke of oxen to return it to its original place, 240 paces away.

*White Castle.* The earliest reference to this is in the reign of Henry II when it was known as Llantilio Castle, but its earliest masonry dates from about 1155 and the white plaster coating to the walls gave it its present name. Its history follows that of Grosmont and especially Skenfrith, the other castles in the trilateral and which were under a united command.

The curtain walls were built in 1184-6 and in 1201 the castle passed to Hubert de Burgh, the great justiciar of King John and the early years of Henry III. In 1234, on his unwarranted disgrace, they passed to Waleran the German. In 1254 they came to Prince Edward when he received all English lands in Wales, and in 1267 to his younger brother Edmund Crouchback, later the first earl of Lancaster.

The castle was fortified against Llewelyn. Later the original keep was destroyed and a large tower was built at each angle of the six sided enclosure, with the outer ward being enclosed too. It is now in the care of the Welsh Office and is open to the public.

*Whitney.* Meaning Hwita's Island, it used to have a castle built on a spit in the Wye, but its last traces were washed away when the river changed course slightly in 1730.

*Wichenford.* Here is a timber framed dovecote in the care of the National Trust. It contains 557 nesting boxes and the birds entered and left via the lantern at the top. Dovecotes were widespread in the late Middle Ages when it was difficult to overwinter stock for lack of feed, and the birds could supply an alternative source of fresh meat.

*Wigmore.* The history of the settlement and castle is very much tied up with that of the Mortimer family, about whom more will be found in the History chapter.

The original castle of Wisingamene, meaning Wcga's moor or big wood was built by Ethelfleda, a daughter of Alfred the Great and wife of Ethelred, Governor of Mercia. She died in 912 and the castle eventually passed to Edric, the Saxon earl of Salop from whom it was seized by Ralph de Mortimer. The existing castle was started by William de Fitzosbern and then granted to the Mortimers. Wigmore was one of the four boroughs in Herefordshire in 1086.

Roger Mortimer was one of Henry III's staunchest supporters against the barons and he made extensive additions to the castle. He rescued Prince Edward from Simon de Montfort during his imprisonment in Hereford, and commanded the third division at the Battle of Evesham.

His grandson fell in love with Queen Isabella, wife of Edward II, and played a leading part in the king's murder. He then assumed the role of regent, until Edward III obtained his revenge when Mortimer was hanged at Tyburn in 1330. The Mortimer lands were forfeited till restored to his grandson. The Roger Mortimer who was born at Usk on 11 April was declared by parliament to be the heir presumptive to the throne on the death of Richard II, should the latter have no issue. However he was slain in 1398 while acting as deputy in Ireland, a year before Richard was murdered by Henry Bolingbroke, later Henry IV.

Roger's son Edmund was committed by Henry IV to the care of his own son, later Henry V. On the latter's death, Edmund was sent as Lieutenant to Ireland, where he died. The Mortimer claim to the throne then passed to the son of Edmund's sister Anne, the Duke of York. When Edward Duke of York became Edward IV during the Wars of the Roses, the castle passed to the crown.

In the Civil War the castle, once reputedly one of the strongest in England, was pulled down on the order of its owner, Sir Robert Harley, who had declared for parliament, because in an overwhelmingly royalist area he could only manage to defend his other castle and home, Brampton Bryan.

**Wilton.** The remains of the castle date from the thirteenth, fourteenth and fifteenth centuries, though the original castle was probably built by King Stephen or Henry de Longchamp.

The remains are on private land but can be seen fairly close to from a public footpath that leads off immediately from the Wilton end of the bridge. Portions of the south-west tower and part of the sixteenth century house were included in the later building standing adjacent to the ruins.

The castle was burnt at the start of the Civil War by the royalists under Viscount Scudamore, as the owner, Sir John Brydges, couldn't decide who to declare for. After the burning he promptly chose the parliamentarian cause.

The six spanned bridge was built between 1597 and 1599 and has an eighteenth century sundial in the middle.

Near the river is the sixteenth century prison house, now part of the White Lion, but some of the barred windows on the first floor can still be seen from the lane behind.

**Worcester.** Originally a Roman frontier settlement, Vertis, the early name for Worcester, settled down to become a small settlement for the next few centuries. Its central position, as a crossing point over the Severn and as an inland port, only came to be recognised by the Saxons who started to settle here in larger numbers from around 670. By 680 it had become the centre of a bishopric. However a brief period of developing trade was disrupted by Danish raids up the river, and it was not until 877 when Alfred the Great restored order and when city walls were built, that the city once more developed.

Towards the end of the tenth century the see was held first by St. Dunstan and then by St. Oswald. In the eleventh century it was held for a while by St. Wulstan who trod carefully and dilplomatically between Saxons and Normans, even rallying support for William II against a rebellion by Robert of Normandy. It was arguably under Wulstan that the bishopric saw its period of greatest influence, for all the abbeys and priories were made subordinate to the bishop. Over the years, as the church fragmented and personal rivalries grew, so the bishopric's temporal power declined.

A small castle was built to the south-east of the cathedral, and this initially appears to have withstood attacks by both Matilda and Stephen in their civil war. However, it must have been weakened, or the town walls strengthened, for in the unrest in John's reign, when the castellan of the castle declared for Louis of France, the earl of Chester was unable to storm the city walls, but took the castle and then entered the city by the back door. Indeed from that time on, the castle fell into complete disrepair, whilst the city walls were maintained through a combination of tolls raised on the markets, and the efforts of the city guilds.

The cathedral did not pass unscathed during this time. St. Wulstan had already replaced the Saxon cathedral with one of stone, of which, essentially, the crypt remains. Three fires damaged the cathedral in the 1100's, and the tower collapsed in 1175. Much rebuilding took place, which was encouraged by Wulstan's canonisation in 1203 and King John's burial in 1216. Prince Arthur, Henry VII's eldest son, is also buried in the cathedral. The tower was once more rebuilt in 1374, and is the earliest in England in the perpendicular style.

In the early 1500's the cathedral saw many comings and goings amongst its bishops. There was a series of Italians who acted as political agents for the English crown at the Vatican. Then came Bishop Latimer, burnt at the stake in the reign of Queen Mary. Bishop Paty was appointed, but was promptly removed when Elizabeth succeeded to the throne. In turn he was followed by Bishop Sandys who had spent several years in prison as a supporter of the ill-fated Lady Jane Grey and her nine day reign.

The city itself was comparatively tranquil till the Civil War, in which it saw virtually the first and the last engagements. The former was a skirmish between parliamentary troops under the earl of Essex, and cavalry under Prince Rupert. Essex was trying to capture the king's treasure which was being moved to safety in the west, and sent a force across the Severn at Powick. This was promptly charged and routed by Rupert. Other skirmishes over the next few years kept everyone on their toes, but the city was essentially royalist held until the end of the first phase of the civil war. Once the king had lost the Battle of Marston Moor, and the parliamentary forces broke the siege of Plymouth and began their victorious advance north-east, it was only a matter of time before Worcester was besieged. This siege began in May 1646, and though resistance was stout, once Oxford, the centre of royalist fortunes, capitulated, Worcester quickly followed suit.

It wasn't long before Charles II chanced his arm at seeking a military restitution of the crown. He landed in Scotland, and whilst Cromwell defeated the lowland Scots at Dunbar, he gathered an army largely of highlanders and headed south. But English support was few and far between, and with parliamentary forces blocking the route to the south-east, Charles headed west to try and bolster his army. At Worcester Charles again hoped for reinforcements, but very few were forthcoming. The city's defences were strengthened in the few days he had before Cromwell's army caught up with him.

Cromwell's army outnumbered Charles' by almost three to one, but Cromwell had to attack. General Fleetwood was despatched to make a pontoon bridge across the Severn at Powick and to drive in Charles' rear. Whilst many parliamentary troops were so engaged, the royalists tried to storm Cromwell's position. But Charles' command was riven with rivalries, and short-term gains were not consolidated. The attack was overwhelmed, and soon Cromwell's troops were entering the city from both directions. Charles, as we know, managed to escape.

At this time the population of the city was some 7,000. It grew as agricultural trade increased and as the city developed into an inland port on the Severn. Much trade was developed with the Americas, via Bristol, and as the War of Independence removed that particular opportunity, so the coming of the canals created others.

However subsequent development has rather marred the city—the Guildhall designed by the local architect Thomas White in the 1720's remains in the High Street, and some of the older buildings remain in Friar Street. There are St. Nicholas's and All Saints churches, the Alice Otley School in the Tything, and the Berkeley almshouses, but much of the rest of the old core seems to have been ripped away.

Other places to visit include The Commandery in the Sidbury where there are both static and audio-visual displays about the Civil War housed on the site of St. Wulstan's Hospital, much of which now dates from the 1500's.

There is The Royal Worcester Dyson Perrins Museum in Severn Street, The Tudor House Museum in Friar Street, where there is also Greyfriars, a house in the care of the National Trust, and also the City Museum and Art Gallery above the library in Foregate Street.

*Yarpole.* The name means a pool formed by a dam, and the church here has a detached belltower, though not as big or as impressive as Pembridge's. The village has a collection of old timber and stone built buildings.

# WALKING LAW AND CODES

## General

On a public path the public has a right of access on foot only, and on bridleways a right of access on horse and pedal cycle as well. On each you can take a 'natural accompaniment' which includes a dog, prams and pushchairs. All dogs should be kept under close control, and always on a lead when near livestock. Some public paths are way-marked by the landowner, and have coloured arrows at junctions and changes in direction to indicate the course of the path. The colours are usually yellow for footpaths and blue for bridleways. The highway authority, being the relevant County Council in this area, has a duty to signpost footpaths where they leave a metalled road. There is no time limit in which to fulfill this duty, and in addition signposting can be considered unnecessary in certain limited circumstances. In effect, most paths are neither signposted nor waymarked.

## Maintenance

County Councils have a duty 'to assert and protect the rights of the public to the use and enjoyment' of paths and 'to prevent as far as possible the stopping up or obstruction' of such paths. It is normally the surface of the path that belongs to the Council, the soil under-neath belonging to the landowner who adjoins the path.

Owners of the land have the primary duty of maintaining stiles, though the Council must contribute a quarter of the cost and can con-tribute more if they wish.

Often County Councils have agreements with District or Parish Councils whereby the latter maintains the path and charges the County Council; but any complaint about non-signposted, unmain-tained or obstructed paths should be sent to the County Council, and can also be sent to the Ramblers Association who may pass it onto a local group to follow up.

### Obstructions

If the path crosses a field, the field may be ploughed and planted, but, in general, the farmer must make good the surface of the path within two weeks of starting to plough, or if prevented by exceptional weather conditions, as soon as possible thereafter. Reinstatement can just involve driving a tractor along the route of the path to flatten the soil. It is a criminal offence subject to a fine of up to £400 to plough a public footpath or bridleway which follows the edge of a field or enclosure, or not to reinstate a path which crosses a field.

If you come across an obstruction on a path, so long as you are a bona fide traveller, in other words if you haven't set out with the specific purpose of removing the obstruction, you're entitled to remove it, but should only remove as much as is necessary to pass through. Alternatively if there is an easy way round the obstruction, you may legally take that route, and would have a defence to any charge of trespass.

### Bulls

It is illegal to keep bulls of a recognized dairy breed (Ayrshire, British Friesian, British Holstein, Dairy Shorthorn, Guernsey, Jersey and Kerry breeds) in fields crossed by a public path, except in open hill areas or if they are under ten months old. Nor is it legal to keep any other bulls in such fields unless accompanied by cows or heifers.

If owners disregard the law relating to bulls and thereby endanger the public, an offence may be committed under the Health and Safety at Work Act 1974, and the police may institute proceedings.

### Trespass

If you stray off a path you may be trespassing which is a civil wrong, not a criminal offence, and the landowner may have a remedy in damages and/or an injunction. If you are trespassing solely as a way of avoiding a blockage on a path, then you automatically have a defence.

If you are unsure of your route, remember always to be polite and find out where you should be walking.

### Definitve Footpath Maps

The County Council is required to keep a definitive map of footpaths. Ordnance Survey maps may show additional paths and it is these, often still public rights of way, which are most likely to be obstructed or overgrown. It is also more difficult to follow the exact line of paths on the larger scale maps as field boundaries are not shown. Copies of definitive footpath maps can be obtained, usually at a price, from the relevant County Council. In the old county of Herefordshire, the maps can be inspected at Hereford library, and similarly at Worcester library for those in the old county of Worcestershire. In Powys, inspection can be made at County Hall in Llandrindod Wells, and in Shropshire at the Council Offices in Ludlow.

All paths on definitive footpath maps are public rights of way and to show that a path is on such a map is sufficient to establish a legal right of passage. To incorporate paths onto the definitive map it is necessary to prove that the path has been dedicated to public use. This can happen by either act or omission—either the landowner may simply grant the public the right of way, or, alternatively and more likely, you must provide evidence that the public have used the route for at least twenty years without an actual or implied prohibition by the landowner. Applications for additions to the map as well as reports of obstructions should be addressed to the relevant County Council.

Once established a right of way does not 'disappear' simply through lack of use, though this may provide evidence in support of an application to extinguish a path. It is normally the County or District Council who will make an application to extinguish or divert a path, and a publicity and consultation process has to be followed before the order may be confirmed or rejected.

### Country Code

Remember when walking to take other peoples' interests in the land into consideration, and remember that you only have the right to walk along the footpaths and not to, for example, use them to carry wood from adjoining land. Remember especially to:

1. Keep any dogs under close control, and you are required to keep a dog on a lead when in a field with livestock. Take additional care at lambing time which normally runs from Christmas to the end of April. If your dog does worry sheep, you may find that not only is it shot, if that is the only way the farmer can stop it, but you may also have to compensate the farmer for any damage it has caused.

2. Leave gates as you find them—remember you may close off livestock from water by closing a gate meant to be open. Always close a gate you've opened to pass through. If it is impossible to open a gate climb over at the hinged end to minimalize the risk of damaging the gate.

3. Always keep to a path unless it is easier to avoid an obstruction by leaving it, which you are entitled to do.

4. Never light fires, and extinguish all matches and cigarettes.

5. Take your litter home.

6. Leave livestock, crops and machinery alone.

7. Make no unnecessary noise.

8. Protect wildlife, plants and trees—remember it may be an offence to damage certain plants and wildlife. It is a simple rule—if you leave them alone they may be there next time for others to look at.

# WALKS INTRODUCTION

The number of the walk relates to the number on the map giving its location. An estimate of the length of time the walk takes is then given. This time only allows for walking at a reasonable pace and not stopping to continuallly admire the view, or identify all the wayside plants!

Then follows a note about the main points of interest on the walk, together with some information on the condition of the paths and tracks to be taken. In the descriptions we use 'path' to describe either a well marked route only wide enough to walk along, or where there is no clearly defined route, for example across or alongside fields. 'Track' refers to a well defined wide route, in all probability used by vehicles of one form or another.

There then follows a description of how to reach the start point by vehicle from the nearest town or large village. The symbol 𝐏 on each map indicates the location of the parking place suggested.

The walk itself is then described and the written directions should be read in conjunction with the sketch map provided. We also recommend use of an Ordnance Survey map of the 1:50 000 series to help identify views. The relevant map number and co-ordinates for the start point of each walk are given above the walk's title. You may of course do the walk in reverse, but then remember to reverse the directions! We have walked all of the walks between November 1988 and February 1990 but cannot guarantee that the countryside remains unchanged. So you may find, for example, that some hedgerows and woods referred to have been grubbed up or that additional fences have been erected and some paths obstructed.

Some notes on walking law and the countryside code have been given in the previous section.

# CLEE ST. MARGARET

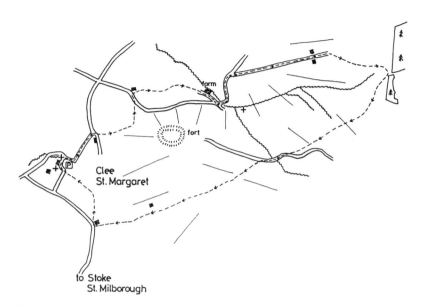

Two hours.

A walk in rolling countryside round Clee St. Margaret and up to the saddle of the Brown Clee Hill, with views towards Wenlock Edge. The climb is fairly long, but the walk is on paths and tracks in generally good order. Some of these can be wet due to their sunken nature.

Park near the telephone kiosk in Clee St. Margaret, this itself being adjacent to the T-junction formed by the road-cum-ford in the village. Walk away from the heart of the village, leaving this ford to your left. Round the first bend a track leads off to the right towards a few newer houses. Take this, but bear left through the gate onto the open land below the ramparts of the hillfort. Once on this land the path shadows the fence on your left, and if you follow this you will come to a gate out onto another minor road ahead.

144

Turn left on this road and almost immediately right onto a track. This leads to an entrance gate to a house, but in front of this follow the older track round to the right. This soon leads over an old stile into a grassy strip running between fields to left and right. Keep to this, later the path crossing out into a field by another stile. Once over this follow the track through the field, a track which shadows the hedge to your right. This will lead you through a small farmyard and thence down a stoned track to a road. Turn left on this and follow it round the sharp bend to the left and uphill. Where the road reaches its crest, take the wide and well formed track off to the right. This leads in an almost straight line uphill, further on passing between two sets of buildings beyond which it gains a grassy surface. At the end of this grassy ride the track emerges onto the open hillside via a gate. Go through this, after which the track bears half right to follow a fence on your right.

It follows this fence for some way before it reaches a gate. Go through this, after which the path becomes less distinct. However you soon come to some woodland on your left, at which point the path turns right to shadow the cut into the hillside on your right. The course of the path is in fact the sunken track which initially rises slightly uphill, then almost stays on the level before starting a gentle descent. However this can be overgrown or water logged in places, so take whichever parallel route you choose. You walk a reasonable distance and cross a few small streams before joining with a gravelled track which runs down the hillside from your left. Join this for a few hundred yards, but when it bears right and towards the hillfort, which you're now above, your old track, still visible with its humps, carries on ahead on much the same line as it has been following for some time. Now keep to this line, for the track gradually loses its clear shape and form. But by the time you may be becoming confused, you should see a house standing in its fenced-off field on the hillside ahead. Your route takes you to the left of this, bearing slightly right to follow the hedge on your left. Once beyond the house and back onto the open common beyond, drop down the hillside to the hedge on the far side of the common, turning left in front of this and its houses beyond, and you'll leave the common through a gate onto a short track.

When you reach the road, turn right, and immediately, between the house and an old barn, turn right and onto a narrow muddy slightly sunken path. Walk down this and when it splits ahead, take the left-hand fork. This will lead you out onto a track on which you turn left. Walk down this, and turn right when you reach the road to return to your vehicle.

# PRESCOTT

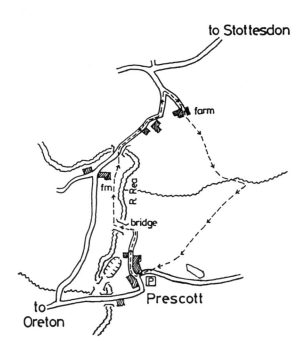

Three-quarters of an hour.

A walk in gentle countryside, mainly on paths which can be awkward due to ploughing and planting. The walk crosses an old stone bridge isolated from roads, and includes fairly extensive views.

Prescott lies roughly 4 miles north of Cleobury Mortimer. If travelling north from Oreton towards Bagginswood, once across the River Rea the road bends sharp left, passes through a bit of a cutting, and then turns sharp right. On this corner there is a public footpath signposted

146

to the left, but carry on along the road and within a few yards there is a second footpath also signposted off to the left. This is the easiest and best place to park.

Walk back down the road to the first footpath sign, and follow it, turning down a track past the farm buildings down to the River Rea. Here you cross the old bridge. Immediately over the bridge, take the stile on your right. The path heads across the field to a stile half way between the river and the farm on the far side of the field. However, depending upon crops growing in the field, it may be easier to follow the river along to the fence and then walk up the fence to the stile, as you would be entitled to do if the path is obstructed. Once across the stile, head to the stile at the top far left corner of the next field by the buildings. Over this bear slightly to the right to leave the third field by a stile above another bridge. Turn right on the road on which you emerge, crossing the river, and walk on up the road, passing the buildings on the right. The road then turns left, shortly after which a track leads off to the right. Walk down this and straight ahead through the farmyard. The track leads to a gate at the far end of the yard, through which you pass and then follow the hedge on roughly the same line, keeping it to your right. Walk down to the stream in the valley bottom, cross the rails at the bottom of the field, cross the stream and then bear left and walk along the bank, following the stream on your left.

When you come to a bridge on the left, the path turns right to cross the field on your right, heading towards the corner of hedge which juts into the field. Walk across to this and then follow the hedge, keeping it on your right to the stile at the far end. Cross the next little limb of field to the clutch of stiles ahead. Over these the path crosses the next field to a stile at the corner of an old hedgerow, to the right of a conifer plantation. Once over this stile, walk along this old hedge come field boundary on your left to the road and your vehicle.

# CATHERTON COMMON

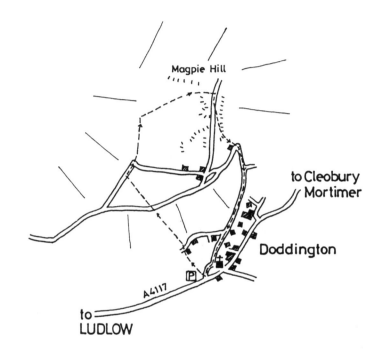

One hour.

This walk, though technically starting on paths, tends to veer off over open countryside. The return is made on larger tracks. It affords good views and passes around many of the old mine shafts and workings of the coal pits.

If travelling from Ludlow on the A 4117, park just before Doddington Church and the cattle grid; or just after if travelling to Ludlow.

Above where you've parked are some houses, and set off up the hillside keeping them to your immediate right, passing old mine shafts as

148

you go. Towards the ridge of the hill head roughly onwards towards the large clump of old mine shafts, crossing one metalled lane en route. From this collection of shafts, bear right to walk roughly parallel with the line of trees much further across the hill. This will lead you above a small pool towards what has the appearance of a disused quarry. Passing across it you come to the edge of the workings, at the bottom of which the hill slopes away to Catherton Common where there are more mine shafts.

Take whatever route you fancy to the right along the face of the workings' escarpment. As you round the hillside, keep a couple of stone-built houses to your right, from which a track leads on around the hill. Take this and it will lead you above a cluster of houses sandwiched between the track and the main road. Keep these houses to your left and, crossing other tracks you come to, this will lead you back out above the church to your vehicle.

# HOPTON CASTLE

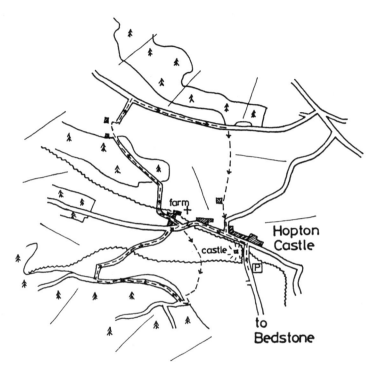

One and a quarter hours.

This walk passes near Hopton Castle and includes some gently rolling border countryside with views towards the Long Mynd. The route is largely on main tracks but involves some field crossings and a stream to ford. The walk can be split into two roughly equal parts if you wish.

Take the B4367 north from the A4113 near Brampton Bryan. Turn left in Bedstone and then right and past the church, following the road along to Hopton Castle. The castle will be seen quite close to the road on the left-hand side and consists of a square stone tower. Park anywhere near the castle, which is listed in the gazetteer.

Depending upon where you parked, walk up to the T-junction near the castle, and turn left through the village. Over a stream and opposite the entrance to Upper House Farm on the right, turn left through a small gate into a little orchard. Cross to the far left-hand corner of the orchard and through the gate into the field beyond. Cut across the right-hand corner of this field to the gate on the far side, through which you pass. The path now curves through the next field to its top left-hand corner at the base of the wood. Cross the stile here into the wood. Turn right on the gravelled track just inside the wood and follow it round. When the track splits, take the right-hand fork which shortly afterwards curves round to the right and out of the wood. It then crosses two fields and emerges on to a minor road. Turn right on this and after 20 yards or so you come back to Upper House Farm.

Turn left onto the farm's drive to start the southern part of the walk. Follow this track past the farmhouse on the left and then between some farm buildings, most of these lying to your right. Once through the farmyard and opposite the end of the last building on the left, turn right to ford a stream and then follow the track, which later curves to the left, uphill into some woodland. Pass through the gateway into the woodland and continue slanting across the hill on the track. Further on the track leaves the wood and enters some fields near a cottage. The definitive footpath follows the hedge behind the cottage but tends to be obstructed by ploughing and crops, so we suggest turning right down the hedge on your immediate right and onto the drive to the road at the end. Turn right onto the road.

Follow this road until it reaches a wood on the left. Almost exactly opposite this you'll see an entrance on the right leading into a field. There used to be a wooden gate here, but on our last visit it was on its last legs and had been partially replaced by a hurdle—it may since have been replaced with something else! Go into the field and follow the hedge on your right. Back over the brow of the hill you come to another gate. At this point the path goes straight over the field ahead, aiming just to the left of a part collapsed brick building on the other side. However if the path is blocked by crops or is ploughed over, you could follow the hedges around on the left and rejoin the correct path near this building. From the left of the brick building the path goes through the left-hand gate and follows the hedge on your right. At the far end you need to clamber down the bank above the minor road. Turn right on the road and then left at the T-junction ahead to return to your vehicle.

# OFFA'S DYKE ABOVE KNIGHTON

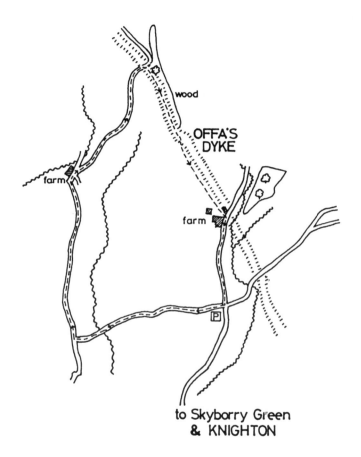

One hour.

This is a walk along one of the best preserved sections of the dyke in this area with its remnant of old larch wood, and affords wide views of the border country. The walk is on good quality tracks and involves a bit of an uphill climb.

From Knighton take the A488 to Bishops Castle and immediately after crossing the River Teme and the railway line on the edge of Knighton, turn left onto the minor road to Skyborry, which starts off by following the railway. After about two miles turn right on to another minor road signposted Selley Cross and Clun, but beware not to turn too early onto a lane which leads solely to a farm. Carry on up this second road for about one and half miles and park when you come to a crossroads of minor roads and tracks.

Take the left-hand metalled track from the crossroads, walking uphill to a small rise and then dropping downhill and crossing a stream in the bottom of the dip. When the metalled track turns sharp left beyond this stream, take the gravel and dirt track to the right which starts to gradually rise uphill. This leads to a set of mainly new farm buildings in a dip in the general rise of the ground. The track keeps to the right of the buildings and then begins a sharper ascent to the dyke itself.

Turn right on the dyke which runs near the crest of the hill, crossing the stiles as you come to them and following the dyke downhill through an old larch wood. At the foot of this wood pass through the gate slightly to the right into the field ahead and follow the dyke and hedge now on your left. At the farm ahead go through the gate to the left of them and onto the metalled lane beyond. Turn right on this and return to your vehicle.

# SHELDERTON HILL

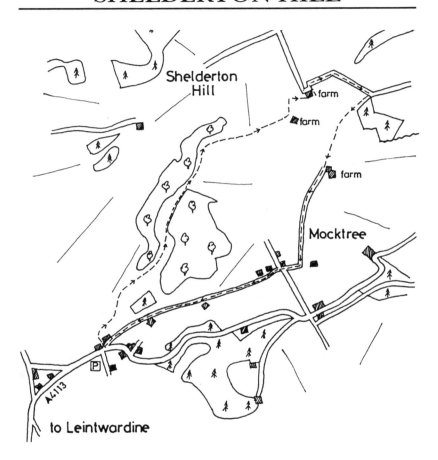

One and a half hours.

The walk can be started from Leintwardine, or if you prefer, take the A4113 north from Leintwardine, passing the two turnings to the left just out of the town which are signposted to Craven Arms. When you come to an unsignposted minor road a short distance ahead on the right, park where you can.

The walk starts on the tracks opposite the minor road, taking the left-hand unsurfaced one of the two. Presently this turns sharp right and about a hundred yards up the track from the bend, you'll see a stile on your left. Cross this and bear half left to the direction you were following along the track, to cross the field to a stile set in the hedge ahead just above a gate in the valley bottom. Cross the next field towards the valley bottom, aiming for the gate at the far end. Beyond this the path follows the bends in the valley, crossing the bottom to meet the right hand area of woodland where a lone thorn tree stands a few yards out into the field.

The path now follows the edge of the wood and eventually meets it. Here you will have to scramble over some fencing to join the path just inside the left hand valley side's woodland. Carry on walking along this path, which soon becomes a track and will lead you up through the wood to a gate near an old quarry, into a field near the valley top. Once in the field, continue following the valley floor, though now more a dingle, and you will soon emerge near the hilltop and see a collection of ruined farm buildings on your right.

Pass through a gate on the left, and follow the fence on your right towards the hilltop, turning right at the corner of this field through a handling area onto a track. This in turn leads towards some dilapidated farm buildings, and turn half left through these, to then curve round the field on your right towards a conifer plantation. Turn right immediately before this, and walk along the field edge with the wood on your left. At the far end of the field the path leads between two hedges and soon becomes a track at Mocktree Farm.

Follow this track over the crest of the hill, shortly after which it turns sharp right. Soon after that it'll pass over a junction of tracks, the one to the left being metalled. Keep straight on and the track soon disintegrates into a path again—but along a verdant sunken route, which can be muddy due to its very sunkenness.

The path will eventually return to the status of a track and later becomes metalled and will lead you back to the main road and your vehicle.

If you want to visit an interesting pub for refreshment, try The Sun in Leintwardine.

# STOWE

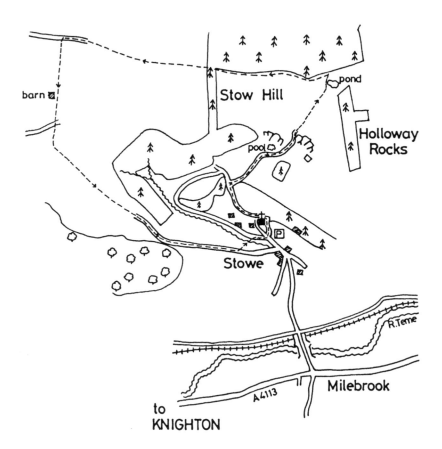

One and a half hours.

A walk with pools and rocks, with views of Caer Caradoc and the Teme Valley. The route is on tracks and paths in good order with a fairly steep climb to start with, but in stunning countryside. It may include one awkward fence crossing.

Take the A4113 from Knighton to Leintwardine. Just over a mile out of Knighton take the first minor road left to Stowe. Cross over the River Teme and go over the crossroads on the other side. Keep on up the lane and bear right up the hill to park in a little car park near the church. (It's marked Church Car Parking—Private, but there's no where else really to park, and whenever we've been the church has been locked in any event.)

Walk on up the lane past and above the church, curling round the hillside to the right. Go through a gate and take the right-hand track which winds up through the hills and rocks, passing a pool on the left. As you come to the top of the hill the track bends round to the left, but you keep walking ahead, leaving one wood on your right and slanting across towards another. You come to a pond between the woods at which you bear left to the wood now straight ahead.

Turn left along the fence in front of the wood and initially follow the wood on your right and then pass another wood on your left. Caer Caradoc now appears like a beret perched on the hill on your right. After this second wood the path enters a series of fields, but you carry on following the line of the fence on your right and eventually you'll come to a gate which leads onto a track. Walk a couple of hundred yards down this track until just before it bends right and more sharply downhill. At this point there are two gates on the left, one either side of a hedge leading off at right angles. Take the first gate and follow this hedge on your right, circling past some farm buildings which you'll soon come to. In the field past these buildings, follow the fence on your right until a track comes up a gully on the right. Join this track beyond the gate at the far end of the field, and keep on straight ahead. The track heads half left across the next field, heading into the left-hand of the two far corners of the field. In this corner you want to pass through the small gate on the left onto the track on the far side of the field boundary. However the last time we walked this it had been fenced across—thankfully with no barbed wire though. Once through this gate and/or across this fence, turn right on the track and follow it across the ridge of the hill, after which it swings gently to the left and makes a steeper descent. After crossing a cattle grid, the definitive footpath turns left down the hill, following the remnants of a sunken track between a few trees and tree stumps. Cross the stream at the bottom and turn right, passing out onto the lane through a gate. Turn left on this to return to your vehicle.

# SOURCE OF THE RIVER LUGG

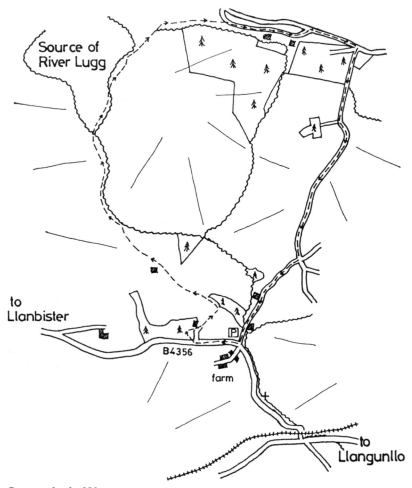

One and a half hours.

A walk across fields, up a rocky gully through which the Lugg flows and then across heather clad moorland, returning via farmland again.

The walk is on a mixture of tracks and paths and involves a bit of a scramble by the side of the Lugg at one point.

From Presteigne take the B4356 to Llangunllo and Llanbister, turning right and then left over the A488. Once through Llangunllo continue on the B4356 turning sharp right under the railway. The road then bends to the right and left past some houses and on the next major bend left you want to park where you see a track going off to the right and another off to the left leading to a collection of farm buildings.

Walk on up the road for a few hundred yards till you reach a sunken lane on the right with a gate immediately past it which leads onto a stony track curving through a field. Walk up this track, which swings right past some stone buildings on your left. Past these the track bends left again and goes uphill, bending left again once through another gate. At the next gate the track appears to end, but go through the gate into the field and follow the hollow in the ground to the hedge on the far side of the field. Turn right in front of the hedge and follow it up to the gate ahead through which you pass and continue to follow the fence round on your left, passing another stone building in a hollow in the ground on your left. Pass through a further gate into another field and ahead you'll see the Lugg's rocky gully. Turn to the right of this and walk down the field, heading for the middle of the boundary down the hillside—you'll eventually see a gate in the fence, for which you aim. Pass through this onto the moor.
Walk up the Lugg, taking the right-hand stream at all major junctions on each occasion. On the last section the cleft narrows, and depending upon how much water is coming down the Lugg you may need to clamber up out of the cleft and rejoin the stream at the top.
Once up onto the open moorland, follow the dip in the ground between the low rises on either side and this will take you in a gentle arc to the right eventually, and fairly suddenly, bringing you to the corner of a wood. Follow this wood along on your right, the paths slowly becoming tracks which pass an old tumbledown lodge. Beyond this you pass through a gate onto a gravelled track. Turn right onto this and it will lead you to another corner of the wood. At this corner turn right (but not sharp right) onto the waymarked Glyndwr's Way, and go through the gate onto a wide track which initially passes between two plantations. This will lead you gently downhill and after about a mile you'll reach a valley bottom. Here there is a crossroads of tracks and you turn right. This track will lead you out to your vehicle.

159

# BWLCH - Y - SARNAU

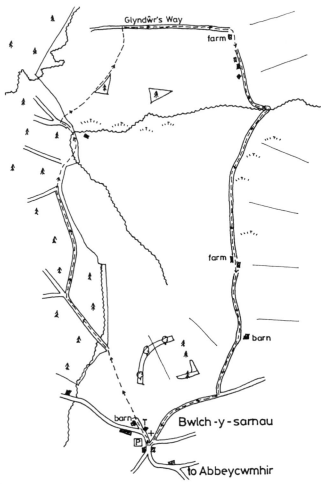

One hour.

A walk in a valley surrounded by soft hills. Some of the walk is on Glyndwr's Way and is in good condition, some on tracks and paths

160

which seem rarely walked. These can be very boggy but are passable with proper footwear.

Park near the school and Baptist church in Bwlch-y-sarnau.

Take the track to the right immediately below the school, itself immediately below the church. Before you reach the barn a short distance ahead, bear right into the field and you'll see your route ahead—it technically follows the sunken track down this field and into the wood ahead by the gate just to the left of its right-hand corner. Initially follow this sunken lane, but when you come to the fence ahead, as there is no stile, turn right along it and cross over the gate which you come to on your left. Now walk towards the gate into the wood mentioned above. Cross over this into the wood and you will find yourself on a wide grassy ride, which can be very wet.

Keep on this till you come a crossroads of tracks, where you turn right. This will gradually lead you closer to the edge of the wood. When it makes a sharp left turn, you take the smaller track through the trees to the right, essentially keeping close to the edge of the wood. Not much further on another track leads left, and once again you keep to the right, soon to follow a stream which flows along the edge of the wood. You pass some rough ground on the right before coming into a larger clearing where the track divides. However just before this division you need to cross the stream on your right and leave the wood by the little gate on the far side. You may need to peer through the trees to spot this gate and find the right place; it is immediately to the left of gate between the two fields to the right of the wood.

Once out of the wood, the path crosses to the near corner of a small triangular conifer plantation on the other side of the field. Here bear left and follow the fence on your right to the corner of the field, then turn to the left and leave the field by the gate you soon come to. Turn right on the major track here and walk up to the farm ahead. You're now on Glyndwr's Way, and this is waymarked to the right and around the back of the buildings on your right. Beyond them the track swings left and right over a stream and then follows a hedge on your right at the foot of a steep slope to the next farm. Here the track passes to the left of some barns and the farmhouse, passing out by a gate immediately to the left of the farmhouse. The track now gains a metalled surface and will lead you up to a road. Turn right on this to return to the village and your vehicle.

# ABBEYCWMHIR

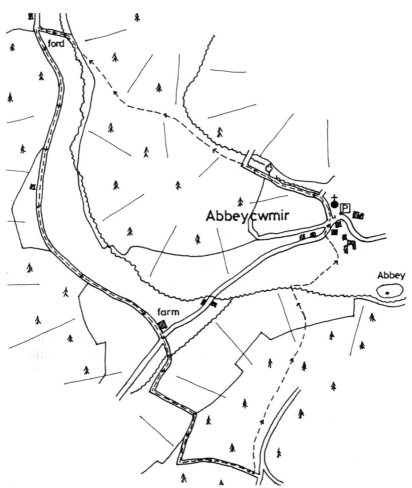

One hour.

A walk on tracks and paths in generally good condition, though with one slightly awkward fence crossing at the end. There is also a section of quiet minor road. It is set in pleasant wooded rolling countryside and includes a path from which it is possible to see the distant-ish remains of the abbey where Llewelyn the Great was buried.

Park near the church in the village.

On the road just to the west of the church take the track which is sign-posted Glyndwr's Way. This will lead you past a newish house and then between the church's graveyard on your right and an agricultural machinery graveyard on your left. The route keeps to a track which follows a fence to the wood ahead. Go through the gate into the wood, and walk on the track ahead, keeping left at the splits in the track. You will quite suddenly breast the rise, and here you cross a forestry commission road and descend the hillside by a track on the other side. This leads down to a stream which you can ford or cross by the bridge provided. Walk up the track on the other side to the road.

Turn left on the road and follow it down to a junction near a set of farm buildings. Cross this junction and go through the gate onto the track which leads down to the stream in the valley bottom. Once over the bridge, turn right through the gate on to another track. This bends to the left beyond the next field and passes between two fences up to the woodland ahead. Once over the gate into the woodland, the track turns right, at first keeping to the field boundary on your right before entering the wood proper. Soon it makes a sharp turn left and then you have quite a steep climb up the hillside. The track eventually joins a large forestry commission road, but immediately before this junction you take the path off to the left which initially appears almost to be heading back on yourself. This will lead you down a fairly dark alleyway between the trees, slanting across the hillside. Presently you will come to a brighter spot at a junction with plantings of different species of trees. Carry on straight down the hillside here to the stile not far ahead into a field.

Once over the stile look down into the valley on the right to see the remains of the abbey. Bear slightly left and downhill to cross the stream by the bridge provided, then turn right along the far bank and enter the field you come to by the gate provided. The path now turns half left heading to the right of a new bungalow and to the left of a small group of barns at the top of the slope. In front of the barns is the awkward fence you have to cross, and then the path keeps to the left of the barns and swings round behind them to emerge onto the road via a gate. Turn right to return to the church.

# GARREG DDU RESERVOIR

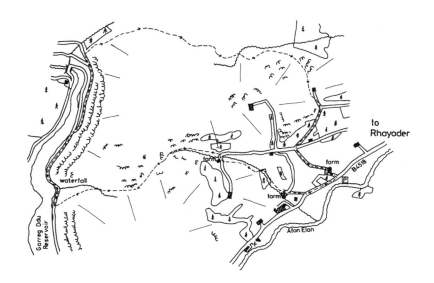

Two hours.

A walk past cascading streams and Elan valley reservoirs with extensive views, and on paths and tracks in generally good condition. However it is worth ensuring wearing waterproof footwear as there are some boggy patches on the hilltops, and after rain many of the paths can become small streams.

From Rhayader take the B4518 Elan Valley road. Out of the town go past one turning off to the right, then over a small crossroads. Go past one farm set at the foot of the hillside on the right, and then park near the entrance track to a white painted farm on the right which nestles by some woodland. If you reach a double bend sign on the road, then you've gone just too far.

Walk on down the road towards the double bend sign, and bear half right through the gate onto the track on the right. This leads to a farm, by the side of which you bear right on the track by the side of the stream, this passing under a bridge further ahead. Yet further on the track ends at a junction in the stream, but you cross the stream on your right and walk up the steep bank ahead, joining another track at the top. Turn left on this and it crosses the stream, then bends to the right in the field on the far side. Follow this track through a total of three fields, at the far end of which it leads out on to a more major lane near some renovated stone farm buildings.

Turn right on this lane, recross the stream and walk up to a gate across the lane. Just before you reach this a grassy track leads sharp left across the hillside, and is marked by a sign which says 'no vehicular access'. Walk up this grassy track, which initially keeps to the right of the stream, before crossing it and then keeping to its left. As you reach the crest of the hill the path swings first slightly left and then right to cross a dip between rocky outcrops. On the far side of this dip it bends left once more and follows the dip into a large bowl in the hillside. Here the path turns to the right again and keeps to the right of the bowl, gradually picking up a stream flowing downhill on your left. As you walk down the path the Elan valley will gradually open up before you. The path crosses the stream, rises across the shoulder of the hill on the far side, and then drops quite sharply to the Garreg ddu reservoir.

Turn right on the road and follow this alongside the reservoir, taking the right-hand no through road at a split further ahead. This will lead you gradually up the hillside, and keep a look out through the trees to your left for you will eventually see the dam to the Pen-y-garreg reservoir further up the valley. This can be an impressive sight if the water is streaming over it. Keep to the right-hand track further ahead, and then turn right in front of the gateway to a house, to shadow the wood on your left. Where the wood bends away to the left a few hundred yards ahead, you want to take the path which clambers quite steeply up the hillside.

Fairly soon however this turns more to the left to shadow the wood and soon meets another track at a hairpin bend. Turn right onto this track, and it will lead you up the hillside. As you near the top you have a boggy patch of ground to cross on much the same line as you've just been walking, but where the track can be slightly indistinct. But on the far side you will rediscover the track, which turns slightly more to the right. Keep on this well formed track on which you will start to make a gradual descent. You cross a couple of boggy patches and then a stream which flows out from the hillside on the right. Beyond this keep to the left-hand track at the various splits it makes, and it will bring you back to the stream further on. Here keep to the right of the stream, ignoring the track which crosses it, and you will gradually swing round the hillside to your right in a gentle arc. As you descend you will pass a cottage on your left and then come to a corner of a wood. Keep to the right of the wood and soon you will be passing by old deciduous woodland  and above another cottage to your left. The track will eventually meet a metalled lane, which you cross and go through a gate onto a track between two hedgerows, a track which takes your route half left. Go down this and you will come to a farmyard. Go through the gateway into the farmyard, leaving it via the left-hand of two gateways to the right of the house. This will lead you back to the B4518 and your vehicle.

# ST. MICHAEL'S POOLS, BLEDDFA

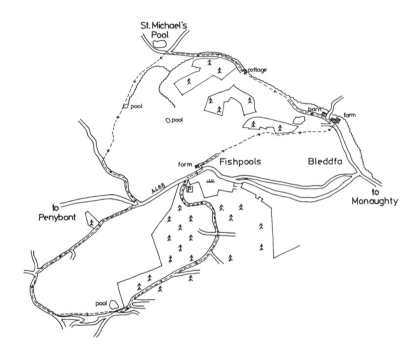

Two and three-quarter hours.

This walk is on tracks and paths to the rear of Radnor Forest, with pools, open country, woodland and intriguingly shaped hills en route. The walk can be cut roughly in half you wish.

Bleddfa lies on the A488 west of Knighton. Travelling from Knighton you pass through Bleddfa and travel round several bends whilst climbing uphill. After the road makes a sharpish bend left and starts to level out, you come to a wood close to the road on the left. There is a large gravelled track into this wood and you can park here.

Walk back down the main road towards the sharpish bend. Just past a driveway to a farmhouse and buildings on the left there is a wooded track with a gravelled surface. Take this and pass through the gates at the top, turning half right on to another track which climbs uphill between two hedges. This leads to a gate at the top into a field. Carry on walking on the same line across the field and you will come to a gateway in the far corner. Pass through this and continue once more on the same line, heading for the wood ahead. When you reach the wood turn half right and keep the wood's boundary to your immediate left, passing through one gateway en route. Presently you come to the corner of the wood, and it drops away downhill to the left. However you cross the field carrying on walking along the line you've just been walking along, and head towards a gate, initially not visible, in the far corner of the field positioned just to the right of the large group of farm buildings in the valley bottom. Through this gate follow the sunken track down to the farm in the valley bottom.

Turn left on the metalled track in front of the farm buildings and presently turn left off it to pass to the left of a modern barn. Keep on this track, which initially follows a fence on your left before entering a field. Keep straight across this field, passing through the gate ahead. Similarly cross the next field, passing out by another gate on to a track, just to the left of a newly repaired cottage on your right. Carry on up this track which continues to lead up the valley, keeping a stream on your right and a wood on your left. Just past the end of the wood you cross the stream and carry on up the hillside to a gate.

Pass through this gate and St. Michael's Pools can be seen by walking on ahead when they will appear on your right. The walk however continues by turning left once through the gate and then dropping down to a stream and following it along on your left. There is a rough track here which can be made out and followed. There are two pools on this stream, the second one being at its source. At the next gate you come to on your right past this pool, go through it and then continue to follow the fence, which is now of course on your left. The track ones more takes a definite form and will bring you to a metalled lane beyond the gate at the end of the field.

Turn left on this lane and it will bring you back to the main road. If you want to follow the shorter version of this walk, turn left on the main road and you will soon come back to your vehicle.

168

The full walk continues by crossing the road and bearing up the track on the far side. This track slopes along the foot of a hill, passing a wood on the right, and further on, once it has passed over a little rise, it divides. A grass covered track leads off to the left and you take this, soon to see a network of tracks crossing each other below to your right. The grass track soon joins one of these and you turn left onto it and go through a gate. The track you're now on gradually swings round to the left and starts to follow a little stream on your right up into the hill. When the track meets the edge of a large wood it splits and you take the left-hand split which passes along the outside of the wood and gradually climbs uphill. Eventually you come to a pool on your left and a gate into the wood on its right. Pass through this gate and join a gravelled track. Keep left on this track which then slants up and down round the back of the hill's summit, before dropping down towards the main road and your vehicle. However just after the track turns sharp left, a grassy track slants off to the right, past some semi-cleared land. If you take this and follow it down, it provides a pleasanter way of returning to your vehicle.

# PILLETH

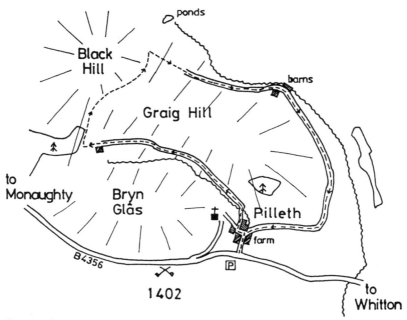

One and a quarter hours.

A circuit of a grassy hill above the battlefield of Pilleth, with views across the border country, along well maintained tracks and gentle slopes. (You can visit the church to see the pieces of armour and weaponry from the Battle of Pilleth. This was fought on 22 June 1401 when Edmund Mortimer was taken prisoner, and Sir Walter Devereux of Weobley and Sir Robert Whitney, Knight Marshall to the king, were killed in a battle against the Welsh forces of Glyndwr. The clump of trees on the hillside above the church marks the burial place of those killed. Henry IV refused to pay the ransom demanded for Edmund Mortimer after the battle, so the latter joined forces with Glyndwr.)

From Presteigne take the B4356 west to Llanbister and Newtown. About three miles west from Presteigne you pass over a crossroads with the B4357 at Whitton and about three-quarters of a mile further on you come to Pilleth, recognizable by the church up on a hillside on the right. Park near the lane at the foot of the hill on which the church nestles.

Walk up the lane to the farmyard and turn towards the church. (The path to the church goes on ahead through a small gate.) The track then turns round to the right and passes through a gate as it turns left once more. The track crosses a stream and then climbs gently up the hillside. It eventually heads towards the lower, left-hand end of a wood on the hillside ahead, below which you come to a gate into a field. Pass through this gate and turn right to take the path along the hedge and into the edge of the wood. Keep the wood on your left and walk steeply uphill.

At the far end of the wood go through another gate and onto the hillside. The track initially follows some fencing on your right, but passing through one gate, it then follows a hedge and fencing on your left. When the ponds in the valley floor are visible the track turns right immediately after passing through another gate. It then follows the valley on the near side of the fence, one field up from the ponds. When you reach some farm buildings, the path actually passes them to their right—go through the gate into the field just above the buildings. Keep the buildings on your immediate left and when you've turned the far corner you'll see a stile on which to cross out back on to the track. This now has a metalled surface and will lead you back round the hillside to the farm you started from.

# CASCOB

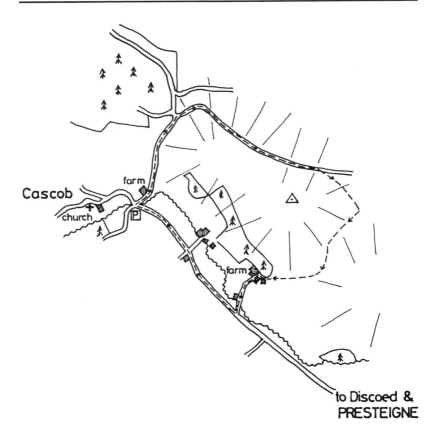

One hour.

A walk up and around a hilltop with views over the border country, with streams and rocks en route. Largely on tracks, though with a section of very minor road.

From Presteigne take the B4356 west to Llanbister and Newtown. About a mile and a half out of Presteigne and immediately before the road crosses the River Lugg, take the minor road left. In the settlement of Discoed, about a mile ahead, take the minor road to the right, then at the crossroads with the B road go straight over on to the no-through road signposted to Cascob. You want to park on this road where it crosses a stream about one and three-quarter miles on.

Take the track that leads off the road to the right and which initially follows the stream to your right. The track passes a farm on the left before curving left itself and uphill towards a rock face which lies just to the left of the path. The path crosses over a small ridge between two hills. Almost immediately across this saddle you take a track to the right which runs parallel to a fence and curves gently up and round a grassy hill. The path goes through a gate onto some bracken covered hillside and continues to curve up and round the hill.

Near the place where the path reaches its highest point it splits, and you take the right-hand of the two paths offered, which then leads downhill into a flattish and wide saddle. Near the bottom of this saddle, when you near the corner of a fence, turn right along a track which leads above and partly around the boggy patch between the hills. At the far side of the saddle, the track bends to the right and descends via a steepish cut in the hillside. It leads down through a gate to some farm buildings, and after passing some sheds on your left, you bear left before the house and follow a track down to the road in the valley bottom. When you reach the road, turn right to return to your vehicle.

A few hundred yards further up the road from where you parked is Cascob Church. This was built on a pre-Christian mound and contains a charm on paper dating from circa 1700, together with a modern translation. The charm itself is a jumble of incantation and invocation making much of the word abracadabra. The church also has a half timbered tower and a rough fifteenth century screen.

# NORTON

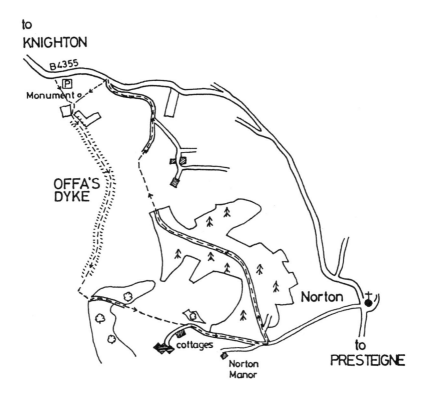

One and a half hours.

This walk includes a reasonably well preserved part of Offa's Dyke with its views over central Wales, as well as tracks through and on the edge of woodland, some of it old oak, some coniferous.

From Presteigne take the B4356 west, and just past the end of the town turn right on to the B4355 to Knighton. After passing through the village of Norton the road starts a long climb uphill. When you

174

reach the top of the hill, park when you come to a metalled area on the left near Offa's Dyke path signs.

Cross the stile on the left and walk across to the track to the left of the gorse strip. Follow the oak waymarking signs of Offa's Dyke path round to the left of the first wood and between it and the second. This leads you on to Offa's Dyke itself which you then follow.

The dyke runs along and then descends the hillside and where it peters out, Offa's Dyke path is signposted to the right. Ignore this and carry on, turning slightly left to reach the gate into the woodland on the left about 200 yards ahead. Pass through this gateway and walk down the track. Pass a narrow conifer plantation on your left and through another gateway you come to an area of open ground above some farm buildings and cottages. Turn left and walk down to the left of the left-hand most cottage, passing through a further gateway on to a metalled lane. Follow this lane round, which overlooks Norton Manor, until a branch makes a hairpin turn to the right to descend to the manor. Immediately past this point you take the stoned track off through the woodland on your left.

Follow the track along and it gradually climbs back up the hill, though when it swings left it becomes steeper. Near the top of the wood it bends to the right and passes out of the wood through a gate. Follow the track, which now almost follows the contour of the hillside, along the fence on your right and eventually the track will become metalled and lead you back to the main road.

However, literally just before you reach the main road you come to a gate into the field on your left. Go through this and walk towards the marble monument, passing just to its left. Shortly afterwards you'll rejoin Offa's Dyke path on which you turn right to return to your vehicle.

# BIRTLEY HILL

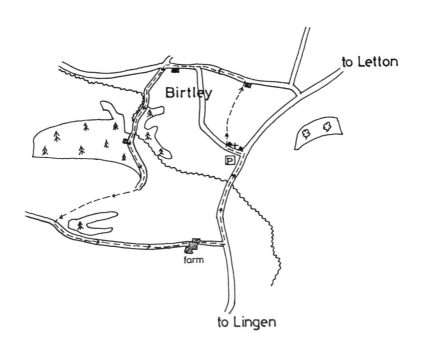

One hour.

This walk is set in rolling countryside with views of the locality, streams to follow and woods to wander by. Most of the walk is on tracks which can be muddy in places in wet weather, but all the slopes are fairly gentle.

Birtley lies between Lingen and Brampton Bryan and can obviously be approached from either. The place to park is on a lay-by on the west of the road between the two, a lay-by situated about a mile north of Lingen at a T-junction, and which has a letter box and a telephone box to help recognition.

176

Walk up the most minor road that creates the T-junction, just to the north of the lay-by. Pass the Methodist Chapel and then immediately past a house on the right, take a path that leads across a stile behind the house. Keep the hedge on your left and the path soon gains the status of a track. Then once more pass through a gate and the track vanishes. Head to the gate to the left of the building at the far right-hand corner of the field, and turn left onto a road.

Walk up the road passing the turning to the left, and the road drops downhill past a couple of houses on the left, after which you turn left through a metal gate and walk down a sunken track—this is the start of the part which can be muddy. Follow this track downhill to a stream at which point it turns left and follows a wood on your left and the stream on your right, crossing the stream further on. Once over the stream follow the track up the hill, passing a cottage on the right after which the track bears left. It then gradually climbs and circles back round to the right, eventually ending at three gates leading into different fields.

Pass through the gate straight ahead and follow the hedge along on your left to the end of the field where it meets a metalled track. Turn left on this track and follow it downhill past a wooded cwm on the left, and further down through some farm buildings and out on to the Lingen to Brampton Bryan road. Turn left to return to your vehicle.

# BURRINGTON

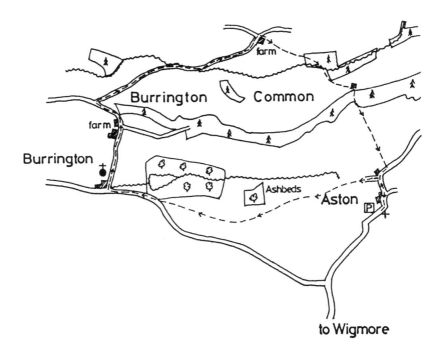

One and a half hours.

A walk on tracks and paths in attractive rolling limestone countryside.

Park at Aston Church (for which see the gazetteer) on the minor road between Ludlow and Wigmore. The church is easily recognized—it's small with a tympanum above the main door, has a neatly kept church-yard and lies on a sharp bend near the foot of the hill leading down from Mortimer Forest.

Walk up the road towards Ludlow, making one bend to the right and another to the left near the castle mound. At the next bend to the right, take the track that leads off to the left. This soon becomes a grassy ride, but don't become too carried away, for once through an old gateway in this ride, go through the gateway into the field on your right. The path then follows the fence on your left up and over the long axis of Bowburnet Hill. Over the crest and above a wood on your right called Ashbeds, walk down the fence you come to for a few yards, and cross over the stile. Walk back uphill to the fence, and keeping it on your left walk down this to the road ahead. Turn right on the road and follow it till you come to a road to Burrington and its church to your right. Take this road.

Past the church follow the track which is an extension of this road, and carry on up past the farm on the left, curving round to the left beyond it. When you come to a gate into a field ahead, continue sharp right on the track, and on uphill. The track then drops downhill into a valley, passes through a gate and then climbs gently up to a farmhouse. Turn right between the red brick farmhouse and farm buildings, walking out through a gateway at the far end of the yard. Now follow the hedge on your right and go through the next gateway. Presently you come to a gate on your right, which you go through and walk down a track through some rough ground.

This track crosses a stream in the valley bottom and passes through another gate. Walk on up to the left of a line of trees ahead, and bear left round the lump or knuckle of ground, passing to the right of some dilapidated farm buildings, to pass through a small gate into some woodland. Turn immediately right in the woodland, and after just a few steps, sharp left down a path which leads down a gully. Go straight across the track you meet and follow a fence down on your left and cross out into a field. Initially keep the wood on your left, walking in the same direction, and at the next corner of the wood, carry on straight across the field to the gate on the other side. Go through this gateway and then follow the hedge on your right to the road. Turn right on the road to return to your vehicle.

# MARY KNOLL VALLEY

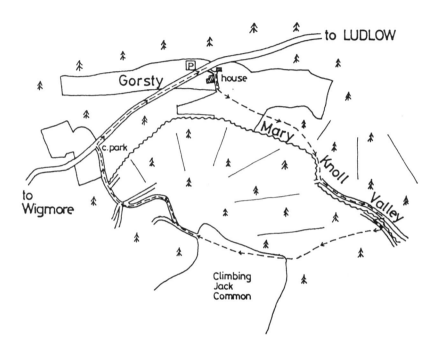

One and a half hours.

This walk contains views of the hills around Ludlow. The paths and tracks pass through a variety of woodland—conifer, old oak and silver birch—and follow a stream at one point.

Take the minor road from Wigmore to Ludlow. After driving along a valley bottom the road starts to ascend a long hill before flattening out in a fairly straight section at the top of the rise. On the right of this section is a collection of buildings, just past which is a wooden footpath sign. Park between here and the bridleway sign a short distance ahead on the left.

180

Walk back to the wooden footpath sign and pass through the gateway at this sign. Follow the hedge on your right, and you'll swing round to the right behind the houses. Here a gate leads left onto a wide track which passes through the middle of a field. Take this track which then enters the woodland ahead by another gate. Walk on down the track in the woodland, following a stream on your right. As you near a clump of conifer wood ahead, the track bears to the left, and you take a path to the right between the wood and the stream. This path soon becomes a track once more and is marked by posts with an incised green painted band. Past a pond in the valley bottom the track joins another even wider one on the outside of a hairpin bend which this new track makes. Here you turn sharp right on to a path marked with posts with green and white bands. The path leads back on you and crosses the stream, then meets a track on the other side.

Turn left on this, then take the pine needled track which gently rises uphill to the right, again marked with green and white incised posts. The path leads round and slowly up the hillside, then out into some old oak and silver birch woodland, keeping some conifer woodland to your immediate right. At the far corner of this the white track leads to the left, the green to the right. Take the green one which keeps a conifer wood on your right, crosses a stoned track and then follows a conifer wood on your left. The track is still marked with the green posts and leads out on to Climbing Jack Common. The track crosses the common, initially keeping a hedge about 30 yards to your left. Further on the hedge leads off to the left and the track bends to the right to re-enter the conifer woods, this time a young plantation. The track is well defined from here on and leads round to the right and then fairly sharply downhill, before making a series of zig zags and leading through a car park to the road. Turn right on this and return to your vehicle.

# CAYNHAM CAMP

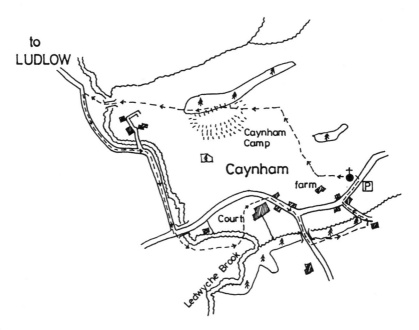

One and a half hours.

A walk on paths and some unavoidable roads. It incorporates the well preserved ramparts of Caynham Camp, its views and its interior seclusion. Wellingtons are a must if you want to cross one stream en route, unless you're happy to spend additional time on the roads.

Park near the church at the eastern end of Caynham. A footpath leads off around the north of the church, though the church's most interesting feature is the remains of the old preaching cross to its south. Inside the church there is an Early English chancel arch. The footpath leads to a stile in the north-western corner of the churchyard. From here the path crosses the field on the same line as you should have passed through the churchyard, aiming for a small gate in the next field boundary about a hundred yards up from the farm buildings. Once through this gate turn right and follow the hedge on your right. You pass through one gate almost immediately, and towards the corner of the next field, pass through a gate on your right. The path continues on the same line, but now follows the hedge on your left. Just over the ridge you come to a stile on your left, and you cross this and go across the next field to the far right hand corner, immediately in front of the ramparts of Caynham Camp.

Cross a couple of stiles and pass into the hillfort. The path now crosses over the right hand part of the central area, and at its far side, you make a steep descent of the banks to join a track which leads to a stile near a gate. At this point aim just to the left of Ludlow church tower, and cross the field to a stile roughly in the middle of the fence opposite. Once over this stile follow the same line to a bridge across the stream, after which the path turns slightly right to cross out onto the road by a stile—not through the obvious gate straight ahead!

On the road, turn left and walk all the way till you reach a T-junction. If not wearing Wellingtons, turn left on the road till the walk rejoins it near a new development on the right. Otherwise go straight over the T-junction and follow the Ledwyche Brook on your left. At its bend ahead, turn left towards a gate above the brook at the far corner of the field. Here, below Caynham Court, you'll see the remains of the old bridge. Go into the next field and within a few yards you can pass down to the river and walk along a small weir of stones where the river is shallower, and up a path on the far bank. Turn left at the top of the bank and leave the wood through a gate. Turn right and pick up a track below the court. This leads you round the court and past some new housing.

Back on the road, turn right, and take the little road to the right just before the lay-by with its telephone and post boxes. This road crosses a stream after which you take the first gate on your left. You then walk along the edge of the field, above the bank which drops down to the stream. You pass through one gate, and then leave the second field by a little gate below a cottage further up the hillside. Once through this gate, bear left and walk down the lane below the bank. When you reach the road, turn right to return to your vehicle.

# NEEN SOLLARS

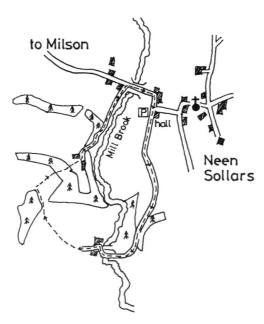

Three-quarters of an hour.

A pleasant walk largely on tracks set in rolling countryside.

Park near the village hall, located at the western end of the village on a sharp bend in the road.

Walk down the track which passes the village hall, this track following the ridge before curving right to drop down and cross a river. Before it does so you'll pass on the left what you may take to be the river, but which is in fact a classic example of an ox-bow lake—though this one may have been formed when the railway was built at its far end.

    Over the river, walk on the track past Sturts Farm on your right. At the crest of the ridge beyond the Sturts, the path turns right through

184

the first of a pair of gates. Now walk along the hedge on your left, passing through one gateway, to the wood ahead. Here turn right in front of it and follow its boundary to your left, passing through another gate. At the far corner of the wood, turn right towards the highest piece of ground in front of the silver birch fronted wood on your right. Here you'll find a stile to cross into the wood, the then better worn path leading down through the woodland to a semi-collapsed footbridge. Over this carry on straight ahead into a field. Cross this, aiming for the little gate between the stables on the left and a house on the right. This gate will lead you onto a drive, down which you walk, it curving downhill to the stream beyond, which it then follows. Once back on the road turn right to return to your vehicle.

# TENBURY WELLS

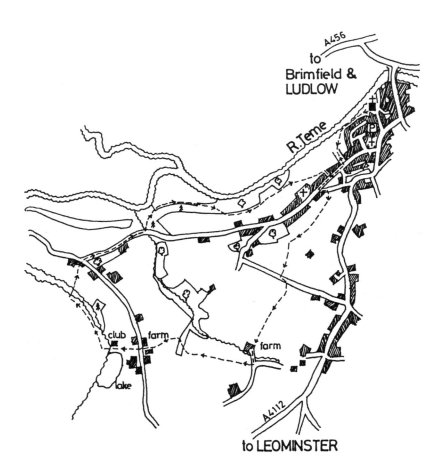

One and a half hours.

A walk mainly on paths in gentle rolling countryside to the west of
Tenbury, and alongside streams and in woodland above the Teme.

Park near the church in Tenbury Wells.

Walk down the footpath to the left of the church, the path following the churchyard, then passing houses on the left before entering a small new housing development. Walk through this to the lane beyond and turn left on this to meet the road ahead. Turn right on this and walk up past the fairly new group of bungalows on the left. Turn left on the road immediately beyond these bungalows, passing the single garage and shed on the right, and turn right through the gate beyond, some hundred yards from the road junction. Once through this, walk up the sunken route into the field, then gradually turn to the right over the rise, and follow the dip in the ground below and to your left. Cross one stile into the next field, and out of it by the stile on the other side. Cross the next field on the same line to the gate on the far side. Through this, drop down to the stream and cross it by the bridge, then head to the far left-hand corner of the field. Here you will find a stile out onto a track.

Turn left on this and after about thirty yards turn right over a small old stile into the field on the right. Cross the field to the gate on the far side. When you reach it you'll find it's a blind, but cross it and walk down the hedge on your right. At the far end of the field go through the next gateway and continue walking down the hedge on your right. Again go through the gateway in the next corner, and pass Manor Farm on your right. You'll soon find yourself on the farm's driveway on which you turn left.

Once through the farm's gateway and over the brook, turn right and go through the entrance into the field. Walk up the old sunken route to the fence above, turning right in front of it and head to the far left-hand corner of the field. Cross the stile here, and then the stile on the far side of the lane, to the left of the hedge ahead. Walk ahead down this field, following a hedge on your right, to the far corner of the field. Cross a stile here, and continue in the same direction, now following a hedge and fence on your left. When you reach a gateway in this fence, turn half right and if you walk across the field you'll soon see a gateway in the fence below and ahead. Go through this, following the sunken route beyond to the right of a tree, after which the path turns left and heads towards the farm buildings. The path technically passes to the right of the new large barn and between it and the old farmhouse. But you'll probably cause less annoyance to the farmer by taking the gate to the left of the new barn and walking out on to the road beyond through the farmyard.

Once on the road, take the stile opposite the farmhouse, and walk down the field towards the lake in the valley bottom. Cross two stiles in the fence above the lake, and turn right to walk above it and past a new golf club house. Cross the weir and turn right on the stoned track beyond. Follow this to a gate at its far end, turning right onto a track back over the stream, and which then bends left and rises to meet a road.

Turn right on this and immediately left at the junction ahead. Once over a bridge in a steep dip in the road, turn left through a gate onto a track. Follow this track as it bends to the right and passes through another gateway into a nursery plantation. At the far end of this cross the stile and clamber up the bank. At the top you'll pick up a path which shadows the Teme on your left at the top of the bank above it. Keep to the edge of this bank, crossing stiles as you come to them, and gradually you leave the edge of the bank further to your left, finally passing out onto the road round some gardens and between some houses. Turn left on the road and retrace your steps to your vehicle.

# SHRAWLEY

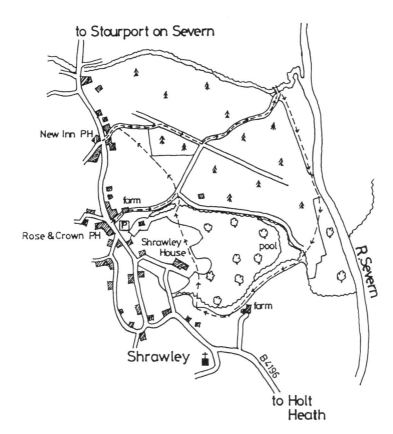

One and a quarter hours.

A walk largely on tracks in varied woodland—young conifer, damp alder and willow to mature oak—and near the Severn for part of its distance. It also enjoys fairly extensive views to the south at one point without involving any major climb, and passes ponds and Shrawley House.

There's a choice of starting places. Parking is not easy so you can choose either the Rose and Crown or the New Inn just north of Shrawley Church on the B4196. Both are Marstons' pubs. If you want to avoid a pub, then it is just possible to park on the roadside opposite the Rose and Crown.

Assuming you're starting from the Rose and Crown (if not then read on), walk up the lane opposite the pub. This quickly leads you to a farm, and you pass the farmhouse and major buildings on your right, the track following a hedge on your left. Further on above a pool on your right, take the track which leads off to the left, this following a field boundary on your left. When it joins the wood on your right, it keeps to the outside of this. Walk into the wood at the far end and turn right on the track just inside the woodland.

If starting from the New Inn, take the track opposite the pub, and when it passes through a gate, take the right-hand track, initially following a field on your right before passing through woodland on both sides.

The two different starts have now met! Walk on along the track and presently it makes an angled crossroads with another track. Turn right. Further on you come to another crossroads where you turn left, this track taking a more curving route through the woodland. At its first major junction you turn right and further on, when a path leads off to the right up a bank, you keep left down the gully heading towards a footbridge. However, before you reach the footbridge you cross a stile into the field on your right.

The path now hugs the edge of the woodland, and gradually your route and that of the Severn on your left come closer together. You pass through a small area of woodland right on the banks of the river, and in the field beyond, once more keep to the edge of the woodland on your right. After about two hundred yards cross the stile on your right back into the wood. The path here initially keeps to the foot of the bank on your right, before slanting up and over it and then dropping down to a pool. Here the path bears left over the dam which creates the pool and then rises up the far bank, eventually leaving the woodland by a gate into the field above the wood.

The track, as it has become, keeps to the edge of the woodland and enters a farmyard. Keep all the buildings to your left and leave the yard by another gate, so as to continue following the edge of the wood on your right. Presently you drop down to the right, crossing a footbridge, and in the next dip take the stile on your right back into the woodland, presently crossing a second bridge. Over this you bear left up a sunken path, emerging from the wood beyond it by a stile into a field. On your left is Shrawley House with its old walled garden. Shadow the boundary of the house, crossing by another stile ahead into some park-like land. Cross the next stile on the same line ahead, and in this larger field bear just slighly further to the left, but still heading for the far boundary. Once over the rise in the field you'll see a pool ahead of you. Cross the stile on your right in the fence above this and walk on the track to the far side of the woodland.

Here turn left to return to the Rose and Crown. To return to the New Inn take the track opposite which follows a field boundary to your left. When it joins the woodland to your right, it keeps to the outside of this. Walk into the wood at the far end and turn left on the track just inside to return to the New Inn.

# WOODBURY HILL

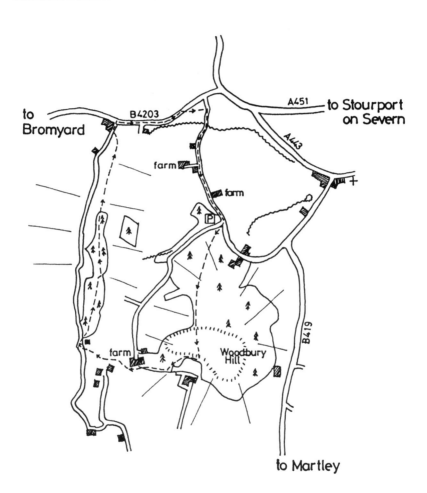

One and a quarter hours.

A walk on good paths and tracks, many of them part of the Worcestershire Way and so are also well waymarked. It takes in

192

Woodbury hillfort and wide views from a thin ridge over much of Worcestershire. It does involve a fairly short section of a relatively busy B road.

At Great Witley, to the south-west of Stourport, take the B4203 west, signposted to Bromyard. Almost immediately, take the narrow unsignposted metalled road to the left, and, after several hundred yards, park in a lay-by on the right at the foot of the wooded Woodbury Hill.

Walk on up the road, and on the corner with another metalled lane off to the right, there is a footpath leading up the hillside through the wood. Take this, crossing another track after a short while, and carry on up the hillside. The path soon joins a wide track, on which you turn left, again to carry on up the hillside. You pass a field off to your right and then enter the ramparts of the hillfort. Carry on through the hillfort and at the far side, pass out through the ramparts and turn right at their foot to walk parallel with them to a conifer plantation ahead. At this the path turns sharply left and downhill, keeping to the edge of the plantation.

At the bottom it joins another path, on which you turn right. Further ahead you come to a gate through which you pass to enter a field below Woodbury Hill Farm. Here the path keeps to the left of all the buildings and yards before crossing another stile. Here you head to the conifer wood down the slope, coming to a waymarked stile and now you follow the Worcestershire Way for a while. The path leads through the conifer wood and then down a gully with wide views, to a gate out onto a minor road. Here you turn right and past the cottage on the right, turn right, still following the waymarks. The path now leads uphill through the woodland, making a zig zag further on, to lead out onto a narrow ridge along which you walk for some distance, with its extensive views, especially to the west.

As the Abberley clock tower comes into view over the hill, so the path bears slightly left to descend the hillside, joining a minor road on the left. Walk down this and turn right on the B road. After passing a pool on the right, and just beyond the first bend in the road, take the double stile over the fence on the right. In the field bear slightly away from the B road and pass out of the field at its far side via a stile. Turn right on the road and return to your vehicle.

# KYRE GREEN

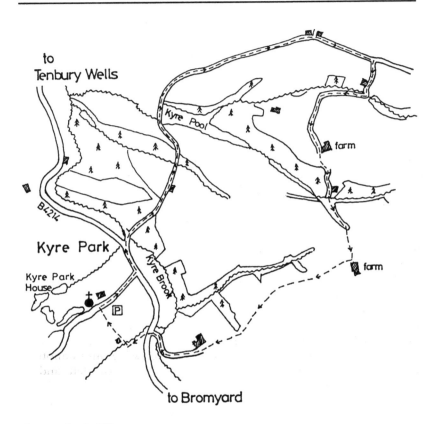

One and a half hours.

This walk is set in rolling countryside with a lake and woods. It is generally on major tracks, though these can be very muddy in some places. Towards the end one path crosses a field, so again can be muddy depending upon the time of year.

From Tenbury Wells take the B4214 south and when well out of the town take the first non no-through road to the right to Kyre Green.

Park when you come to Kyre House a few hundred yards up on the right-hand side.

Walk back down the road up which you've just driven to the B road, on which you turn left for a couple of hundred yards before turning right onto a wide bridleway. This leads you through some woodland and later past an artificial lake before traversing farmland on each side. Keep to the main track which gently swings right, passing some houses on the left and which then rises to a junction with a lane on the right. Turn right down this and follow the lane as it bends right past a cottage on the right, cross over a stream and then follow the track as it turns gently left. Further on it passes a white painted cottage on the left and then comes to a farm.

Pass through a gate on your right immediately before the farm buildings so that they are all on your left. Follow the fence on your left down between two orchards. At the bottom you turn left through a gate onto a wide sunken and probably muddy track. Follow this through the wood passing one cottage undergoing restoration. You turn right on to its approach drive, and after some twenty yards left on to a path across the stream and up to a gate on the other side. Beyond this the path eventually leaves the wood and emerges into a field. Follow the hedge along on the left and then pass through a gate in the fence ahead into another field and follow the fence on your right this time, heading directly towards the old farm buildings ahead.

Immediately in front of the buildings turn right through a gate and follow the hedge on the left, passing an old moat and go down to a gate in the bottom left-hand corner of the field. Pass through this and cross the next field on roughly the same line, crossing out by another gate into the next field. Again follow the hedge on your left, and in the bottom left-hand corner pass through the gate and go into a large field. Keep on walking on roughly the same line, heading just to the left of the farm buildings which lie further down the slope, picking up a track near the farm. (Recently it appears the farmer may be leaving a headland on the edge of the field if you follow it round to the right. It's a longish diversion and the choice is yours!) Once you join the lane on the far side of the field, follow it past the farm and round to the right to meet the B road.

Go straight over the B road into the orchard and follow the hedge on your right till you come to a footbridge. Cross this and head up past the cottage on the left to a track which will take you back to Kyre House, past the walled garden.

# TEDSTONE DELAMERE

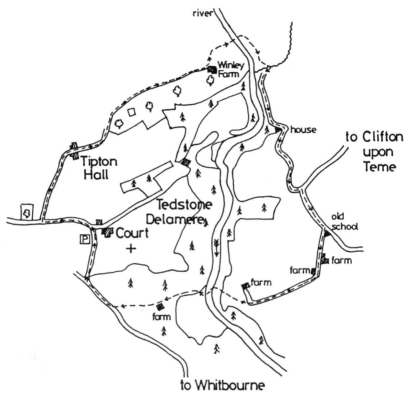

One and three-quarter hours.

A walk in rolling countryside following streams at times. Mainly on farm tracks and bridleways so generally is easy to follow, but can be muddy and difficult in places because of horse use of the bridleways.

Park in Tedstone Delamere in the lay-by at the church entrance.

Walk along the road, keeping the brick walls of Tedstone Court to your right. Round the corner and over the brow of the hill turn right on the no through road. This leads to Tipton Hall Farm, the bridleway then passing through the farmyard with most of the farm buildings to your right. Go through the gateway at the far end of the yard, and follow the hedge on your left round to the left. Go through the next gate ahead, and though the track carries on ahead before dropping gently to the right, the public bridleway on which you should walk, turns hard right and follows the hedge on your right to a gate in front of you. You can see the line of the old track by the dip in the ground. Go through this gateway and follow the hedge on your left, passing through another gate but continuing to follow the hedge. This will lead you through a break in the hedge to rejoin the track you left those few fields ago. This now leads down to Winley Farm.

Before reaching the farm buildings, turn left through a gate and follow the hedge on your left, before following the dip of the track to the right to the woodland ahead. Pass through a gate into the wood and follow the track down to and across the stream and up the far bank. The path bends to the left to pass near the cottage above the bank, where you turn right and follow the path along the top of the woodland. This path soon bears left and right over a small stream flowing into the valley. Beyond this stream you come to two gates on what is now a track, the one straight ahead leading to a house. Take the one to the left and walk alongside the fence, passing out through a gate onto another track beyond the cottage on your right.

Carry on along this track, round another house and stables, and later on it turns left to join a minor road. Turn right on this road and turn right again in front of the old red brick brick school building onto the lane to Woodhall Farm. This track leads to the right of Woodhall Farm and to the left of May Farm. The track then bends round to the right and passes Primrose Cottage on the right. When it makes another turn to the right to lead to a farm, go through the gate into the field ahead and follow the sunken track along the hedge on your right. This leads to a gate in the far right-hand corner of the field, through which you pass to another gate ahead on the edge of the woodland. Through this gate turn left and downhill, the track bending right further on to ford the stream. Once across the water walk almost straight up the hillside to the left of a little gully that leads down to the stream. Higher up this crosses a new track and resumes its sunken appearance, bending right and emerging at Pizhill Farm. Keep to the right of the farmhouse and buildings and walk up the track to the road ahead. Turn right on this and return to your vehicle.

# BACH CAMP

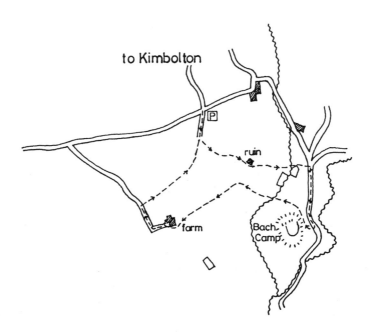

Three-quarters of an hour.

A pleasant walk in rolling countryside, passing another of the area's hillforts. Many of the tracks and paths are in good condition, whilst others cross fields and may be obstructed by ploughing or crops. One of the least convenient walks for parking.

Take the A4112 Tenbury Wells road from Leominster, and once above Kimbolton, turn right on the lane signposted to Bache. This presently reaches an unmarked T-junction, and you want to park tight in here.

Walk up the farm track which, if surfaced, would turn the T-junction into a crossroads and this soon leads to a gate into a field. Go through the gate and walk along the field edge on your left to another gate.

198

Go through this and across the right-hand corner of the field you'll see another gate. Cross this field to this gate. (If badly obstructed, it's not too much further to follow the field boundaries round on your right.) Once through this gate walk down the tongue of the field and past the well grown over ruins of a building on your left, after which the field opens out. Walk down to a point about fifty yards to the left of where the hedge on your right meets the stream below. Cross the stream and walk on up the field opposite on the same line, emerging onto a metalled lane through a gate. Turn right on the lane and walk along it for a while, gradually nearing the banks of Bach Camp.

When the lane just starts to diverge from the banks, you'll see a signposted stile in the hedge on your right. Cross this and walk up to the stile above. The track now bears right, travelling between the two banks, eventually emerging on the far hillside. The path then crosses down the field to the left of the far right-hand corner, where you cross the stream by a bridge and come back on to a track once more. This now leads left up the hillside and then swings harder left, later leading through Upper Bache Farm, before turning right and gaining a metalled surface.

Walk along this lane and turn right through the first gate just beyond the first hedgerow that meets the lane on the right. Keep this hedgerow on your right and pass through another gate into the next field. Keep to the hedgerow to the next gate, and again follow it till you come to a place where the hedgerow forms a point jutting into the field. Here, if you turn half left, you should spot the gate by which you initially entered this field at the start of the walk. Cross to the gate and return to your vehicle. (Alternatively if the the field is badly obstructed, follow the hedgerow round on your right.)

# CROFT AMBREY

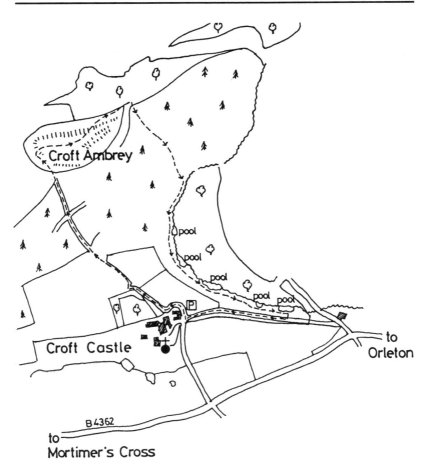

One and a quarter hours.

This walk includes Croft Ambrey hillfort (see the gazetteer) with its one particularly fine rampart, views across to Wales and a walk down the wooded Fishpool Valley. Virtually all the walk is on major tracks none of which have too steep a slope, but they can be quite muddy.

Park near Croft Castle which is signposted off the B4362 Mortimer's Cross to Ludlow Road towards the Mortimer's Cross end.

Follow the metalled lane round the rear of the castle and then turn right at the crossroads of tracks behind the castle and head up the hill. The footpath is waymarked in blue at various points and you keep going straight ahead through a gate and into a field with some twisted chestnut trees. Carry on up this field to a gate at the edge of a wood and continue on the same line through the woods, crossing over a track in their middle. Pass through another gate at the end of the wood and out onto the bracken covered hillside. Carry on walking along the track and presently you'll come to a stile over the fence on your right. Take this and follow the track which zig-zags its way through the ramparts, before crossing the internal area to the scarp slope. The track will then lead along the scarp face and out of the hill-fort and over a stile. A short distance further on you'll come to a small gate back into the woodland.

Go through this and down the track down the hillside till you reach a stony track. Turn right on this for just a couple of steps and then turn left onto the path down the slope. This will lead you to another major track on which you turn left and continue downhill. It eventually meets another track at a T-junction. Turn right here and then almost immediately right and left and over a stream so that you end up following the stream downhill with the stream on your left. Here you initially follow blue, red and green waymarking signs, though at further splits always keep to the track immediately above the stream and ponds. This is later just waymarked with red and further on still, with no colour at all. You pass a total of five pools, with an old water-mill at the far end of one. Above the fifth the track bears up to meet the metalled lane to Croft Castle. Turn right on this and follow it back to your vehicle.

A pleasant pub to visit is the Bell at Yarpole, a village south of the B road.

# SHOBDON

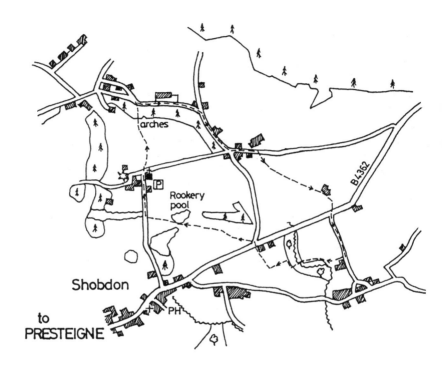

One hour.

A walk on good tracks, minor roads and paths, some in good order some unlikely to have been reinstated by the farmer. (However there is an alternative using minor roads to avoid the worst places.) The walk includes Shobdon arches, some of the nearby grounds and pools and a length of old protective dyke.

Turn into Shobdon Park opposite the Bateman Arms in Shobdon and park near the church near the top of the drive. (Even for non church lovers this one is well worth looking inside. For more information refer to the gazetteer.)

Walk north from the church, leaving the church on your right and the main buildings on your left. Carry on up the grass avenue to the arches re-erected from the old Norman Church. Turn left at these and walk around the edge of the wood to emerge onto the road behind. Turn right on this and walk round to a crossroads formed with another entrance to Shobdon Park. Turn left at the crossroads and just past the last cottage on the right and opposite the main farm on the left, go through the Public Footpath signposted gate on the right. Cross to the corner of the ditch and dyke on your left and follow this and the resultant fence on your left down dale and uphill to the B road. Cross this and walk down the lane ahead.

You pass a fairly large field on your right, and at its far end, just before a cottage, cross into the field. (The County Council and landowner may not have organised new stiles on this next section, so if you want a longer but slightly easier route from here, carry on down the lane rather than enter the field. At the T-junction ahead turn right and walk up to the B road. On this turn left and then right at the park entrance to return to your vehicle.) Follow the field boundary on your left and pass through a gate on the far side and over a small stream to another gate. Through this, turn right and follow the field boundary to the next hedge at which you turn left and walk to its far end. Then cross the hedge you've been following. Walk down the hedge on your left to the road, and cross out onto it. (If this is dificult, turn right in the field and walk along till you reach a gate onto the road.)

Turn left on the road and almost immediately go through the gateway on the far side of the road, just beyond the junction of a minor road with the B road. On the far side of this field is a wood and you want to aim slightly to the left of the left-hand corner. Once you've crossed the crest of the field look for a small break in the row of evergreen trees, about eighty yards to the left-hand end of the wood. Go through this break and join the track through the hedge and above the Rookery Pool. Turn right at the end of the pool and cross the stile, then walk up the old avenue to the gate onto the lane. Turn right to return to your vehicle.

# STAUNTON - ON - ARROW

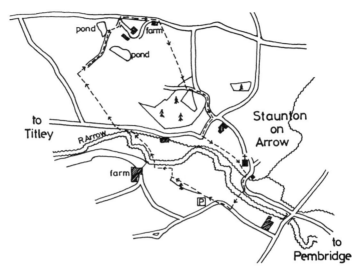

One hour.

Largely on paths through permanent pasture, with a short stretch of minor road, passing pools and following the River Arrow for a short length. Set in undulating morainic country it also passes Staunton motte. However there can be areas of mud created by cattle at certain times of the year, and some shaky stiles at some crossing points.

From Pembridge take the road to Shobdon, and turn left once over the river, past the old railway station. At the crossroads outside Staunton, turn left to Lyonshall and Kington, turning right onto the unsignposted road very soon, just past the Georgian Court of Noke. Follow this road till it makes a right-angled turn to the left, and park on the side of the road on the right.

Just before where you've parked, on the same side of the road, you should see a little gate into one field, with an overgrown stile to its left into the neighbouring field. Cross the stile and walk along the right of

204

the high ground, later following the length of the wooded slope on your left. At the field boundary ahead, turn right down it and go through the gate into the next field. Follow the river bank to the left and presently below a farm and its wooded hillside you come to a footbridge over which you cross the Arrow. Follow the river on your left and cross the next field boundary at the stile. The Arrow makes another bend to the left and right again, whilst the path cuts diagonally across to the second bend, crossing the mill race above the weir at the bend. Follow the river round to the left and cross out of the field by the gate on your right onto the road.

Cross the road and go through the gate into the field on the other side. Pass immediately through the hedge on your left. The path now runs up and slightly across the gentle hillside, heading to the left of the main bank in the field. It will lead you up to a gate in the top left hand corner of the field. Pass through this gateway and walk on the same line following the hedge on your right. At the end of the field you come to one of the worst field crossings, but once over the wire and ditch, turn right and follow the hedge passing through a gate into the next field. Keep the boundary on your right, and you come to a wide track which leads past Staunton Park on your right, and a fishpond on your left. Follow the wire fence on your left past the pond and cross out onto the road ahead by the stile, with the drive to Staunton Park farm buildings just on your right.

Turn right on the road, passing Staunton Green on the left and Staunton Park Farm on the right. Past the stone wall beyond Park Farm, go through the gate into the field on the right, then follow the metal fence on the right. Pass through a gateway between woods at the end of the field, then follow the edge of the trees on your left, and go through a gate onto a track, which will lead you to a road. Turn right on the road and walk down to the junction below. Turn right, and when the road bends to the right, take the footpath to your left. This leads via a stile across a garden, so take extra care here for bear in mind your thoughts if a path crossed your garden. Cross out over the stile on the other side, and keep straight ahead through the small fields to the motte. Walk round between the motte and the church and then head across the next field down towards the cottage in the dip below. Cross out of the field via another collapsed stile opposite the cottage onto the road.

Turn right and at the next bend take the footbridge back over the Arrow. Go straight over the next field to the gate opposite which returns you to your original road. Turn right to return to your vehicle.

# PEMBRIDGE

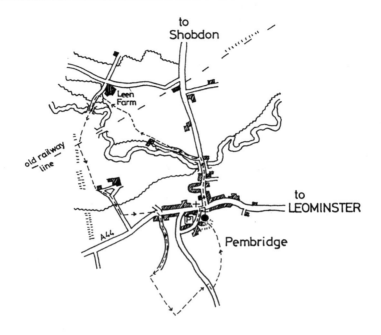

One and a half hours.

A walk largely on paths in the fields around Pembridge. But because some paths cross fields which tend to carry crops and where paths haven't been reinstated in the past, they can be difficult to walk at ploughing or before harvesting. There is also one rather overgrown stile and one low fence to cross, though these can be avoided by resorting to a section of minor road.

Park near the old market behind the New Inn, a pub which can provide a good ending for your walk!

Walk down to the main road and turn towards Leominster, turning left on the minor road to Shobdon opposite the village stores. Cross the River Arrow, and then take the track to the left. This leads round a bend in the river and then enters a paddock in front of some old mill buildings. Here the path follows the fence on your right, crossing stiles and gates to the right of the buildings you approach. Carry on following the fence on your right beyond these buildings and beyond a gateway you'll come to a stile into the field ahead. Over the stile turn right and follow the hedge to the stile onto the old railway line. Cross this and the stile on the far side, then bear half left to follow the hedge on your right. This path will lead past The Leen farm on your right and through gates onto a track.

Turn left on this and you'll soon cross the Arrow. Once across head for the far right-hand corner of the field you're in. Here you'll find a stile back onto the railway line and once more you cross it to another stile. Over this look for the building on the rise beyond the field boundary on the far side. Below this you'll see a gate and your route leads to and through this. Once through, follow the hedge and later the wall on your left and this will lead you round onto a lane. Turn right on this and you head down to and over a stream. Go through a kissing gate on the left and walk up across the slope to the far right-hand corner of the field. Here you leave the field by another kissing gate.

Turn left on the main road and almost immediately right onto the public footpath signposted track. This leads you past some new houses and then between fields. The track swings to the right and eventually ends at two gates just past a large shed on the left. Go through the left-hand gate and the path now follows the hedge on your right. At the end of the first field, carry on on the same line to cross the next small field, and then similarly the next larger field, still keeping to the hedge on your right. At the end of this larger field go through the gateway to your left, and then turn left to follow the hedge now on your left. This will lead you to an overgrown gate on to a road.

Here, if you want to avoid obstructions which may not have been repaired, turn left to return to Pembridge. Otherwise turn right and cross the stile on the left which you come to after about seventy-five yards. The path has been over-planted with fruit bushes, so walk along the strip below the fruit trees on your right to the far side. Then turn left and walk down the hedge to the bottom corner of the field, where you cross the fence on your right into the field beyond. Then turn slightly right and walk over the rise, to head for the gateway to the right of a pond in the dip on the far side of the field. Once through the gateway turn left to follow the hedgerow to a kissing gate into the churchyard. Walk through the churchyard to return to your vehicle.

# HERROCK HILL

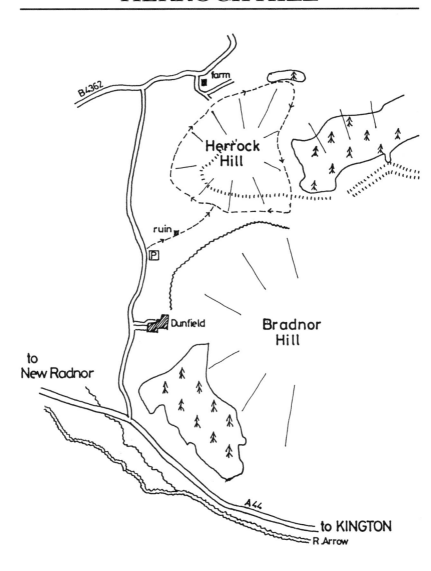

One hour.

This walk incorporates part of Offa's Dyke path, with views over the hills around Kington, and the valley of the Hindwell Brook. It is all on major tracks, and there is one long but not too arduous ascent to make.

Take the A44 west out of Kington and take the first minor road on the right which is signposted to Dunfield House and Dunfield Farm. Follow this road, bearing left at the farm driveway, to the top of the rise which you come to quite suddenly, and park here.

On your right as you come to the top of the rise in the road there is a gate which you go through and then follow the track which keeps to the hedge and fences on your left. This track soon comes to the remains of a ruined building at which point the path turns slightly left and crosses a field to a gate at the foot of Herrock Hill. Go through the gate and then turn left along a sunken track and follow it round the hillside.

Towards the far side of the hill a track leads down down to the left to some farm buildings—ignore this and carry on round the hill, keeping the fence to your left. A little further on another track joins yours from the left—this is Offa's Dyke path. Carry on walking along round the hill, now following the Offa's Dyke path and the acorn way-marking signs. A little further on you come to two gates and Offa's Dyke path is waymarked through the right-hand gate. Past some farm buildings the path divides again, and again it is the right-hand path you take, slanting up the side of the hill. At the crest of the hill Offa's Dyke path is signposted to the left; you should continue straight on down the far side of the hill. This will lead you to an elbow of fencing, in the far corner of which is a gate. Turn right onto the track which leads back to the gate at the foot of the hill. You then return to your vehicle by the same route as you approached the hill.

# EVENJOBB

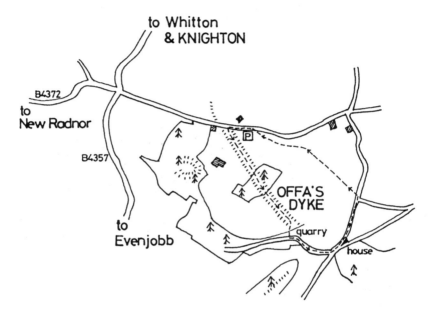

Three-quarters of an hour.

This walk includes a short section of Offa's Dyke, but over relatively flat ground. It is all on good paths and tracks, with views over the surrounding countryside.

Take the B 4357 north from Evenjobb and turn right at the first crossroads you reach. Go for about half a mile down the minor road until you come to the second wooden Offa's Dyke path sign, just over the crest of the rise. Park near to this.

Cross over the hedge to the right of the road and walk along Offa's Dyke uphill to the wood ahead. Continue on the dyke through the wood, following the waymarking signs, and when you come out of the wood the path follows the fence on your left downhill. At the end of the field cross the fence by the stile provided and drop straight down to the track below. Turn left on the track, pass through one gateway-and then you come to a junction of several roads and tracks. Take the left-hand track, leaving a house to your right in the apex of the split. Walk on up the track and when, just over the brow of the hill, another track meets it at right angles from the right cross over a stile on your left. Follow the hedgerow along, keeping it immediately to your left the whole time so that further along you bear sharp left and pass out through a gate onto a road. Turn left and you'll soon come to your vehicle.

# ROUND THE WHIMBLE

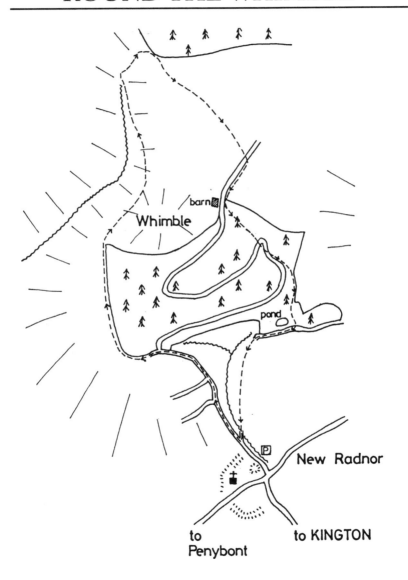

One and three-quarter hours.

This walk includes the moors of Radnor Forest, with wide views of a variety of countryside ranging from the valleys of the borders to a deeply cut gorge on the moor itself. The walk is on tracks with the exception of narrower paths through some woodland.

In New Radnor take the B4372 to Knighton and immediately take the minor road off to the left up to Radnor Forest. Park where suitable just up this lane, and certainly before it divides with a track leading off to the right.

Carry on walking up the metalled minor road, taking the left-hand metalled lane of the two branches referred to above, heading towards the wood ahead. Later the road turns slowly to the left and, becoming a track, keeps to the left of the wood before passing through a gate and out onto the moor. The track keeps close to the edge of the wood and bears right up the hillside. The Whimble itself emerges from behind the wood as you walk on, and then the track turns right and passes along the foot of the final lump of the hill, before following a gorge in the hillside on your left and a fence on your right. The stream that feeds this gorge and the track itself eventually almost meet, at which point you come to a gate. You turn right and loop round two man made water holes, and keep to the right of the fence to head towards a tongue of forest which appears over the crest of the hill.

Just before you reach the forest you turn right onto a grass track through the heather and follow it across the top of the moor, keeping a fence on your left. Later the track drops down and you pass through a gate on to a gravelled track, over which you cross. Then you then follow the track to your immediate right, crossing two stiles in the process, and heading towards a wood and new barn. The track then leads to the left of the barn and into the wood. After continuing for about a hundred and fifty yards in the wood, a path leads off to the left straight down the hillside. Follow this path down, twice crossing gravelled tracks. The path eventually leads down the hillside just inside the wood itself and with a fence to its left. Later it comes to a pond on your right and thence out of the wood by a gate and onto another track. Turn right on this track and follow it as it initially keeps the wood on your right and then swings to the left and slants across the hillside to the minor road on which you parked.

# WATER - BREAK - ITS - NECK

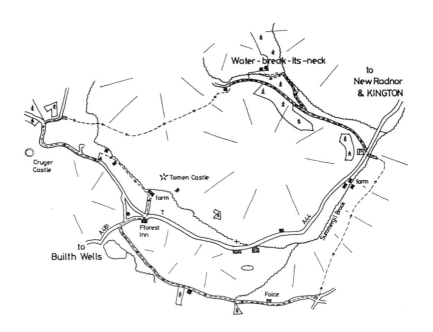

Two and a half hours.

This walk is on a mixture of paths, tracks, a metalled lane and two short sections of A road. It includes a tall waterfall, woods, moors, a lake and often has sweeping views of the surrounding countryside.

Take the A44 west from Kington towards New Radnor. As you drive along a fairly straight section of road past New Radnor, a limb of Radnor Forest on the right seems to hang over the road. As you start to ascend slightly to round this limb, there are two track entrances on the right, and a track off to the left almost opposite. Park on the verge beyond this left-hand turning.

Walk up the track off to the right into Radnor Forest and follow it along the hillside. Before you reach the wood the track divides. Take the right-hand fork and enter the wood. When the track reaches a small stream flowing out from the left, turn left and follow the path which starts on the near side of the stream. This will lead you into a gorge and to the waterfall itself. This is obviously the more impressive the wetter the weather has been in the recent past.

Return to the fork in the tracks outside the wood referred to above, and turn right up the track leading up the side of the hill to the woods above Water-Break-Its-Neck. Once out of the wood on the other side, you keep on the track to the right till you come to a new barn. Follow the track to the left of and round the barn, and then take the first gate on your left once past it. You now follow the line of an old track which swings first to the left and then to the right leading up to a fence. When you reach this fence, bear right, keep the fence to your left and follow it along. You pass through several gateways, but always keep the fence to your left—the line of the old track sometimes diverging slightly from the fence if you keep a sharp eye out for its line on the ground. You gradually drop downhill and eventually cross a stream, after which the route bends slightly to the left and then right to run in front of a wide V shaped wood. In front of the far part of the V, the track gains a stoned surface and bears left to meet the main road.

Turn left on this and walk round the bend, past Cruger Castle on the right, past a parking area and then a lay-by on the left until you come to a drive off to the left which leads down to a couple of houses. Turn left down this, turning to the right before you reach the stream in the valley bottom. Pass in front of one house after which the track enters a field through a gate. Go through this and head towards the farm ahead, passing through another gate into the farmyard. In the farmyard you turn right onto the farm's drive and follow it up to the main road.

Turn left on the road and immediately right onto the main road to Builth Wells. Not far up this road turn left onto a metalled lane, which has a no through road sign and which may also be signposted (depending upon the time of year) to a dog kennels and cattery. Walk for some distance on this undulating lane till eventually you walk up the side of the hill ahead, passing the kennels and cattery at The Foice on your left. Past this the lane reverts to a track and soon bends slightly to the left. Take the first gate on your left past this slight bend, which leads onto a track with a stone base. Very shortly over the brow of the hill you should find yourself aiming straight at a large farm in the valley bottom. Carry on down the track to the corner of the field, where you turn right through a gate, to then follow the fence on your left, still heading towards the farm. Keep following the fence and later a hedge, crossing some field boundaries, and you'll soon pass above the farm and join a major track. However you stay on this for only a hundred yards or so, for when it bears right you yet again keep following the line of the fence on your left. Roughly adjacent to where you parked, a wide track leads off to the left between two fields. Take this, crossing the stream below, and walk up to where you parked, turning left on the main road to do so.

# CEFNLLYS

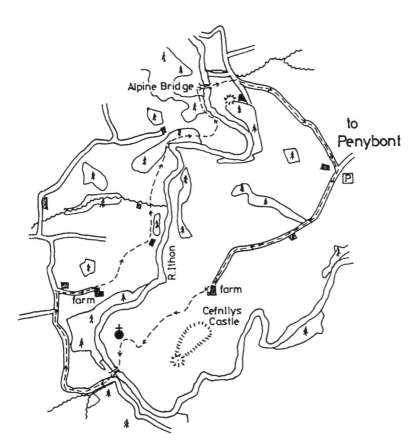

One and three-quarter hours—with the addition of a nature reserve if you so wish.

A walk in rolling countryside, including part of the scenic River Ithon and passing the old and orignally Welsh castle site of Cefnllys. This has been the site of a stronghold from very early days. In the tenth century it was held by Elystan Gladrydd; in the twelfth by the

217

Mortimers who strengthened the castle in 1262 only to have it stormed by the Welsh twenty years later. Roger Mortimer and Hugh de Bohun recaptured it only to be besieged themselves and to be starved into surrender after a total of 800 deaths on the two sides. The English were allowed to return home under a pledge of good conduct. Years later the castle was garrisoned by 12 spearman and 30 archers against Owain Glyndwr, but it was burned and wasted by 1406 and in ruins in 1540. The walk is largely on lanes and tracks, together with some paths on the far side of the river. All are in good condition.

In Penybont take the A44 west and immediately over the bridge over the Ithon, take the minor road to the left. After about a mile take the turning to the right, and when the road turns sharp right again park near the no through road sign which stands at the beginning of the metalled lane leading straight ahead.

Walk on down this lane, which passes a new house and older buildings before heading towards another older farm. Shortly before you reach this second farm, take the stile on your right and follow the new track round to the right, passing out by another stile at the far end. Over this you turn right onto the track which leads downhill and passes the site of Cefnllys Castle on your left. When you reach a gate into a field in which stands Cefnllys Church, go through this gate and walk towards the church. Before you reach it, however, you will see a path off to your left which leads downhill through old hedgerows. Take this and cross the bridge at the far end.

Immediately over the bridge is a nature reserve in the care of the Radnor Nature Trust which you may want to visit before continuing the walk.

From the bridge bear right and uphill on the metalled lane. This will take you round to the right, and at the first junction on the crest of the rise, you keep straight ahead. However at the next junction, in a dip just in front of a bungalow, turn right. This track will lead you into the farmyard of The Pentre. In the yard keep to the right of the newer buildings and to the left of the house and older buildings, and walk out of the yard past new sheep handling equipment and with the tump on your right. The path now follows the field boundary curving round to your left, and when you reach a gate, pass through this into the next field. Now follow the hedge on your right. This will lead downhill to a gap in the hedge in the corner of the field, where you turn half right and walk down the hillside to the left of the house in the valley bottom. As you near this you will see a stile with its middle timber painted with a yellow bar. All the remaining stiles on this walk are so marked, helping you to spot them across field boundaries.

Cross this stile and go over the track to the one on the far side. The path now keeps almost straight ahead, crossing stiles as you come to them. Presently you will come to the foot of a wood, and here the path keeps to the field and follows the wood's edge on your left. When you come to the Ithon, you cross into the wood over the stile provided. Here the path involves a bit of a scramble up the river bank before diverging from the course of the river and leading through the woodland. At the far end of the wood you cross a wooden gate, and then follow the footpath signs. These will presently indicate a right-angled turn to the left and this will bring you back to the banks of the Ithon at another gate. Cross this, and follow the river. After you cross a stream flowing into the river the path climbs a bank and leads out through a little gate onto a track near some barns. Turn right on this and almost immediately right again through another little gate. This will lead you over a gorge by the Alpine Bridge. Once over this the path leads out across a field to a gate which leads onto a minor road. Turn right on this, bearing left at the split you almost immediately come to, and this will bring you back to your vehicle.

# BUILTH WELLS

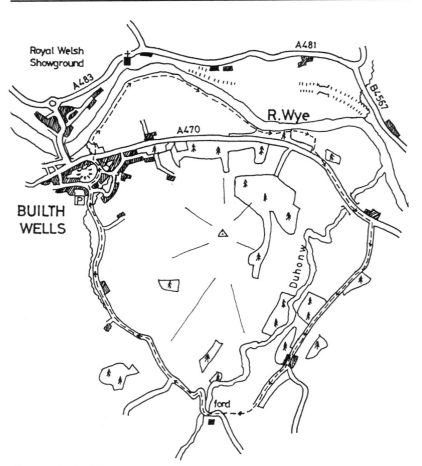

One and a half hours.

This walk includes a section of the River Wye, some of Builth itself and gentle valleys to the town's west. It is generally on good tracks, though there is also a four hundred yard or so length of main road to walk along.

Park in Builth and walk out of the town on the A470 Abergavenny/ Brecon road. Just past the garage on your right near the edge of town, turn down the farmyard entrance on the left, following the tarmac and concrete that winds through the buildings and leads down to the Wye. Go through the gate at the end of the concrete and turn right onto the track that runs parallel with the Wye.

This eventually peters out but the path follows the banks of the river as it bends around. There are a couple of fences to cross—one with no stile but still fairly easy, one with a tentative stile but barbed wire as well. The Wye eventually draws close to a bank and in the corner of the meadows at the foot of this bank there is a gate-cum-stile which you can cross into the recently replanted woodland. Don't be too put off by the sight—what we saw immediately ahead was the worst of the next two hundred yards that we had to face. Carry on following the river on your left and you will come to a good stile out into the field beyond the wood. Walk along the river to the fence at the far end, and turn right up it to leave the field by the gate onto the main road at the top of the bank.

Turn left down the main road, cross the stream and opposite a farm on the left, turn right up a little metalled drive with a letterbox on its corner. This leads up a valley to a farm and you enter its farmyard. At the yard's far end two gates lead out of it. Take the right-hand one into the field beyond and the track follows the edge of the wood on your left and leads along to a gate into the next field. Through this turn slightly right to the opening opposite into the further field, and once in this field bear downhill to the far right-hand corner where you'll pick up a track which leads down to a gate.

This is overgrown and easier to climb over, but once across, follow the hedge on your right and you'll soon join a better path which leads to the house ahead. Immediately in front of this house the path turns right between the house's boundary fence and a hedge and will lead you to a choice of ford or bridge over the river ahead.

The track now gains a metalled surface and zig-zags up the hillside before dividing. Take the right-hand fork and this will lead you gently back to Builth. When you meet the major junction in front of the old castle mound, if you bear right and look out for a stile on your left you can clamber up the old mound and its two ditches.

# ABEREDW

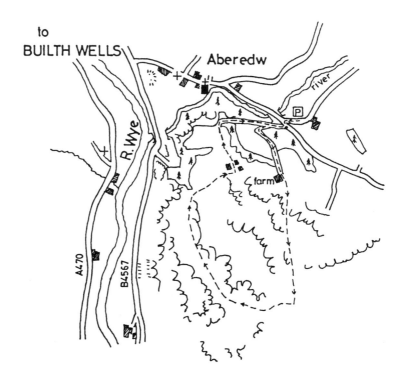

One and a half hours.

A pleasant walk past rocky outcrops and with views over the surrounding countryside. It's on a mixture of paths and tracks, generally in good condition.

From Builth take the A481 to New Radnor, turning right onto the B4567 to Aberedw after a mile or so. Turn left off the B road to Aberedw as signposted, go through the village and past the church and park just over the bridge.

Take the the right-hand metalled lane beyond the bridge, and after a hundred yards or so turn right through a gate onto a track. This stoned track zig zags through the trees and up the hillside before heading more directly up the slope. Eventually you reach a farmhouse on the right of the track. Go through the gateway adjacent to the farm and rather than continuing on the stoned track which turns to the right and carries on zig-zagging across the hillside, your route follows the grassy track straight ahead of you, keeping to much the same direction you've just been walking.

This grassy track leads on up the hillside passing through various crags, and before the summit of the ridge it splits in two. Take the right-hand split which leads you past a couple of small pools on the top on your right, and then curves round under an impressive rock face beyond this. Here it meets another better marked track on which you turn right, but when this begins to swing round to the left look out for a less well marked track which shadows the scarp face on your right, so that you start to walk back in the direction of Builth.

Bracken may obscure this path, but once you've found it follow it and you will gradually close on the scarp face, eventually passing right under it and above a cut into the hillside. Here, ahead of you, is a gate and fence. Go through the gate and follow the fence on your left, walking back into the hillside. At one point you come into a little stony dell between the rocks, but keep following the fence on your left till you come to a group of buildings. Go through the gate onto the track which leads between them and out through the gate at their far end.

Follow the track down to the next gate, keeping the fence on your right. In the next field walk down the fence on your right to the gate (not visible at first) in the far right-hand corner. Once through this gate you are once more on a well defined track which leads through various paddocks with views down into the Edw below, eventually rejoining your original track above where you parked.

# COLVA

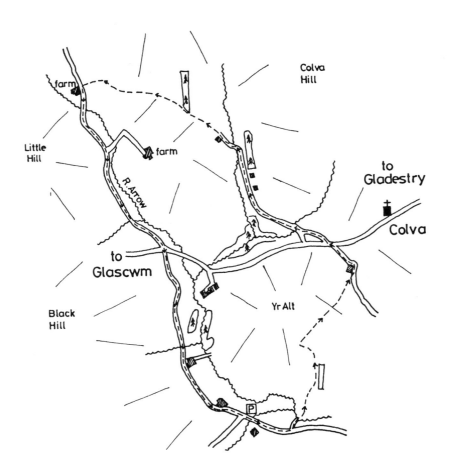

One and a quarter hours.

A walk in fields on the edge of open hillside, and sometimes in that open hillside. It includes streams, old sunken tracks, metalled lanes and some paths and minor road.

From Newchurch on the B4594 Painscastle to Gladestry Road, take the minor road to the west and carry on till you come to another minor road off to the left just past a farm and over a stream. Park near the junction.

Walk back down the minor road past the farm, now on the right, for a few hundred yards and take the track off to the left which leads down to the stream. Cross the stream by the footbridge and then walk up the slightly sunken and rather stony path slightly to the left of straight ahead and follow it up the gentle hillside. You pass a wood on the right and then the path bends round to the left and meets a track at a T-junction. Turn right on this track and follow it up to a metalled lane. Turn left on this lane, which rises uphill passing a house on your left, and then drops down to a crossroads.

Go over the crossroads and keep following the track. This will lead you to the right of one farm and then to the left of another house. Beyond this the track deteriorates—as do the buildings. The track will lead you over a stream, immediately over which you keep to the main track on the right, and not many yards ahead still to the main track, but this time to the left. This will lead you past an old house on your left, the course of your route then being marked by the sunken track which slants up across the hillside. At the top of this you pass through a gateway onto the open hillside. Your route still lies straight ahead, and you cross many other tracks. Almost on the crest of the ridge your track bends slightly left and starts to descend the hillside, bending slightly right again further on. The track becomes more indistinct and may become obstructed by bracken, in which case you could drop down the hillside to your left and pick up a clearer path which follows the field boundaries on your left. Whichever route you choose, you will come to a gate ahead, which leads into a field above a farm in the valley bottom. Go through this gate and diagonally cross the field to the gate opposite the farm.

Once through this turn left on the lane. Follow this along to another crossroads. Again go straight over and the road will lead you back to your vehicle.

# HERGEST RIDGE, GLADESTRY

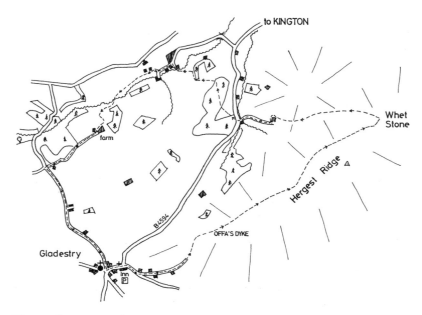

Two and a quarter hours.

A walk on good quality tracks and paths, including a section of Offa's Dyke path over Hergest Ridge, with good views, rolling countryside, open hillside, woods and streams.

Park at or near the Royal Oak in Gladestry.

From outside the pub turn right on the road and almost immediately right again on the minor road. Offa's Dyke path is soon signposted off to the left; take this following a good track past some houses and then through a gate out onto Hergest Ridge. Keep to Offa's Dyke path, ascending the hill in stages and passing a triangulation pillar away to the right. Just before you reach the summit, Offa's Dyke path meets a broad grassy track and you bear left on this. As you circle the summit

226

watch for the Whetstone on your right—a not particularly large rock a few yards into the vegetation. (Refer to the gazetteer under Kington.)

Here, making a hairpin left turn from the track you've just been walking along, is a smaller track heading downhill and aiming to the left-hand edge of Hanter Hill. Take this track, crossing the pass between Hergest Ridge and Hanter Hill, shortly after which the track bends left and follows a fence. Carry on downhill, the track gradually swinging right and becoming more of a path. It will lead you above a house, your route then turning left and crossing an old stile adjacent to one of the gates in front of and to the side of an old barn. The path then crosses in front of the house and you walk down the track which leads from the house to the B road in the valley bottom.

On the road turn right and adjacent to the first field you come to on the left, turn left up a small path and cross a stile into the field. (The end of the path is marked by a public footpath post which has no sign!) The path now slants across the field to a stile on the far side into the wood ahead. Cross this stile, the path then slanting right, up and across the hillside in the wood. Cross the track you come to almost immediately in the wood, and towards the top of the hill, the path bends left to a stile on the far side. Cross this stile and then diagonally cross the field you're in to the far left-hand corner. You'll see a gate as you approach, and cross this to emerge onto a path on the other side. This path initially follows a gully on your right, before bearing half left and dropping down to a stream in the valley bottom. Cross this by the footbridge provided, go through the gate ahead, and then turn left at the road junction not many yards further on.

Walk on along this road till you come to a gate across it to a house. Go through this. Bear left shortly afterwards to keep to the left of the house and follow a new fence on the left which runs alongside the track. This will bring you to a gate at the far end; once through you keep straight ahead and this will lead you back onto a track. Turn left on this and cross the stream either by the footbridge or the ford. Follow the track from the ford to the wood ahead and then to the right. This leads across the hillside to a gate into a field. Once through this the track zig-zags up the hillside to a farm. Go through the gate into the farmyard, in which you keep right to leave it by another gateway. Walk down the track you're now on between two hedges before entering a field, when you continue to keep to the track as it stays close to the hedge on your left. Through the gateway at the far end the track will lead you past a house to a crossroads. Turn left here onto a lane and this will lead you back to Gladestry.

# MICHAELCHURCH
# ON ARROW

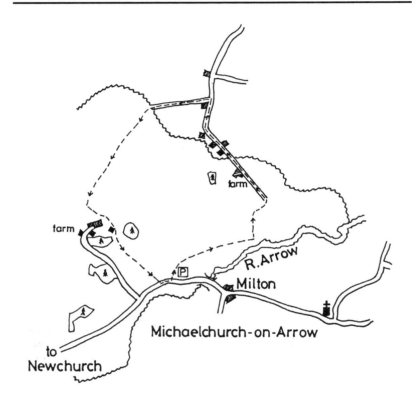

One and a quarter hours.

A fairly gentle walk on the border, on tracks in good condition, some on open hillside, or on paths on the edges or across fields.

From Newchurch on the B4594 Painscastle to Gladestry road, take the minor road east to Michaelchurch. About a mile along, near the end of a section of narrow road, there is a metalled lane that leads up to a

228

farm on the left, and a newish house on the right. Just beyond this there is a track which leads up onto a bank above the road at a point where the road bends to the right. You want to park in the area just below this bank. If you reach the River Arrow itself you will know you've gone just too far!

Walk up the track onto the bank above your car and go through the gate on the left at the top, and then turn right along the hedge on your right. You cross several field boundaries at or just up from the hedge you're following until you enter a field where the hedge comes to an end. Cross this field on the same line to the gate ahead, by which time you're on a bank above and quite close to the River Arrow. Once through this gate, the path turns left up the hedge and fence on your left, following the field boundary round when you come to the corner of the field. Pass through the gateway you come to in the top corner of the field, so continuing to follow the hedge on your left. This will lead you to a track off to the left, and you take this. This passes some farm buildings to the left, and later crosses a stream and passes other buildings on the right.

Keep on this track, which has gained a metalled surface, until you come to a stone cottage on the left with a track off to the left immediately behind it. Take this track which leads almost straight at the hilltop ahead. Once you've passed through the gate onto the open hillside, continue up the track ahead, taking the left-hand branch as soon as you come to a split in the ways. This leads round the hillside, bearing right at the next branch and then crossing another track. The track then nears and shadows a fence on your left and shortly before you reach a farm and its collection of farm buildings below you and to the left, you leave the open hillside through a gate. Now follow the field boundary on your left, and you'll cross a stream and join a more major track as you pass to the left of the farm buildings. However don't enter any field but keep on following the fence on your left, passing round behind a derelict farm shed. Further on you cross the stream and enter a field by a gate perched immediately above the stream, on the far bank.

Once in the field head slightly to the right of the line of telegraph poles and as you cross over the field you'll see a gate in the fence below you. Go through this, after which the path heads to a gate in the far left-hand corner of the field. Through this turn left on the road to return to your vehicle.

# ALMELEY

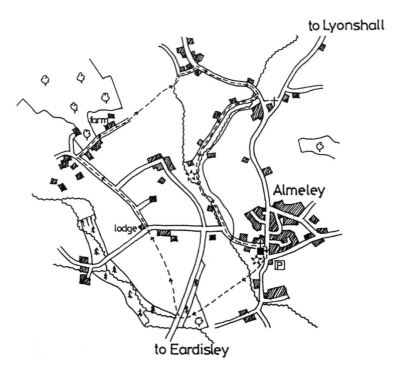

An hour and a quarter.

A walk on a mixture of paths, tracks, minor roads and lanes, mostly in good repair. It includes a stream fed and wooded valley, the Almeley 'twts' or motte and bailey castles, and general views across to the Black Mountains.

Almeley lies to the north of Kinnersley which is on the A4112, to the east of Eardisley which is on the A4111 and to the south-west of Lyonshall which lies on the A480, and is signposted off all these roads. Park near the church in the centre of the village.

Walk down the lane to the east of the church and take the footpath across the stile towards the obvious motte to the south of the church. Keep to the left of the motte and go down towards the stile and footbridge in the corner of the field, passing the remnants of two fishponds on your right. These used to provide the castle with some of its food. (For more information refer to the gazetteer.)

Over the bridge, cross the next field on the same line to the stile in the hedge ahead. Cross this and go over the next field on the same line to the gate on the far side. Over this still keep on the same line through a corner of the orchard to another stile; similarly through the strip of wood and a narrow field beyond, to cross out onto a minor road. Cross this and go over the stile adjacent to a gate and into the field. Walk up towards the fence on your right and then along it. When you come to a gate in the fence, pass through it. Now head across the corner of the field you're in to the right-hand of two gates in a line between you and a white painted farmhouse. Go through this gate, and then walk along the fence on your left, crossing a couple of stiles before emerging onto another minor road in front of an old lodge.

Take the metalled lane to the right of the lodge. This leads to a large Georgian house which is now a home for Latvians. As you reach the house on your left you come to a crossroads of lanes, at which you turn right and walk past the old walled garden on your right. The lane presently leads past some farm buildings and a house on the left to a gate into a field. Go through this and follow the hedge on your right to the next gate ahead. Cross the track beyond this gate, going into the field opposite through another gate. Here you bear slightly more to the left to the far left-hand corner of the field, aiming for the right-hand of two gates. Through this follow the hedge on your left and this will lead you over a bridge and up to a gate onto another minor road.

Turn right on this. After a few hundred yards it drops down as it enters the hamlet of Almeley Wootton. Take the gravelled track that leads off to the right in the dip and which shadows the stream. When the track swings right and uphill towards the second 'twt', turn left on the path which continues to follow the stream. This path leads you round the bottom of the 'twt' and across a couple of bridges to another gravelled lane. Follow this down to the road ahead. Turn left on this and it will lead you back to the church.

# WEOBLEY

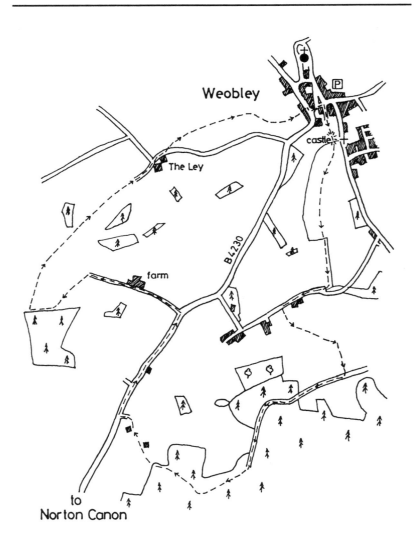

Two hours.

This walk includes crossing the remains of Weobley Castle, views from Burton Hill over north-west Herefordshire and passes two old farmhouses. One of these is The Ley, a fine example of a timber framed building. The walk includes a gradual ascent of Burton Hill and a steeper descent, but otherwise is fairly flat. It is on a mixture of paths and tracks, which can be muddy, and a short section of B road.

Park in Weobley.

Walk up the lane to the left of The Salutation Inn, past the telephone kiosk, to the castle mound. Go through a gate into the castle area and walk through the middle passing out over a stile at the far side. Head across the field towards the gate opposite, walking roughly parallel with the hedge on your right. Go straight across the next field to the gate on the far side and then follow the fence up on your left across the third field to the trees ahead. At the trees, which shelter the remains of Garnstone Castle, turn right on the track and follow it till you reach the end of a tall brick wall, at which point you cross a stile on the left and cross the field to an old metal revolving gate where you cross into the next field. The path then turns half left and you cross the field diagonally to the far corner.

In the far corner of the field, go through a gate and almost immediately turn right through a second one. Go straight ahead up the hill, until you meet a large track on which you turn right. When this track splits, take the right-hand fork and follow it through a gate into the wood. Carry on through the wood, where the gravelled track becomes a grassy ride. This ride passes through woodland, then runs just above a field on your right before re-entering woodland. After a while it splits, and again take the right-hand fork. Follow this track which swings downhill. When the path splits yet again as it nears the edge of the wood, you bear right and carry on downhill. Shortly after this split the path emerges from the wood and makes a dog-leg left and right to join a metalled track which you follow down to the B road.

Turn right on the B road and pass a cottage on the right. A little further on you take the gravelled track signposted with a public footpath sign off to the left and which leads towards a farm. Go past the old farm and an orchard on the right, shortly after which the track comes to an end at a gate into a field ahead. At this point turn left through another gate and follow the track along the hedgerow on your right. At the far end of the field go through a gate on the right into the next field and walk down along the edge of the wood on your left. Walk on to the gate ahead, pass through it and turn right along the new fence. Cross the next field boundary and then follow the old hedge on your right. You cross two field boundaries and when you come to the third boundary bear right and then immediately left through two successive gates. Cross the next field on roughly the same line as you've been walking, aiming just to the right of a little wood. As you approach the far side you'll make out a footbridge and stile, which you cross and then carry on up the path straight ahead keeping to a hedge on your right, and going through a gate at the end of a long field and onto a lane.

Turn left up the lane towards the farm buildings, passing round them to their left and you'll come back onto tarmac in front of The Ley. Opposite the house and just past a pond on the left, cross into a small triangular field and follow the hedge up on the left. Go through a gate at the end into a long field and this time walk along the hedge on your right. At the end of this field you cross a stile into another field, which you cross over and then turn right down the hedgerow ignoring the stile immediately ahead. After about a hundred yards, you come to another stile on your left. Cross this and walk downhill across the next field to an old stile. Across this walk to the corner of the fence on the far side of the field, and cross the stile here. Now follow the hedge on your right, which will bring you round in a curve to a gate beside a partially timber framed, partially brieze block building. Walk through the gates adjacent to this into Weobley, heading up the road almost opposite to return to the castle entrance.

# BUSH BANK

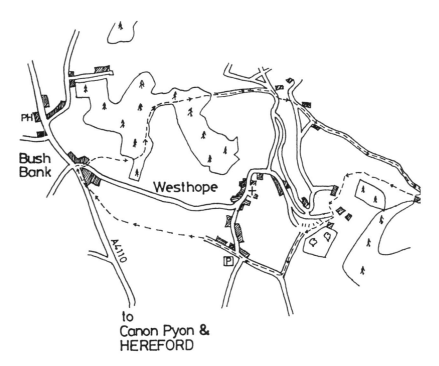

One and a half hours.

A walk through apple orchards, woodland and fields, with views over the Hereford Plain. This walk is on a variety of well marked and not so well marked paths, some of the latter slightly overgrown in places.

On the A 4110 at the northern end of Canon Pyon and opposite Pyon Hill, turn right where signposted to Westhope. At the T-junction ahead turn left and park anywhere suitable.

Just after you turned left at the T-junction the road bends right towards Westhope. At the bend there is a metalled track leading straight on with a public footpath sign pointing down it. Walk down this lane and pass through the gate at the end. Follow the wide track that swings gently through the orchard, till you meet an internal corner in the field.

At the corner you'll see a footbridge just on your left and you cross this and then follow the hedge on your right. You cross the next field boundary by a stile and then pass through a small gate and over a stile onto the other side of the hedge. Turn left and cross the stile with the next field. Turn half right once over this stile and you should see what looks like a public footpath sign pointing straight at you from a gateway, and that's because it is a public footpath sign! Walk across the field to it and leave the field via the stile. Turn right on the main road for about two hundred yards, turning right at the crest of the hill on the little road signposted to Westhope.

After about fifty yards this road bends to the right, but your route lies through the gate on the left at this bend. Walk up the side of the farm buildings, and towards their far end you go through a gate on the right into a field. Then aim for the right-hand of two gates in the fence further up the hill. Through this gate carry on up the hill to the edge of the wood, and then turn right and follow it along to the far left-hand corner of this field. Cross the stile here into the wood.

It now looks like hard going—but don't despair—it's the worst section! Cross over towards the fence on the right of the wood and you'll soon spot a level, if overgrown, path which follows the fence above the orchard on your right. The path soon broadens out and after climbing for a while meets a large grassy ride on which you turn right. This carries on climbing the hillside and soon meets another grassy ride. Turn left this time and after about twenty yards, turn right and cross out of the wood by a stile onto a farm track.

Turn right on this and it will lead you across an area of common to the first of many tracks which lead up to the common from Westhope. For the next few hundred yards you largely follow the contour of the hill—don't take any of the tracks which lead up onto the hill or down from it, though occasionally you have to go a few yards down one of these before taking the track which heads straight on.

After passing an area with several farms and cottages on your left, you come to another split where 'School House' stands in the apex. Take the left-hand route which soon leads out between fields on both sides, and you'll appear to be heading towards a radio mast. When you've drawn up to some further farm buildings, turn right in front of them, follow the fence and then the hedge, keeping it on your left, so that you seem to be walking back almost parallel to the way you've just come, though in fact your route gradually diverges.

Look out for an old gate in a small gap in the hedge on your left about a hundred yards before the end of the field. Cross this and the strands of barbed wire beyond, and walk down to the stile in the far right-hand corner of the field. Cross the two stiles and follow the hedge on your left till you come to another stile in the hedge. Cross this and walk down a short section of overhung path before emerging by a house. Carry on downhill on a better path which soon itself meets up with a wider, deep sunken path crossing it an angle. Turn left on this, following the field boundary on your left. This path leads you out between two houses onto a dirt track. Take the track leading downhill from this area—it soon crosses yet another track, becomes narrower again and passes bang by another cottage, before once more meeting a larger track—but all this while following much the same direction. However it now presently swings left and leads down to a minor road. Turn right on this to return to your vehicle.

# STRETFORD

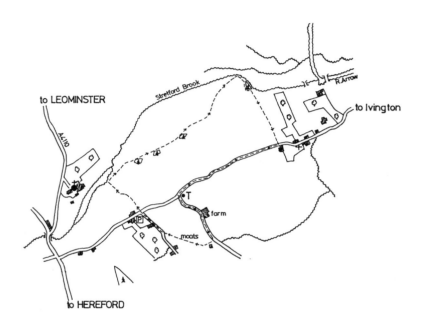

One and a half hours.

A walk on paths, and roads where alternative paths are obstructed. A fairly flat walk for once, but with paths running along the edges of fields some of these could be hard to traverse at times of the year, depending upon how much headland the farmers have left. There is also one awkward stile. A good autumnal walk, with extensive views depite being in the valley of the Stretford Brook. Two old moated sites are included on the walk.

From Leominster take the A4112 Brecon Road west, and turn left at the first major crossroads and take the A4110 to Hereford. Take the first road left after about a mile and near the top of the gentle rise, park where a metalled lane leads off to the right.

Opposite this lane are two gates on the road you've driven along. Take the right-hand gate and follow the hedge on your left. Once you can see the Stretford Brook in the valley below, the path leaves the hedge and turns slightly to the right to join the brook at at its furthest ingress into the field. Turn right on the bank and walk along the brook to the next field boundary. Cross this and follow the hedge on your left to the next field boundary ahead. Once across this you enter a large field. Walk towards the left-hand corner of a small spinney in the top right-hand corner of the field. The boundary here is not so easy to cross, but the path crosses the fence just to the left of the spinney. Now follow the fence on your right along the next field to a small evergreen wood. Go through the gate in the corner of the field, turn left, and then right through the next gate a few yards ahead and once more follow a fence on your right. This again leads to a small spinney and you cross the rails to its immediate left. Once more you're in a large field which you'll presently cross a couple of times.

Carry on walking along the hedge on your right till you come to the second tree, adjacent to where a hedge leads off at right angles up the slope on your right. If you then look left towards Monkland's church, you'll see a stile almost immediately on this line in the hedge on the far side of the field you're in. The path crosses the field to this stile and once over it you turn slightly more to the right than the line you've just been walking on and head towards a collection of gates and a bridge over the brook. However you turn right once you reach this, following the brook on your left. When you reach another spinney, the path technically crosses it. However its entrance is not easy, and exit less so, so it's advisable to follow the boundary of the spinney, pass through the gate at the corner of the field, and then turn left along the top side of the spinney. When half way along the spinney's length, turn right and cross the field to the gate opposite. Through the gate follow the track up and over the ridge to the road beyond.

Turn right on the road and walk along it till you pass a telephone box. Then turn left up another road. Walk up this past a farm and down into the dip beyond. Just beyond a moat on your right, turn right up a short track and pass out through a gate. The path now leads first between some old farm buildings and the moat, then swings to the right through the apple trees to a corner of the field where there are some rails. Four fields meet here and you cross the ditch and rails diagonally, leaving a field to both your left and right. Cross this next field diagonally to the far corner, and cross out over some rails onto a lane. Turn right on this and walk back to your vehicle.

# IVINGTON

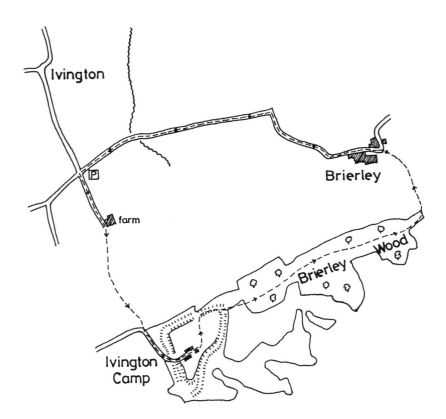

One and a half hours.

A walk largely on tracks and minor road, but which also includes a couple of field boundaries and much of the walk can be muddy. It includes Ivington Hillfort and a stretch of dark coniferous woodland. The hillfort covered some 24 acres but has suffered from ploughing and quarrying. However there are still some impressive remains,

240

including a double rampart on the north side, where the walls rise some twenty feet above their enclosure.

From Leominster take the A4112 Brecon road and turn left onto the first minor road outside Leominster. Turn right at the T-junction ahead, and keep left through Ivington further on. Park at the crossroads you come to half a mile from Ivington.

Walk on up the track from the crossroads towards the hill, passing the farm on your left. The track becomes a grassy ride and runs between two hedges before entering a field. Carry on up the hedgerow on your right towards the right-hand edge of the hill, crossing a part of the field when the hedge veers off to the right.

Walk along the metalled lane at the edge of the wood, and which then curves left through the embankment of the hillfort and through a collection of farm buildings into a field. Pass through the gateway into the field and follow the embankment on your left. This leads you to a fence on the other side of the field at which you turn right and walk along to the gate into the wood. This gate leads you onto a track through a short section of wood and out through the ramparts, to a gate into another field. Pass through this and walk along the fence on your left to the next gate ahead. Now carry on through the wood to another field, where the track hugs the edge of the wood, before once more returning to the wood proper. After a longer stretch of walking in the woodland, the track drops to the left and leads into a field through a gate.

Follow the track which curves through the field and you'll come to a gate to the right of the majority of the buildings in the valley bottom, and which will lead you to a minor road. Turn left on this and it will lead you back to your vehicle after about a mile's walk.

# RISBURY

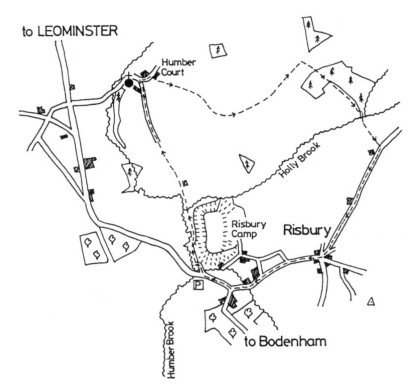

One and a quarter hours.

A walk on paths, tracks and a short section of minor road. There is one arable field where paths aren't reinstated. The walk passes the banks of Risbury hillfort, and is in gently rolling countryside with old farms and wide views.

From Leominster take the A44 to Worcester. At the top of the hill above Leominster, turn right at the crossroads signposted to Stoke Prior, Humber and Risbury. This road, being an old Roman one, is fairly straight to start with, but after a mile or so bears left and drops down to cross the Humber Brook. Park anywhere in the dip.

Walk up the drive of Risbury Mill with the brook on your left and pass between the house and the sheds to its left. Beyond the mill the path is clearer and passes between the brook and the ditches of the hillfort. As you near the stream ahead you'll see a derelict cottage, interestingly called Gab's Castle, in the field on the far side. The path passes to the left of this but first you have to cross the stream via the bridge.

Then follow first the stream and then a hedge on your left up past Gab's Castle on your right, and over the first rise to a gate in the far left-hand corner of the field. Go through the gate and then through another gate about a hundred yards ahead in the hedge on your right. The path then follows the hedge on your left and becomes a track at the next field boundary. Walk down the track till it meets another.

Turn right on this which leads round Humber Court. When opposite a large range of farm buildings on your left, and just before some newer ones on your right, turn right through some gates and into a wedge shaped field. Walk up to the far point of the wedge, where a gate leads out into the next field. Here a track leads you down a hedge on your left to a gate into a field. Here turn right in front of the gate and walk down the hedge to the bottom of the slope to a small gate and bridge into the next field. Here the path bends hard left along the fence to another gate. Go through this and following roughly the same line, cross the next field to a gate opposite. Similarly cross the next field. At the far end of this field, go through the gate and turn right. Walk down the hedge and cross into the wood by the gate. Then take the path which goes through the wood, called The Roughs, and which emerges into a field beyond by a gate. Walk down the field adjacent to the wood, and at the bottom bear left through a gate, and then right over an old footbridge. (The farmer may have erected a 'keep out' notice here, but the county council assures me there has been no diversion of the path.)

Here could be the awkward field to cross. The path carries on marginally to the right of the direction you've been walking on down the previous field, rising up to the line of trees ahead. When you make this far side of the field, you'll probably have to follow the fence on your left for a short while before coming to a gate through which you pass onto the track on the other side. This track, later gaining a metalled surface, will lead you down to a road. When you reach this, turn right to return to your vehicle.

# PENCOMBE

One and a quarter hours.

A very pleasant walk on an old bridleway and a less well marked path over pleasantly rolling countryside, with views towards the Malverns and elsewhere.

244

Park near the school and village hall just to the east of the church in Pencombe village.

Just beyond the village hall from the church there is a signposted bridleway leading northwards, and you take this. It is well marked and leads past a farm on your right, after which it leads through a gate and into a field. Here it follows a hedge on your right, and turns slightly to the right. It clambers up the hillside and leads round towards the large red brick Durstone Farm with its oast house on the hilltop. The route passes through the farmyard, bearing right through it, and leaves it just to the left of the block which contains the farmhouse. The track now leads downhill and curves round to the right to follow a stream on the left. Further on it splits, but you carry on ahead, crossing the stream and walking up to another farm, Hawkhurst.

Here the bridleway ends. The path now leads right through the farmyard, leaving the farmhouse and old buildings on the left and new ones on the right, passing out between them through a gate. The path now bends slightly left through two further gates in quick succession and over a stile into a larger field which slopes down to a stream. Aim for the bottom left-hand corner of the wood on the far side of the stream. Here you'll find a bridge to cross the stream. The path then leads up the hill on the far side, diverging slightly from the wood on your right. Once over the crest of the hill you'll be able to see a gate just to the right of the far corner of the field. Head for and pass through this gate and then turn left, to follow the hedge down to the next stream in the next valley bottom. Turn right at the stream and then left over the bridge and through the gate into the next field. Here aim for the oak tree over the rise and when you reach it, turn right along the short section of hedge and pass out through the gate on to the road. Turn right on this to return to Pencombe.

# SUCKLEY

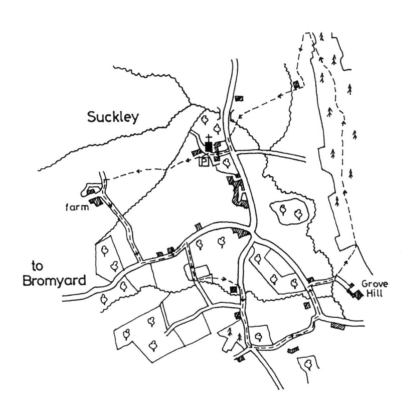

One and a quarter hours.

A walk in flattish countryside around the hopfields to the west of the village, but returning, after a steep but short ascent, via a neck of hills and part of the Worcestershire Way. On a mixture of well worn and not so well worn paths and minor roads.

Park near the church in Suckley.

Walk on up the road on which the church lies till you come to the Victorian school building on the left. Walk down the track immediately before this, passing out through the gate into the field beyond. Follow the hedge on your left till you reach the corner. Here the path bends slightly more to the left, heading for a junction of hedgerows on the far side of the field. Just to the left of this junction is a bridge which you cross, then pass through the hedge on your right and walk down it, keeping it to your left till it too bends away to the left. Here you aim for the middle of the far boundary to the field, again turning slightly to the left to achieve this. As you near this boundary, head for the left-hand of the two gaps in it, and once through this turn left onto the wide track beyond. This curves round the farm and buildings on your right to join the farm's drive. When you meet this, turn left onto the drive and walk away from the farm down to the road ahead.

Turn left on the road and pass a few houses on the left, and follow the road as it bends to the left. When you reach a metalled lane off to the right through a large gate, go through this. Don't be put off by the 'PVW—Keep out' sign—the hopyard this refers to lies beyond the route you will be following. (In any event the county council has assured me that any footpath through a hopyard takes precedence, and they accept modern research which intimates that it is highly unlikely for walkers to spread the hop wilt disease.)

This lane will lead you through plantings of trees and before you come to the stream in the dip below, beyond which the hopyard lies, turn left onto the track on the near side of the stream. This will lead you to a corner of a field, and you cross over the railings into the orchard ahead. Turn right in this narrow orchard and follow the boundary on your right, passing a large collection of farm buildings, and cross out onto the road by the stile in the far corner.

Turn right on the road. The route now follows roads for a while as many paths are obstructed by hop plantations. Keep following the road till you come to a crossroads where you turn left signposted to Worcester. This road will lead you to a T-junction at which you turn left.

A few hundred yards up the road you turn right on the private road to Grove Hill. Once over the stream you go through the gate on the left at the point where the road bends to the right. Once through this gate go through the next gate ahead, after which you diagonally head up the hillside, to the top left-hand corner of this field. Here you will find a stile which you cross, and then walk along the path which follows the ridge. Further ahead it meets the Worcestershire Way from the right, but you still follow the path ahead. This continues to follow the hilltop, dropping down into a dell at one point before rising again. Past this point it meets a wide track made by forestry vehicles. Cross this and immediately take the path slanting downhill to the left.

This will lead you out of the wood via a gate, the path still keeping to the edge of the wood, and bear round to the left when you come to the corner of the field. Once opposite the gate you quickly come to on your right after making this turn, turn left across the field, aiming for just above the red brick house which is dug back into the hillside. Immediately past the house, the path turns right between the house and barn and joins the track which leads to the house. Here you cross straight over the track and walk down to the bridge. The path now turns half left to the corner of the orchard ahead, crossing into this by the stile provided. Now follow the left-hand edge of the orchard, crossing out by the stiles in the next corner. Walk down the edge of this paddock to the footbridge and then across the next field heading to the left of the church and cross out onto the road by the stile provided. Turn left on the road and right past the farm buildings to return to your vehicle.

# ALFRICK

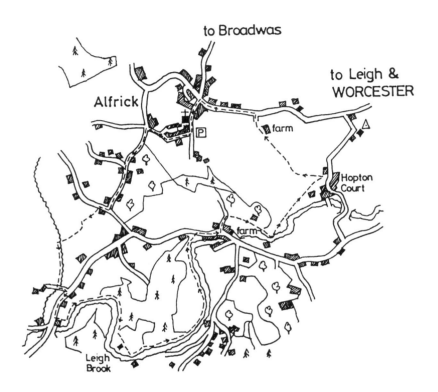

Two hours at a gentle pace, which allows you time to dawdle in the nature reserve en route.

A walk on a mixture of minor roads, small paths, tracks and which includes a nature reserve, The Knapp, managed by the Worcestershire Nature Trust. Towards the end of the walk near Hopton Court, the farmer is extremely unsympathetic to walkers and even though the paths are definitive you may have to put up with verbal abuse if he is around. If this happens just try to retain your calm and know that you are entitled to walk the paths—we have double checked their routes with the County Council.

Take the A4103 to Hereford from Worcester. Once over the Teme turn right to Leigh and follow the road into Alfrick. Turn left in the village and park near the church.

Carry on walking on the road round to the right till you reach a crossroads near a converted oast house. Turn left signposted to Alfrick Pound and Suckley. Carry on walking down this road, past one turning to the right and then take the second road to the right. After about thirty yards along this second road, you come to a set of barns on the left. Go through the gate beyond these barns and walk across to and through a second gate in front of you, keeping the barns on your left and coming out into a second field. Now walk down the field boundary that's on your right to the gate in the right-hand corner of the field. Pass through this and turn left along the hedge. After about twenty yards you come adjacent to an oak tree standing in the field on your right. This marks the line of an old hedge and if you look down into the valley bottom beyond the tree you should see a bridge across the stream. Walk on the line of the old hedge to this bridge, cross it and the stile beyond and then turn left to follow the stream on your left. You cross two more stiles before then coming out onto a farm drive. Turn left on this and walk up to the road ahead.

Turn right on the road and walk along towards the Leigh Brook which runs through the valley ahead. Just before a house on the left which is immediately above the brook, you come to a set of steps and a signposted path to the left which you take. This first follows a hedge along the side of the house and then a field boundary at the top of a bank above the brook. At the end of the first field the path drops down the bank to a stile above the water and the path now follows the brook for a while. At the end of the field the path enters the wood ahead by a gate and continues to follow the brook. Further on it enters the nature reserve by a stile and then clambers up a small bank to enter an old meadow. Here the path keps to the left of an old barn and where it diverges at the stile beyond, take the left-hand branch which leaves the meadow through a gate. You're now on a wide track which you keep following—through woodland, scrub, along a field boundary, more old meadow, through an old orchard and up to the road. All this time the brook is on your right.

When you reach the road, go out on to it by the way that's sign-posted so that you can read about the reserve and its work. Turn right when on the road, and almost immediately left up a track, initially metalled, and signposted Knapp Farm. Where the track bends to the left at the bottom of a small slope, turn right through a gate which leads onto a cart track in an old plum orchard.

Walk along this track and at the end of the orchard you turn right into another field—following the hedge on your right to a small bridge about thirty yards along the hedge. Cross the bridge and keep to the left—there are some yellow painted waymarking signs to help you here—and pass through the field gateway on the left. Now cross this field heading towards the river bank at the far end of the field, passing out over a stile between two oak trees. Now follow the brook's bank to the corner of the next field where there is a slightly more run down stile to cross.

Once over this you're on the territory of the angry anti-walker. The path crosses the corner of this next field to the left-hand corner of the sheds you can see opposite—but if the footpath has not been rein-stated after ploughing or planting, keep to the field boundary till you rejoin the path. Follow all the buildings round on your right till you almost reach the road above Hopton Court, then turn round and head to the left-hand of two gates above the farm buildings. Once through the gate follow the hedge on your left up to the field boun-dary at the far end of the field where a stile will lead you to the calmer waters of Luckalls Farm. Keep the hedge on your left and this will lead you to the farm's drive. Walk down this to the road on which you turn left and this will quickly lead you back to Alfrick.

# CRADLEY

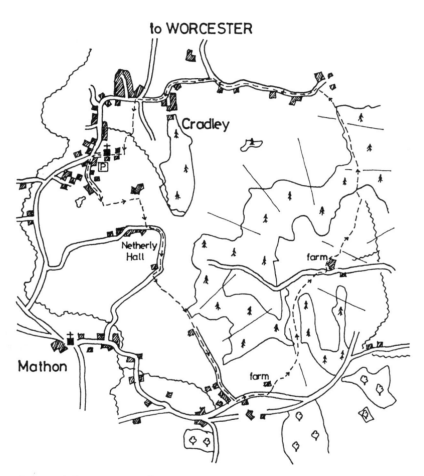

One and three-quarter hours.

A walk on tracks and paths in generally good condition through rolling and wooded countryside, with the Malvern Hills as a backdrop.

Park near the church in Cradley.

Walk in a southerly direction down the track which forms the fourth arm of the crossroads with the road through Cradley and the approach to the church. At the first fork a short distance ahead bear left. This will lead you round past a long white painted house on your right. Don't go through the gate immediately past this house, but through the second one and into the field beyond. Turn left up the hedgerow, right at the field corner and then go through the gate you soon come to on the left. The path now crosses the next field to the right-hand top corner of the house beyond the trees, the route roughly keeping to the bottom of the major rise to your right. At the far side cross the hurdles and then turn right up the hedge on your right. The path leads to a gate in the top corner, through which you pass to emerge onto a stoned track.

Turn left on this and follow it right around Netherly Hall, the track leading past Overley Cottage further on. It swings right and then left again past the cottage, but when the stoned track swings right once more to descend the hill towards the village of Mathon, you bear left through the gate into the field ahead. Follow the hedge on your left and as you near a tongue of woodland, cross some hurdles on your left to emerge onto the line of an old track. This passes through a gate into a small field before running along the foot of the woodland to pass out into a small narrow field. You walk through this to the cottage ahead at which point you join a track. Then you follow this ahead, between hedges, all the way down to a minor road.

Turn left on this and at the first farm you come to on the left after a few hundred yards, turn left up its drive and immediately right through a gate onto a sunken track. Follow this round the buildings, take the next gate on the right and keep on the sunken track now walking away from the buildings. This leads out and up into a patch of hummocky ground and initially you keep following the same line over the rise. (Don't bear sharp left.) The track then swings left to shadow the cwm on your right. the direction of the track is still easy to pick out, and at the far side of the field it passes inside the bottom of some woodland. At the far side of this wood, you come out into another field, and here aim for the stile opposite, just to the right of a small wood. Once over this the path slants down to follow the cwm bottom, passing through a gate into the next field. Carry on towards the farm buildings ahead, still following the cwm bottom, passing out through a gate on to a gravelled track.

Follow this round to the right and when you come to the farm building ahead of you, turn left and right through the gate to walk in front of the farm and out onto the patch of ground beyond, crossing the stile ahead into a field. Here turn right to follow the hedge on your right down to the bottom corner of the field. Turn right and left through the gates here, and continue swinging gently left, eventually walking alongside a fence on your right and again near the bottom of the slopes to each side. Follow this fence to a small gate in the far corner of the field.

Through this bear half right and follow the path which runs inside a fence at the foot of a larch plantation. This will join with a bridleway on which you turn left. This itself will later join a metalled lane on which you again turn left.

Follow this for some way and you'll come to a split in the lane where you turn left once more. Further on you meet a main road near a small housing estate. Turn left and after some thirty yards turn left through a gate into a field. Follow the line of the path through the field—roughly parallel to the hedge on your right. At the far end of the field turn right and walk to the bridge and stile ahead. Walk up the next field following the hedge, and turn right to join the track which leads past the church and to your vehicle.

# UPTON - UPON - SEVERN

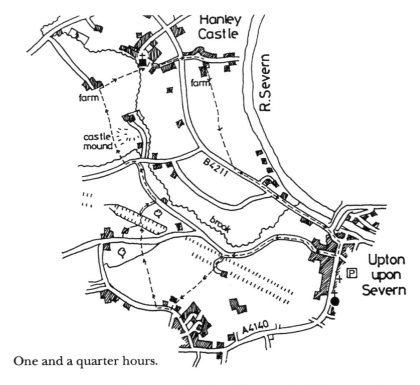

One and a quarter hours.

A walk which includes Upton, Hanley village and which passes the old mounds of Hanley Castle. The Malvern Hills provide a backdrop to the west. The walk is on paths in a variety of conditions, also some minor road and a section of B road at the end.

Park in Upton. Walk down New Street, which heads west from the High Street. Follow this out of the town and look out for a willow fringed brook on your right. The road and this eventually come quite close together, and when the road bends right, take the signposted footpath off to the left. This is initially a wide track and, by-passing some locked gates, crosses the old railway line and then bends left,

256

but you keep straight ahead, passing through a gate, and walking up the line of the fence on your right. Further on you also follow a hedge on your left. Over the crest of the rise you enter a field, where you turn slightly to the right to head for the gate into a farmyard, itself to the right of a modern house. Walk through the farmyard to the road.

Turn right on this road and after a hundred yards or so, take the public footpath signposted off to the right. This crosses a narrow neck of field, and then follows a hedge on your right. Over the rise the path bends slightly left of the line of the hedge, which comes to an end, to enter the orchard ahead. Here walk half right up any of the avenues of trees to the far end of the orchard and out onto the road beyond. Almost opposite is another path. Take this, passing through a further orchard, at the far end of which it leaves by a concrete stile in a dip in the ground. A stepped path then leads down into an old railway cutting. Turn left in the cutting, cross another stile, and then bear right up the far side, crossing another concrete stile. The path now bends right and leads out onto the minor road ahead.

Turn left on this and walk up to the T-junction. Turn left here and then take the first gate on your right, some hundred and fifty yards on. A fairly well worn track leads away from the road through gates, over a brook, and up the rise on the far side. If you look to your right here you can see the old earthworks of Hanley Castle. Ahead the track emerges into a field. This you cross to the far right-hand corner, aiming to the right of the buildings ahead. Turn right at the end, passing through an old metal kissing gate in the corner and then through the next gate a few yards ahead. The path now crosses the field on the same line, heading for Hanley churchyard. At the far side of the field you cross a footbridge, then a small plantation, another bridge and then climb up a bank. Turn left at the top of the bank and you enter the churchyard via a gate. Walk through the churchyard to the southeast corner, in front of some newish building, where you join a lane.

Walk along this to the crossroads with the B road. Go straight over and then take the path signposted right at Herberts Farm. The path enters the farmyard, but then turns immediately left through a little gate to pass round the outside of the buildings, crossing a slatted fence. Beyond this, pass through the gate on your right, and then follow the fence now on your left. The path technically sticks close to this line—emerging back onto the B road nearer Upton by a gate with its accompanying footpath sign. But if part of the field is obstructed by crops, it may be worth keeping to the field boundary for as far as practicable. Once on the B road turn left and walk back to Upton.

# SWINYARD HILL

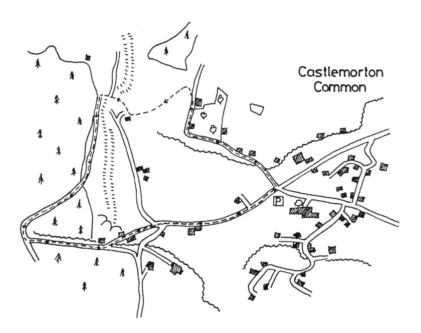

Castlemorton
Common

One and a half hours.

A walk mainly on tracks to the south of the Herefordshire Beacon on and around the Malvern Hills—so plenty of views to be had, along with tracks through old oak and coppice woodland.

From Ledbury take the A 438 to Tewkesbury. Beyond Eastnor the road crosses the line of the Malverns. As it starts to descend the hills on the east you pass a brick retaining wall on the left. Beyond this you come to a crossroads with a couple of minor roads. Turn left here. This will lead you through woodland and over a stream before rising and emerging onto Castlemorton Common. Carry on along the road till you come to a road off to the right. Park near here.

Walk up the wide track which would make this junction of roads a crossroads, heading towards the Malverns. This track snakes around before turning right beyond a wood. The track passes Dales Hall on the right, beyond which it emerges on to the common once more. As it does so, take the left-hand grassy fork and then turn left just beyond the electricity pylons and take the path which climbs up around the hills.

As you breast the first rise, you can have good views to the east if you walk out to the rocky crag. The walk continues along the path which drops down into a dip behind a house to your left. Here take the path which climbs up the gully to the right, crossing the ridge as soon as you reach it and taking the narrow sunken path down the other side.

Within a short distance, this meets a track on which you turn left. Now follow this track, which first shadows the wood on your right, then further on it bears right and slopes more downhill into the wood. Further on you come to a gate and stile on your right, but stay on the track you're on and this soon swings round to the left. Not much further on you come to another gate on the right, and here you turn left more sharply downhill, following the stream on your immediate left.

Towards the end of the wood, you take the path to the immediate right of a deep pool filled quarry, this passing through a small car park and then down a lane to rejoin the road you drove along to park. Take this, or shadow it, to return to your vehicle.

# BOSBURY

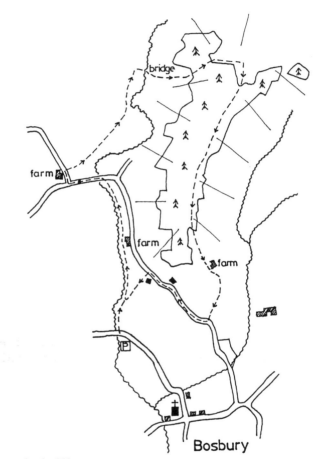

One and a half hours.

A walk in gentle countryside along and over streams, through old woodland and newer conifer plantation, with views to the Malverns. Some of the tracks through the woodland are muddy, and many of the paths cross old pastureland.

Take the road to the east of the church, past the old gateway to the bishop's palace, and park just before a little bridge, about half a mile from Bosbury.

Cross the stile on the right just before this bridge and walk alongside the stream on your left, crossing the various field boundaries by the stiles provided, and pass through the old orchards below Bentley's Farm. Eventually you reach a gate onto the road beyond, on which you turn left. Walk up the hill and turn right on the metalled lane at the top. After a hundred yards or so the lane bends to the left and you pass through the gate on your right, opposite the farm and its buildings. Walk across the field to the gate below you in the hedge opposite, and in the next field gradually slant up across the slope to meet the hedge on the left. Follow this hedge round to a gate through which you pass and then keep slightly further left through the next field to a gate above the stream. Now walk along the line of the old field boundary, marked by a bit of a bank and some trees, diverging slightly from the stream on your right. When immediately above a footbridge over the stream, walk down, across and up the bank on the far side.

Here you'll meet a track which you cross, and turning slightly left walk up to the wood ahead. In an internal corner of this wood you should eventually see a little gate, through which you enter the wood. A path now leads through the wood to a gate on the far side. Once through this gate turn right along the edge of the wood, turning right again at the corner ahead towards another small gate which leads back into the wood.

Go through this gate and take the track through the wood, initially past conifer plantations and later back into older woodland. The track crosses several others, but keep straight ahead. Eventually it divides in front of what looks like an old hillfort. Take the left-hand sunken track which now leads downhill and slants across the hillside, eventually leading out of the wood between fields on both sides. The last section is fairly well blocked, so you may prefer to cross into the field on your left and shadow the track down to a gate in the corner of the field. Whichever route you choose, you will emerge at some farm buildings, through which you pass on the track and out at the other side, continuing to follow the track down to the road.

Turn right on the road, pass some houses to both left and right and after a black and white cottage on the left, turn left through a gate into a field. Walk down the hedge on your left and you will rejoin the path you started out on. Turn left to return to your vehicle.

# SHUCKNALL HILL

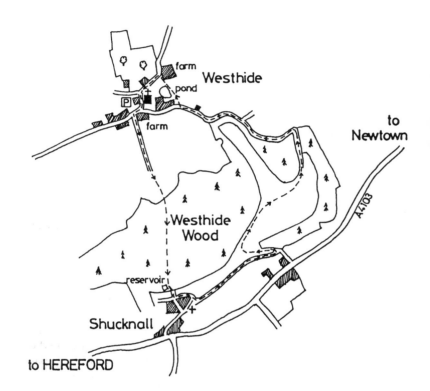

One and a half hours.

This walk offers views over the Frome valley. It is in the main on major tracks, though can be fairly overgrown at points.

From Hereford take the A4103 to Worcester and about one and a half miles out from the River Lugg crossing, turn left to Westhide. Park near the parish church, which is itself about one and a half miles along this road.

From the church walk along the road back towards Hereford, and when you pass the farmhouse on the corner near the church, turn left up a track. This track leads gently uphill between a brick wall on your left and a hedge to your right. Carry on up this track till you come to a field. Go through a gate into the field and keep on heading up roughly the same line you've been walking on towards the wood ahead, crossing into it by a stile you'll come to in the fence.

Once in the wood the path generally bears ahead, first being a little path, then a major new track on which you walk down to the bottom of the next small slope, before changing to an older track which continues up the next slope. This track nears the crest of the hill by a reservoir and houses, emerging onto common land through a small gate.

Take the track to the left in front of the houses, following it downhill as it curves round to the right, almost doubling back on yourself. Shortly along this downhill stretch take the track that leads off to the left along the hill. There are cottages to the left and right along this section, and later on an old quarry on the left as well. Gradually the track and the main road road on your right converge, but where the track does a sharp right turn to go and meet the road, another path leads sharply left and uphill and this is the path you take. The path slants across the hill slope, eventually reaching two derelict cottages. You pass these and turn right in the wood just beyond, this path shortly after emerging onto a track outside the wood and which runs around the field ahead.

Turn left onto this track, following it round the field and then across the hillside between two fields and back to the edge of the wood again. Keep following this track, keeping the wood on your left, and later it first gains a gravelled surface and later still a metalled one. The track turns left downhill and then left again having passed through a short section of wood. Further on a track joins from the right, and later on still you pass uphill through a tongue of wood, coming out to the other side to see a cottage on the right of the track. You pass this and just before you come to the barns further on on the right, you turn right down a track, passing a large pond on your left. This track leads you back to the road, on which you turn left to return to your vehicle.

# SUTTON WALLS

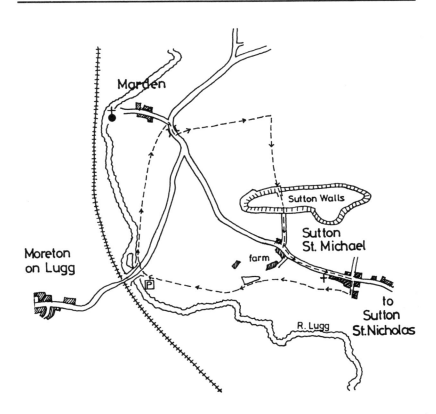

One hour.

This walk is mainly on paths, which can be ill-defined on the ground
in places, and includes Sutton Walls camp and old water meadows.

Take the A49 north from Hereford and turn right about two miles out
of the city to Moreton-on-Lugg. Drive through the village, over the
railway line and park just beyond the bridge over the Lugg.

Cross the stile to the east of the bridge and north of the road and take the path which starts by following the Lugg on your left. Presently the path diverges from the banks to cross another stile at the next fence. Carry on across the next field to the gate in the opposite fence, and which is halfway betwen the river and the road. Cross the next field on the same line to the gate opposite, and then continue on roughly the same line to the gate out of the field and which is near the road on the right.

Turn right on the road, and just over the bridge, about twenty yards along, take the unfenced track to the left and keep straight ahead, eventually following the hedge which starts to appear on your left. Further on the hedge turns at right angles to the left, but the path carries on straight across the field to the hedge on the far side.

At the other side of the field turn right up the hedge and follow it and the line of trees on your left to the wood which runs around Sutton Walls. The path crosses into this wood and carries on through the banks of the old encampment. Cross the middle of the fort where you join a track which leads out of the fort on the far side and down to a road. Turn left on the road and watch out for a chapel on the right. Beyond this chapel you turn right down a metalled lane. Just before the end of the tarmac on this lane, turn right through a gate and walk across the field to the gate on the far side, below the chapel.

Head across the next fields, aiming at the left-hand end of the farm buildings ahead. When you reach these buildings, go through the gates and bear half left to follow the field boundary and a small wood down on your right. Cross over a ditch by the footbridge provided and then turn right and pass through a gate into the next field. In this field, follow an old ditch along on your right, passing through one gate and then across a large field to another gate which will lead you onto the road near where you parked. As a double check that you're heading in the right direction on this last stretch, Marden's church tower should be slightly to the left of the direction in which you're walking.

# EATON BISHOP

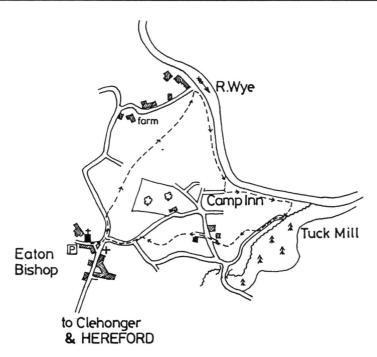

Three-quarters of an hour.

A walk in pleasantly rolling countryside, and which follows the Wye closely for part of its length. There is even a pub en route, not visited by us, if you wish to have a break. Mainly on paths, but which are fairly well marked and seem well trodden even where they cross fields. There is one short sharp ascent.

Park near Eaton Bishop church.

Walk down to the road through the village and turn left, keeping left at a road junction in the village. Just round the first bend out of the village a footpath is signposted off to the right. Take this, heading to the right of the clump of farm buildings on the rise, looking out for the bridge in the hollow ahead which is your target. Over this bridge, keep walking on the same line over the rise and cross the next field boundary by the stile provided. Cross to the far left corner of the next field and over the stile head to the far left corner again of the next field. Leave this at the gateway and walk down to the Wye, the path then turning right and travelling along the bank of the river. The path eventually leads out into a field below a bank on the right. Carry on following the Wye on your left, and at the wood at the far end of the field, turn right to make the steep ascent to the Camp Inn.

The path turns left in front of the inn and traverses the wood, leaving it via some steps. At this point you're just above the Wye again. Keep to the right of the MEB station ahead, and on the track beyond it, turn right. Shortly after passing through a gateway, a path is signposted off to the right. Take this and for a few yards it shadows the track, crossing another stile, before bearing right and up the slope. At the foot of a scar face it bears left and becomes hedged both sides before emerging onto a stoned track, where it turns right. Follow this track downhill, cross a metalled lane and pass through a gate to the right of a house. The path now initially follows the hedge on your right, before crossing it by a stile and then following it on your left. Further on you cross another stile and continue following the hedge still on your left. Over the next stile the path bends to the right through the field, leaving it to the right of a pair of red brick cottages.

Turn left on the lane, and then right on the road to return to the church and your vehicle.

# MONNINGTON AND
# BROBURY

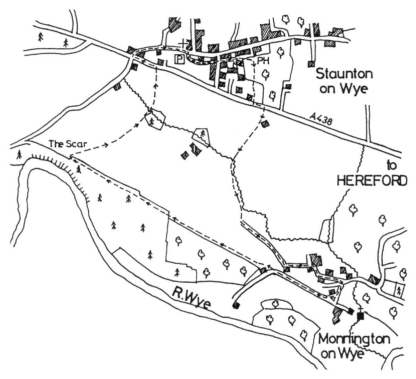

·One and a half hours.

This walk includes the wide avenue of Monnington Walk and views over the Wye in the beechwoods above Brobury Scar. The walk is largely on tracks or alongside field boundaries.

From Hereford take the A438 to Brecon. The village of Staunton-on-Wye lies off to the right of the main road and at the small crossroads with the main road at the western end, turn right and park by the

Methodist Chapel which you'll come to on the left after a few hundred yards.

Carry on walking up the road towards Staunton, and just past the telephone box on the right, walk up the track to the right which slightly diverges from the minor road. This leads across another road and through a small housing estate. At the far end of this you pass through a kissing gate into an orchard. Carry on along the top of the orchard until you are adjacent to a little stile on your left not that many yards into the orchard. Turn right here and walk down between the rows of trees. At the far end you should be almost adjacent to a stile across the fence in front of you. Take this and cross into the field. Pass round the corner of the hedge which juts into the field at the right-hand corner ahead. Then walk down the hedge on your right, passing through a gate near a house and walking down its drive to the main road.

Turn left on this and right onto the bridleway signposted not far ahead. This leads up the side of the hedge on your left, then through the gappy hedge at the far end. Keep following the hedge on your left and you come to two gates on the left. The path technically carries on ahead (the route shown on the map), but because it is blocked, it is best to make a diversion. Go through the second of the two gates on your left, and turn right to follow the hedge. Cross the next field boundary over the rails, and keep following the hedge on your right to a stile and bridge near an oak tree. Over these you return to the definitive footpath route. Leave the field you're now in by the gate in the far left-hand corner. This will lead out onto a track on which you turn left. Walk past one farm to a junction with a road. Turn right on this.

The walk continues by taking the avenue off to the left opposite Monnington Court Farm. Walk down this avenue, passing through gates as necessary, and eventually you will come out beyond a conifer plantation in the beech and oak wood above Brobury Scar. Here a path leads off sharp right, following a hedgerow on your left once it emerges into the field. Cross the first fence you come to and at the far end of the next field, cross the stile provided. Then follow the ditch on your right down to and round the wood ahead, passing through an opening just to its left. The path then crosses the next field aiming just to the left of the cottage on the far sde of the road beyond the field. Cross out onto the road through the gap in the hedge, and turn left on the main road. Turn right at the crossroads to return to your vehicle.

# MEREBACH HILL

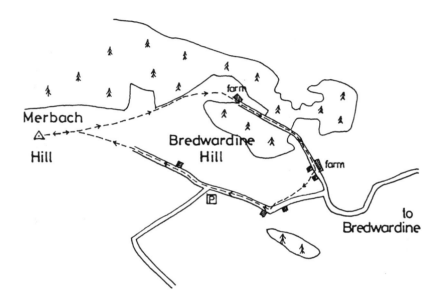

One hour.

This walk contains extensive views over the meandering Wye and away to the north. The hill is approached by a large easy track with a gentle slope as you start from a height close to that of the summit.

Take the minor road up past the Red Lion pub in Bredwardine and follow it up the hill. After about half a mile and after a steep climb, a no-through road leads off to the left. Keep on the minor road and follow it round sharply to the left a few hundred yards further on. When it makes another sharp left turn about a mile further on, you'll see a track leading off straight ahead. This is the start of the walk and so you should park anywhere near here.

270

Walk up this track which soon comes to a gate which opens onto some common land. The path continues across the common, bending slightly to the left, until it reaches the summit of the hill. The best views can be obtained by walking on past the triangulation pillar.

Take any of the paths which lead off to the right from the quarry area, and these will soon join on a path which leads close to the edge of the steep slope on your left. The path itself angles towards the right-hand edge of the woodland ahead. At the end of the common you pass out into a field through a gate. Walk across to the stile at the far right-hand end of the fence ahead, and then follow the hedge on your right to the next gate. You are now on a track which leads along the edge of the wood, then swings round some farm buildings and, passing through another gate, fairly steeply descends across the face of the hillside, leaving the field by another gate into a farmyard.

Turn right on the track here and this leads gently downhill to the right of one field and then through some woodland, before rising uphill to another farm. On the right, opposite the end of the farm-house, is the start of an old sunken lane. Go through the gate at its start and walk up the lane out onto the hillside beyond. Ahead and below you is the road, and the path now swings round to the right and gradually drops down to meet it at a gate in the bottom far corner of the field. Go through the gate and turn right up the road to reach your vehicle.

271

# THE RED HILL

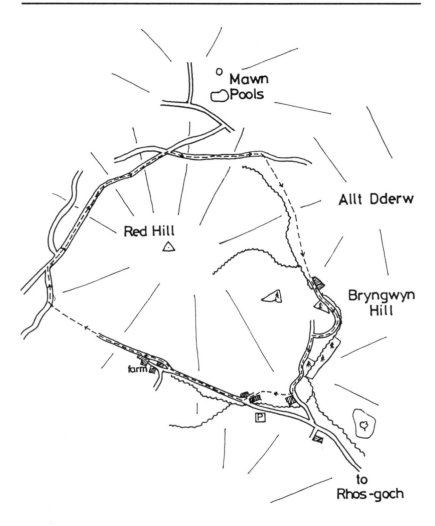

One and a quarter hours, but longer if you wish to see the Mawn Pools.

This is over rolling hilly country between Radnor Forest and the Black Mountains with streams and Mawn (peat) pools. It is mainly on tracks and lanes, one short secton of which is overgrown, though several can be slightly obstructed by bracken in the late summer and autumn.

Take the B4594 from west of Kington to Painscastle. In Rhos-goch take the no-through road next to a chapel off to the right. Follow this for about one and a half miles, bearing right at the first split in met-alled lanes and left at the second. You want to park immediately after you cross a stream with some farm buildings on your right and a bun-galow on your left. Here you are near the foot of the Red Hill.

Walk up the lane which leads half left from where you've parked and this soon brings you up to another set of farm buildings. Take the track to the right of all the buildings and this will bring you out on their far side. Carry on up the gravelled track, keeping the stream on your right, and cross two fields on the line you're walking, coming out onto the moorland via another gate. The track keeps going straight ahead and once you've crossed a crossroads of paths near the crest of the hill, turn right onto another track. This will lead you to a fence at which you turn right again and follow the track along into the small valley between the hills.

In the little valley the track forms a crossroads with another track which roughly follows the valley bottom. (If you want to see the Mawn Pools, carry on up the hillside opposite; the pools are near the sum-mit of the hill on your right). The circular walk continues to the right at the crossroads in the valley bottom, and then past the stream on your right which bends away downhill, you turn right again onto a path and walk down keeping the stream on your right.

The path leads you to a gate just above the stream, which you pass through and continue to another gate a hundred yards ahead. Through this gate you pick up a stoned and later metalled lane to the left which shortly passes by some farm buildings, crossing the stream. It then rises up and drops down the hillside passing through another gate. Further on it turns left and then gently drops towards a collec-tion of barns and cottages. Almost before you reach these, but in fact just past a Dutch barn in a field on your right, you turn right onto a slightly overgrown track which passes between two hedges. After a few hundred yards this track will bring you back to the farm buildings near which you parked.

# LLOWES

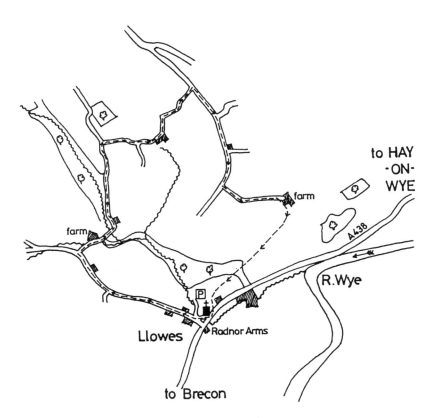

One and a quarter hours.

A walk largely on main tracks and very minor metalled lanes, with views as you descend over the Wye Valley between Hay and Glasbury, with the Black Mountains beyond.

In Llowes turn away from the Wye opposite the Radnor Arms, and then almost immediately right to park near the church.

Walk on up the lane away from the Radnor Arms. You pass one turning to the left and further on a house on your right immediately on the road. Past this the road bends to the left and here you take the drive off to the right. This leads down past a farm and alongside a brook, before turning left up the hillside. Past the next set of buildings on your right the drive becomes a track. Keep following this up the hillside, and where it divides further ahead, take the right hand turn. Further on it meets a surfaced track, and you turn left onto this (in essence to carry on walking roughly on the same line ahead) and this soon gains a metalled surface.

You pass a farm on the right and the lane still keeps gently ascending round a series of bends. Then it bears sharp right where a track leaves to the left, and starts to gently descend the hillside. You pass two tracks off to the left, one with a bungalow on your left and part of its garden to your right at the junction.

Take the third track off to the left, this leading you to a gate into some rough grazing. Walk on down the track to the farm ahead, bearing right through the farmyard, keeping all the main buildings to your left. On the far side of the farmyard you pass alongside one field at the end of which the semi-sunken track turns left, but you take the footpath through the gate ahead. This follows the hedge on your right to a stile at the next field boundary. Over this you pick up the course of another track which leads rather more through the field and through the woodland on the far side after which it heads straight for Llowes Church. Near the end of this last field it swings left and leaves through the gates in the bottom far corner. Return to your vehicle through the churchyard.

Refreshment can of course be had at the Radnor Arms.

# CUSOP

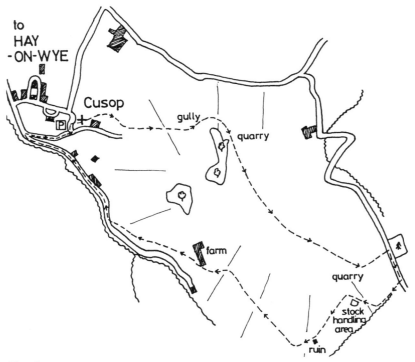

Two hours.

A very pleasant walk over hillsides with views over the border country.

Mainly on paths which cross open fields and hillside and so aren't well defined, but also on some tracks and small sections of minor road.

Park near the church in Cusop. Walk through the churchyard to the right of the church to the gate at the far end. Turn right in the field and follow its boundary on your right to the gate ahead. Pass through this gate, then bear left to follow the field boundary and deep rutted track on your right round the next corner. From this corner head up

276

the hillside across the corner of the field to another gate. Through this gate the path bears left above the gully and angles up across the hillside to a number of gates in the far corner of the field. Go through the gate on the right, and the path now bears to the right climbing and diagonally crossing the next patch of ground. When it flattens out slightly you can see the remains of old quarry workings on the skyline. The path ascends this by a brief section of track after which you follow the edge of the slope on your right, continuing to ascend and curve round the hillside. Presently you'll come to some fences, in the corner of which a stile leads over into the next enclosure.

Bear slightly to the left once over this stile, continuing to ascend the hill, reaching another stile in the next fence. Cross this and carry on for a while on the same line, and when you near a second batch of old quarry workings on your right and a metal gate at the foot of a clump of trees lies to your immediate left, the path turns left and heads to the gate through which it passes onto a minor road.

Turn right on the road and when you come to the next gate on the right into the following field, turn right through it. Head to the left of the trees which mark the site of a spring and follow the watercourse down till you reach a point where you join a track which follows the emergent stream. At this point you are roughly adjacent to some rough ground on your immediate left. Cross the stream and head over the field, ascending slightly, to a gate above a stock handling area. Pass through this gate onto a plateau-like field. In the woodland on the left you'll see a track which slants down the hillside, following a cleft on your left. Take this track and it will lead you down to a couple of wrecked cottages and barns. Beyond these lie a fence and a gate. Here the path turns right before the fence and you follow it on your left to a stile at the next fence. Cross this and, bearing slightly left, continue following the fence on your left through some bracken, this path soon becoming better defined and swinging right to more parallel the contours of the hillside.

Follow this path, taking the path off to the left when you emerge onto more open hillside, and drop down to the hedge below. Follow this to the gate in the corner. Through the gate follow the field boundary on your left to the next field which the path then crosses to meet a track leading into a farmyard. Keep on the track, passing the farmhouse to your right and it gains a metalled surface as it bears left and downhill to join a minor road. Turn right on the road. When the road meets another on the right after a piece of conifer wood, bear sharp right onto it and follow it back to your vehicle.

# BLACK MOUNTAINS ABOVE TALGARTH

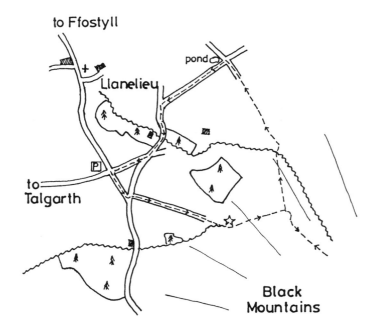

Three-quarters of an hour for the circular walk, but longer if you continue up into the Black Mountains.

This walk has extensive views along the Black Mountains, northwards over the borders and east to the Brecon Beacons. It is mostly on tracks or well defined paths.

From Talgarth take the minor road uphill from the crossroads in the centre of town and which is signposted to Llanelieu and Ffostill. Bear right past the church in Talgarth and turn right on the edge of town on the road signposted to the hospital. Cross the stream and pass the hospital. Take the right-hand fork where the road splits, and carry on uphill and cross over a cattle grid. Park where you come to a crossroads on the flat area of land ahead.

Turn right at the crossroads and walk up the road until you come to two wide tracks leading off to the left. Take the second of these which bears half left and passes between two field boundaries aiming directly towards the Black Mountains. This track leads out onto the mountains, presently to swing left across the face of the slopes and slant across them uphill. Further on it bears sharp right and heads up into the mountains.

At this point you can choose to lengthen the walk and carry on up into the Black Mountains, to return to this point by the same route, or keep to a shorter walk and from just beyond where the track turns right, take a smaller path down the slope. This heads down to and crosses the stream below you and then heads towards a pond on the flat allt ahead. At the crossroads of tracks just before the pond, turn left and follow the track along the field boundary on your left. Gradually the field boundary on the right comes closer to the track, and the track bends left and drops down to cross a stream. Over this it rises again and as you come to the top you should find your vehicle straight ahead of you.

# CRASWALL

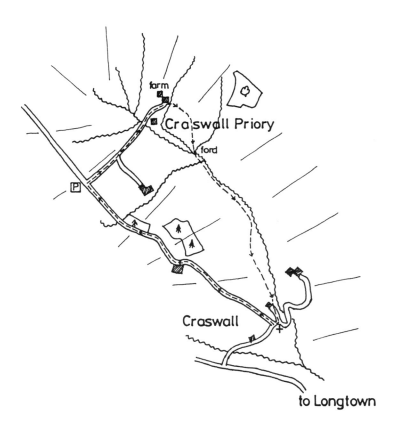

One and a quarter hours.

On generally good tracks and minor roads, but can be very muddy at one point around some farm buildings. Good views towards the flank of the Black Mountains, and bluebell woods in spring. The remains of Craswall Priory can also be seen.

280

From Hay take the road south to the Black Mountains and keep left at all the junctions, following signs to Craswall and Longtown. The road winds round the edges of the lower slopes of the mountains and after a sharp hair pin bend to the left, does a few more wiggles before straightening out, rising to the top of a slope and starting on a straight gentle downhill slope. Park on this last stretch of road where a farm track leads off to the left, which also happens to be opposite a gate into a field on the other side of the road.

Walk down the farm track, which drops down into the valley, crosses the stream and passes the remains of Craswall Priory on the right. The track continues up to the farm buildings. Pass through a gate into the complex and turn immediately right through the gate in front of the first barn and follow the probably muddy section of track to the gate into the field. Once in the field, follow the hedge on your left to the gate ahead. Once through this, walk diagonally across the next field towards the valley bottom, aiming for a group of trees in the bottom corner. When you reach these, carry on to the stream and cross the ford and then pass through a gate on the other side. Now follow the stream on your left, crossing another smaller stream which flows down from your half right. The path now follows the bottom of fields, passing through two gateways before emerging onto a broad flat grass track set high above the stream. Here there are banks of bluebells in spring. The track continues for a while before emerging through a gate into a field.

Continue to follow the woodland on your left till it comes to an end, and then bear slightly right of straight ahead and head for the gate on the other side of the field, just to the right of a hedge which meets the opposite field boundary at right angles. Go through this gate and then follow the hedge on your left to the far side of the field. Pass through the next gate and carry on walking on the same line which will bring you to a gate near a new barn. Here you will join a track, following still much the same direction, which hugs a hedge on your right. This brings you out on to the Craswall to Longtown road. (If you want to call at a pub, turn left and walk on till you come to the one in Craswall itself.) Otherwse turn right on the road and walk back to your vehicle.

# VOWCHURCH COMMON

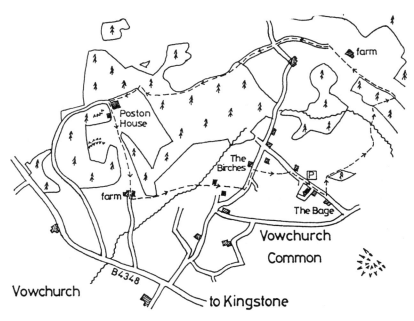

One and a half hours.

This walk has views of the Golden Valley, especially when descending one cwm, and is mainly on tracks and paths. Some of the latter involve field crossings where the paths don't seem to be reinstated.

To reach Vowchurch Common in the Golden Valley, turn up the no-through road just west of the junction of the B4348 and B4347. Follow the main metalled road uphill and after it has made a sharp right turn at the top, park beyond the first house and farm that you reach.

Continue walking along the tarmac lane and take the footpath sign-posted to the left, just beyond a group of stone built and white painted buildings on the right called The Bage. Cross the field aiming for the left-hand corner of the small wood just ahead, and the path

282

continues inside the left-hand edge of this wood. At the far end climb over a slatted fence and cross the field ahead following the base of a bank. Pass through a gate and carry on down the hillside for a while, then slant half left across the hillside aiming for the nearest of two footbridges which cross the stream in the valley floor. Cross the next field to the wood, aiming slightly to the left of straight ahead. Enter the wood via a stile and walk on the path through the wood to the far side, crossing out over another stile. Then turn left on the track which leads towards the left of a set of dilapidated farm buildings and house. When you enter the field in the right-hand corner of which these buildings lie, follow the track round to your right and past the buildings, where the track then gains a greater impression of permanence.

Bear left on this track and further on cross over a track which leads to another set of farm buildings on your left. Shortly after this you pass through a gate into a wood. Follow the path-cum-track straight ahead into the depths of the wood. As you approach a gate at the other end of the wood the track crosses another. Turn right on this new track and after a hundred yards or so take a path to the left which leads out into a field over a stile. Cross this field towards the buildings ahead, passing to their rght and then turning left between them and the grander Poston House on your right. Go through the little gate to the left of Poston House and across the next field. You're now at the top of a cwm and a track leads down to the cwm bottom.

At the farm at the end of the cwm, cross the stile between the buildings, go through the little gate on your left, and then walk out of the farmyard, bearing left once you've done so. Walk up the fence on your left to the next stile. Cross over it and walk down the next field, passing through a gate and cross the stream by the bridge provided. Then bear slightly left and head to the left of a greenhouse at the far side of the field, crossing out of the field by a stile. You'll find yourself on the bend of an overgrown track. Take the uphill branch, but after literally just a few paces, bear left straight uphill on a little path which passes just to the right of one cottage, and to the left of another. This path continues straight on uphill over various stiles before making a little bend to the right and joining the lane you drove up.

Turn left and walk up it for a while till you come to a house called The Birches on your left. Cross over the stile, or through the gate, on your right and walk across to the slatted fence in the angle of the field boundary on the far side. Cross this and follow the fence on your right to the gate at the far side back to the lane. Turn right on the lane to return to your vehicle.

# ST. MARGARETS

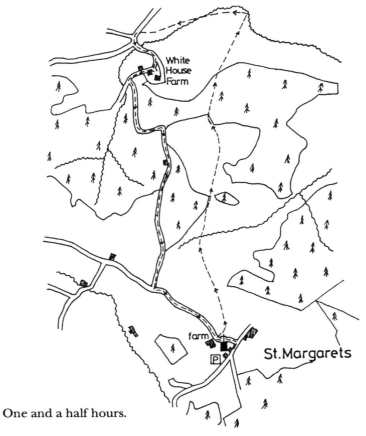

One and a half hours.

A walk on tracks and paths in generally good condition through wood-land and along field edges, with views both to the edge of the Black Mountains and over the Golden Valley.

Park near the church. (This is well worth a visit—for details please refer to the gazetteer.) Walk along the road keeping the church to your left till, opposite the stone built farm set below the road and to

284

the west of the church, you take the track opposite off to the right. This soon leads into a small field and you bear round to the left to leave it by a wide grassy ride between two hedges. At the end of this you come to a gate. It's important here to look across to the wood on the other side of the little valley, for your route follows roughly a straight line in the direction you have been walking across the valley from where you are to that wood. Having a fix will help you in the valley below. If you look carefully enough you may even be able to make out the stile you will be crossing on the fence in front of the wood.

Now, walk across the field ahead, crossing a stile to the right of a clump of trees marking the line of old fence on the far side. Then bear slightly left to cross the first little stream and then to the right to cross the larger stream. Then walk on up the next field to its far right-hand corner. Here you meet the wood and cross the stile into it, to then turn right to roughly follow what is now its right-hand boundary and at the far side, cross another stile which takes you out into a field to the left of a hedgerow. Follow this hedgerow on your right, passing round an area of scrub. Cross the stile in the corner of the field and keep following the hedge on your right and into the wood at the far end of this field, passing into the wood via a rather overgrown gate.

Here be careful not to take the wrong path. You bear slightly right, follow the line of the old quarry on your left and go downhill. (Turn too much to the right and you stay more on the level.) As the path descends it meets another on which you turn right, emerging from the wood over a stile into a corner of a field, with a hedgerow running at right angles away from the wood on your left. Cross this field diagonally to the far right-hand corner. Cross the ditch on your left in this corner and then head towards the stream on the far side of this field, crossing it in front of some rails, which you then also cross.

Then follow the stream on your left until you see a gate leading to the road at the field's far side, and for which you then aim. Through the gate, turn left on the road and left again up the drive to White House Farm. The public right of way leads through the farm buildings, leaving the house and older buildings on your left. Once out of the farmyard, the track divides, but you carry straight ahead, and the track later bends to the left. At the next division of the ways, take the left-hand track and walk uphill through the wood. The track eventually leads to the corner of a field where you turn right, still staying in the woodland and keeping the field to your left. Now just follow the track, passing through some gates, all the way along till you reach the road. Turn left on the road to return to the church.

# ABBEY DORE

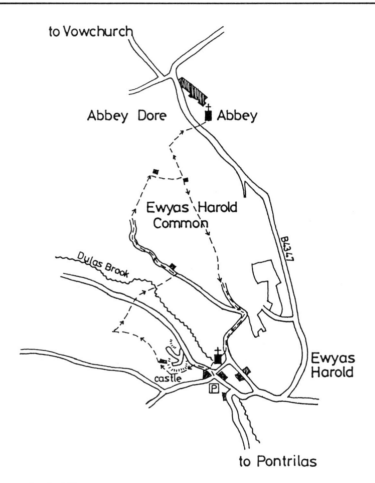

One and a half hours.

A walk which includes Ewyas Harold church and castle, Abbey Dore church and the rolling expanse of Ewyas Harold Common. Largely on tracks and paths generally in a reasonable state.

From Pontrilas on the A465 turn northwards up the B4347 and Ewyas Harold is reached shortly. Turn left just over the brook and park near The Dog public house, a good place for later refreshment.

Walk on up the road you've parked on, and when the road bends to the right after a few yards, turn left over the stile below the castle mound. The path initially follows the fence on your left, but at some point you need to clamber up the bank on your right and onto the outer bailey. Cross this, aiming for the left of the still higher motte and walk alongside a collection of farm buildings to the left of the motte, emerging into a field beyond. Now walk along the hedge on your left, passing through a gate into the next field. Continue following the hedge on your left and cross over the stile at the far end of this field. Now turn right and walk along the hedge on your right, crossing a rather overgrown stile in the corner. Continue following the hedge on your right, and when above a sharp descent to the road below, continue straight down the hillside. If the stile which should be in front of you hasn't been replaced, turn left and walk to the gate out of the field onto the road to which you'll quickly come. Turn right on the road to where you should have emerged!

Across the road from where you should have emerged there is a stile into the field. Cross this and bear half right, aiming just to the left of the far right-hand corner of the field. Here you cross a bridge and then go through a gate into a field on the far side of the strip of land beyond the Dulas Brook. Cross this field, heading to the right of the cottage on its far side, crossing out by the stile provided. Now cross the stile to your immediate left and walk along the track in front of the cottage, called Weaver's Place on the old maps. Beyond the cottage the path joins a semi-metalled lane and swings to the right. Through the next gate which leads into another property, you turn left through a further gate and the path continues on round the hillside. Further on it has been recently stoned and leading past other smallholdings it eventually leads up onto the common.

Once on the common land, take whichever path you like the look of slightly right, up to the crest of the common where you will come to a track laid with blocks. Head over this track to the cottage on the far side of the common, and then turn right down the common boundary till you come to two cottages close together, which themselves form the middle of this clump of houses on the common. Just before you reach these two cottages you'll come to two gates on the left. One is only about four feet wide, the other is a 'normal' farm gate. Go through the 'normal' gate which leads off between two hedges into a field. Once in the field proper, follow the field boundary on your left. When you're immediately adjacent to Abbey Dore Church on your right, turn right and head down across the field. You should come to a wide, rail slatted area in the hedge ahead, which you cross and from this you pass straight across the next field towards the church's lych gate, which is at the right side of the church as you look at it. In the hedgerow here you'll come to a stile to cross.

After exploring Abbey Dore, return by the same route to the common and then turn left and walk down any of the tracks which lead slightly to the right of the summit of the hill and houses ahead. You'll cross a stony track and walk down a sharpish slope to a metalled lane. Follow this down and round the slope, taking the metalled lane to your right which will lead you to the church. Walk through the churchyard and back to your vehicle—or The Dog.

# LONGTOWN CASTLE

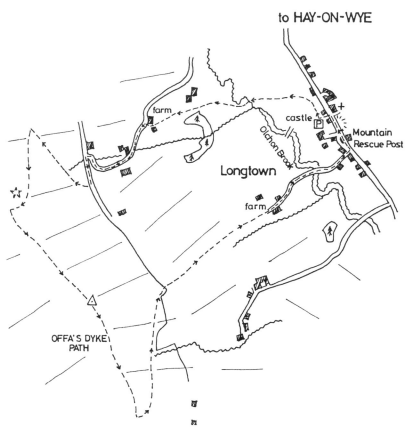

to HAY-ON-WYE

Two and a quarter hours.

This walk has good views from the Black Mountains and is also in pleasant rolling countryside along their flank and foot. It also offers the opportunity to see Longtown Castle. The walk is on paths across and along the edge of fields, and more clearly defined paths up, along and down the Black Mountains. As virtually all the ground is permanent pasture, crops and ploughing pose no great threat.

Park by the castle in Longtown, which is signposted by English Heritage. (More information on the castle is included in the gazetteer.)

Walk up the road with the keep on your left, turning down the track to the left immediately past the group of houses which lie at the foot of the castle. In the corner ahead, turn right through the gate into the field. Follow the hedge on your right to the gateway into the next field. Once through this, turn half left and walk through the gateway approximately half way along the hedge opposite. Through this the path turns slightly more to the left and crosses out of the this next field at the lower boundary. There is a stile here which leads you into the corner of a field. Now diagonally cross this field to a point some twenty yards up from the stream in the valley bottom. Pass through the gap in the hedge and head to the stream on the same line. Here you will find a footbridge which you cross.

Now head up to the stone stile across the field opposite, over which you bear half right through the overgrown hedges into the field above the field which lies alongside the stream. This you cross diagonally to the far corner, where you turn half left and walk straight up the next field to the far boundary, and where you come across an old sunken track. Here you turn right and follow this as it soon swings left, the bank to its right at this point providing the best path. This track leads via a gate into an old farmyard, and you walk through this, keeping the house to your right and barns to each side. At the far side you will come out onto a road.

Turn left on this and it will lead you up the hillside. Further on it swings right, crosses a cattle grid and then swings left. Where it turns sharp right not many yards ahead, you take the track off to the left and after about a hundred yards you come to unfenced hillside on your right. Your route now leads up this, taking the path which crosses the brook on your right outside the top corner of the field on your right. Now follow this path across and up the hillside till you are adjacent to some trees standing in a bracken infested field on your right—these fields themselves forming the outer corner of cultivation on the hillside. Near this point you meet another path slanting down the hillside from your left, and continuing downhill to your right. Turn left on this, and follow it to the summit, walking on across the hill till you reach the wide track of Offa's Dyke path.

Turn left on this, following it past the trig point and downhill onto a narrow neck of the ridge. Here you meet a track which leads back on you to the right, and a narrower track which leads back on you downhill and to the left. This latter is the track you take, following it all the way downhill. It briefly follows an old field boundary but beyond this, keep to the left-hand fork. You pass another little field and then at the corner of the next big field downhill from you, turn right and walk down to the gate by the side of this field, a gate which leads onto a wide grassy track between fields.

At the end of this, turn left into a field through the gate, and walk down to the far left-hand corner of this field. Here the fence may have no stile, and if you find it difficult to cross, turn right along it till you come to a gate, returning to this point on the far side of the fence. However you've managed it, once across follow the hedge downhill on your left and when this comes to a corner, keep heading for the farm below you and you'll soon follow a hedge on your left once more. Pass through the farmyard, leaving the house and buildings to your right. Leave the yard by the farm drive, crossing the stream in the valley bottom, and then walking uphill to meet the road. Turn left on this to return to your vehicle.

# LLANTHONY

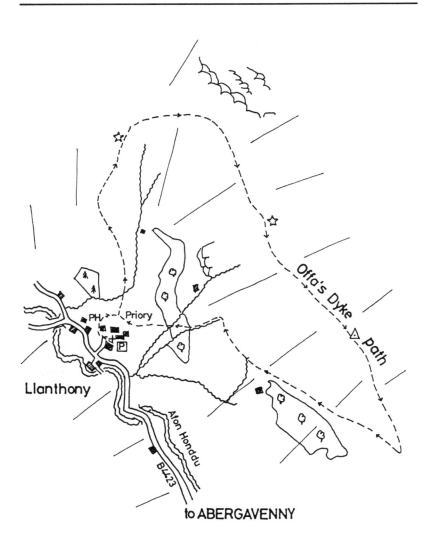

Two hours.

A circular walk from Llanthony Priory leading up to Offa's Dyke path on the ridge above, from where all round views can be had. Much of the route is waymarked and is largely on paths, some of which can be very wet with spring water. It obviously involves a good clamber up the Black Mountains.

You can park in a free car park at the priory.

Walk back past the priory and hotel on your right and cross a stile by a gate straight ahead. Follow the wall on your right to another stile and then walk up the track across the field ahead. When you come to a stream you cross it and turn half left to head towards a shoulder of the Black Mountains. Cross another stile and then walk towards the top corner of the wood on the far side of the field. Here there are two stiles to cross in close succession to bring you out to the other side of the wood. Walk directly on up the hillside—the path is still way-marked—to another stile on the other side of the field. Once over this carry on up the hillside, bearing slightly right when you reach a trio of windblown bushes to stay on the main path.

The path gradually fades into a series of sheep walks on the hilltop, but if you follow the slope round on your right and then cross to the top of the main ridge you'll join up with Offa's Dyke path—a major track. Turn right on this and walk along it, passing a triangulation pillar, and carry on till you reach a dip in the path on a narrow neck of the ridge, where you take a large path which leads off to the right and which slants back down across the hillside towards the priory.

After a while the path flattens out and follows a fence on your left. When you reach a small section of dry stone walling you'll see another waymarked stile just before it on your left. Cross over this and walk beside the fence on your left to the wood ahead, crossing over the stile into the wood. Walk down the track through the wood and out the other side into a field immediately above the priory. The path path follows the edge of the field to the right and then round to the near corner of the priory. Cross the stile to walk along the wall alongside the priory, returning to the start point by the same two stiles you first crossed over.

In the summer months the cellar of the priory provides a good pub.

# PARTRISHOW

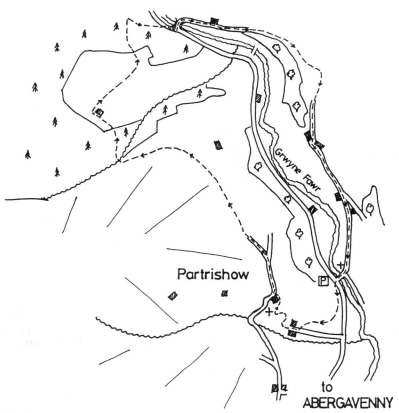

Two hours.

This is a walk of streams, moor and woods coupled with a visit to the unusual church of Partrishow at the southern end of the Black Mountains. The walk is on well maintained paths and tracks, and though it is up and down, is never very steep.

From Llanfihangel Crucorney on the Abergavenny to Hereford road, take the minor road north to Llanthony Priory. Out of the village of

Crucorney, the road drops into the valley bottom. Here there are two turnings to the left in quick succession, and you take the second, just after passing a telephone kiosk on your right. About two miles along this road you come to a junction of five roads in total, but you stay on the road you're on which now bears right and up a valley. Almost exactly a mile from this last junction you want to park when you come to a parking place on your left by a stile, whilst to your right a metalled track leads down across the stream on the right.

Cross the stile by which you've parked and follow the waymarked footpath across the hill passing some ruined buildings on your left. Beyond these the path swings more to the right and enters another field by a gate. Your route then lies to the left of the old farm ahead, in front of which you pass out via a gate onto a track. Turn right on this, and keep to it as it zig-zags across the hillside. On the relevant bend, take the path to Partrishow Church ahead if you want to see it. (Some information about it is given in the gazetteer.)

Return to the track and keep going uphill, eventually passing out by a gate near an old stone barn onto a metalled road. Turn right on this and after a few hundred yards, where the metalled lane drops downhill to the right, turn left on another track and then follow the stone wall up, passing through another gate and out onto the open hillside. Your route now follows the field boundaries on your right, and eventually you will swing round to the left and drop gently downhill to cross a stream. Over this you enter woodland and the path goes along the hillside, later to emerge into a group of farm buildings. Turn right in the farmyard past the house, the track then dropping down to cross a stream. A few hundred yards across the stream, the track then bends to the left.

Further on it meets a wide forestry road. Turn right on this and at the junction of plantings of different tree species on the right, take the yellow waymarked path off to the right and downhill. This will lead you out onto a road, on which you turn right. Almost immediately you turn left onto another metalled lane and cross a bridge. Continue up this lane which turns right and then becomes a stony track once past some houses. It climbs up through a gate onto the hillside and later emerges onto a flatter part of the hillside after a short but steeper climb. Here turn half right and in the corner of some stone walls, pass through another gate onto a track. When this comes to some farm buldings, turn right and left through them, and then carry on down the now metalled lane to the minor road and your vehicle.

# GARWAY COMMON

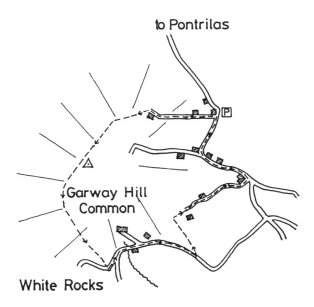

One hour.

A walk on common land, tracks, paths and minor roads in rolling countryside with wide views to the south-west of Hereford. The paths and tracks are generally in good order and there are no steep climbs.

From Pontrilas take the B4347 Grosmont road. Whilst still in Pontrilas turn left onto the minor road which heads east towards Orcop. Take the second road right after about two miles and which is near a stone house and just after another turning to the left. When the road divides a bit further on up the hill, bear to the right of the chapel wedged between the roads. Presently the road swings left and straightens slightly, passing a group of houses on the right. Slightly further on

296

still the road makes a small double bend and you want to park just beyond this—near a red brick house on the right and above some farm buildings on your left.

Walk up the lane which leaves the road on the inside of the bend on the corner with the red brick house, which is now on your right. Towards the top of the hill you come to another house. Follow the boundary of this house's grounds round to the right and cross over a stile onto the common land behind it. Bear half right to the top of the hill for a view of Kentchurch Court.

Return to the main track which stays to the east, or left, of the hill's crest and then branch off to the right on a path which leads to the hilltop near a brick structure. Just past this is a triangulation pillar and then a path, which becomes a bit wider, goes along the hill and then slants slightly left and downhill. Follow it down, initially adjacent to a bank, turning left on to a gravelled track which it meets, and then left again on the minor road which the track joins.

Walk up this road, and further on where it bears right and slightly downhill, you'll come to two gates set back from and above the road on the left. Go through the right-hand of the gates and follow the field boundary on your left back onto the common. Once on the common turn right and walk along the fence passing two buildings and you'll come to a gate ahead which leads onto another track. Walk down this and then turn left on the minor road and walk back to your vehicle, under half a mile away.

*Green man on the Chancel arch, St. Michael's Church, Garway*

# KILPECK

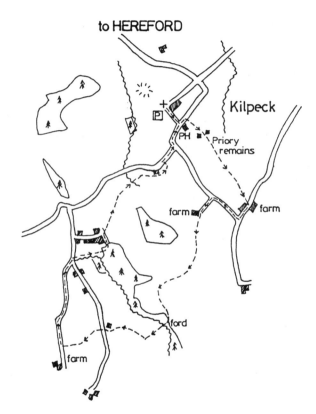

An hour and a quarter.

A walk largely on paths which aren't in the best of order, despite some problems being reported to the County Council a year before publication of this book. However the paths are usable with care, and they cross rolling countryside with its scattering of old farms and small streams.

Park by the church in Kilpeck. (Refer to the gazetteer for more information on this and the adjacent castle remains.)

Walk south-east from the church on the road towards the centre of the village. At the junction in front of the pub turn left, and then almost immediately right up the drive beyond. This drive leads to a house which is built on, and no doubt from, the remains of the old Benedictine priory. The path passes between the house and the barns, entering the field beyond through the gate. The path now shadows the field boundary on your left to the fence opposite. Here you have to cross the fence by the point you find most suitable, unless a new stile has been provided. (It may be that the directions given in the rest of this paragraph can be amended in the light of new stiles provided since publication.) Once across this fence cross the next field to the stile below the strip of wood that runs along the hillside. Turn slightly right through the wood to find the stile on the other side, and once over this cross the next field to the corner of the hedge opposite, and then follow the hedge up to the gate out of the field. Pass through the farmyard and out onto the road beyond.

Turn right on the road, turning right again at the crossroads ahead. When you reach an old Dutch barn on your left, take the track immediately beyond it. Before you reach the farm ahead, take the gate into the field on the left, and walk to the far corner of the field, your route slowly diverging from the line of the barn on your right. Go through the gate in the corner, and cross the next field to its far top left-hand corner. Here you will find a sunken track, but if it's still comparatively obstructed, cross the fence to its left into the field above it, turn right to follow the track and cross into the next field by the gate ahead. Once in this field (which the sunken track will lead you into if you have managed to follow it), follow the hedge along on your right.

Cross the fence at the far end, which will lead you into a field near a tin shack. Initially walk down this field on the same line you've been following, but after some thirty yards gently swing to the left across the hillside towards the wood and here you will find, across some wooden rails, a path which leads down through the wood to the stream below. Before you come to a small stream flowing out from the hillside on your left, you want to turn right and cross the stream in the valley bottom above a pool.

Once over the stream head straight up the hillside opposite and cross the fence you come to by the stile provided. Turn right over this and follow the fence on your right, turning onto the track when this starts a little way ahead. This will lead past a house on your right to a T-junction of tracks. You cross over this junction into the field opposite by the rails to the left of the hedgerow which leads downhill to the next stream. Cross diagonally over this field to the far left-hand bottom corner, crossing the stiles and fences and then the stream, before following a hedge uphill on your immediate right. This will bring you to a gate in the top right-hand corner of this field. Through this, turn right onto a good track. Follow this along and then down the hillside, where it crosses a stream and meets another track.

Go straight over this junction to the stile in the corner of the field on the other side. Over this follow the hedge on your right, and when this turns away to the right, turn slightly left and cross to the rails which you see in the far left-hand corner of an arm of the field. Once over these, cross the ditch on your right and join the path that soon gains a more major prominence. This follows the ditch, then bends left and crosses it by a bridge and leads out onto a track to the side of some houses. Walk uphill till you come to another track which leads off to the left. Here you'll see a stile in the fence on your right. Cross this and head for the far left-hand corner of this field. Cross the ditch and fence here and then follow the fence on your left to the footbridge ahead. Over this keep on the same line, following the hedge on your left, bearing to the right through a gate and round past a house. Keep following the hedges and boundaries on your left and you will come to a gate out onto the road. Turn right on the road, left at the junction ahead and left by the pub to return to your vehicle.

*The doorway, Kilpeck Church*

# ACONBURY

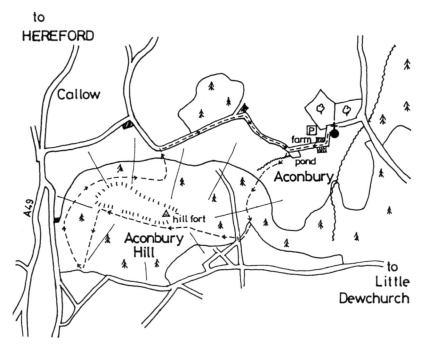

One and a quarter hours.

A walk around Aconbury Hill on paths and tracks, in old oak woodland, past old chestnut coppices and by newer larch and conifer plantations. It has views across to Hereford (time of year and leaf cover permitting!) in the north, and towards the Forest of Dean in the south. Included are also the remains of the old priory at Aconbury and the hillfort at Aconbury Camp.

Park near Aconbury Church, for details of which see the gazetteer.

Head west on the minor road, leaving the majority of the farm buildings on your right. At the bend in the road beyond these buildings,

302

and just past a pond on your left, go through the gate and across the little stream on your immediate left. Then bear right to follow the stream to its spring head in the field at which point you turn slightly left and head up the hillside to the gate into the woodland on the far side of the field. Through this follow the path ahead up the hillside and bank, at the top of which you emerge onto a wide gravelled track.

Turn right on this and immediately left to slant up across the hillside. As the path starts to level off you reach a field just above you to the right. Look for the stile in the field corner and pass over it in to the field itself. Now walk on up the hill, keeping the wood to your immediate right. This is where you gain the views to the south. Near the top of the ridge you turn right onto a track leading almost back on yourself into the wood, but after only a few yards, turn left onto another track which meanders gently upwards through old oak woodland.

Further on it bears to the left and passes to the left of the ramparts of Aconbury Camp. The path now starts to go generally downhill. Keep pretty well straight ahead, crossing various tracks, and eventually the track you're on resumes more the appearance of a path and passes between a conifer plantation on the left and old chestnut coppice on the right. Beyond this it meets another track on which you turn left and walk downhill to meet a wide gravelled track.

Turn right on this and it leads you gently up and round the west of the hill above the main Hereford to Ross road, and then drops down on the north side of the hill. About a hundred yards after it has bent into and back out of the hillside, look for a track off to the left. Take this and it will zig-zag your way down to a gate at the wood's edge. Pass through the gate and walk along the hedge on your left to the road ahead. Turn right on the road to return to your vehicle.

# BOLSTONE — HOLME LACY

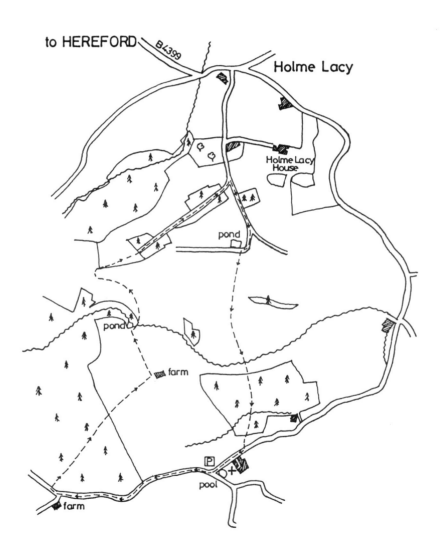

to HEREFORD    B4399

Holme Lacy

Holme Lacy
House

pond

pond

farm

pool

farm

One and three-quarter hours.

On paths crossing fields, on tracks and paths through woodland and on some road, this walk includes views to Fownhope, Dinedor and the surrounding countryside, and incorporating views over Holme Lacy House and gardens.

Take the B4399 Holme Lacy road from Hereford and in Holme Lacy, on the corner with the agricultural college, turn right on the road to Bolstone and Ballingham. The road to Ballingham itself turns left off this road and you keep straight on. About a mile beyond that junction another metalled lane leads off to the left. Here there is also a pool on the roadside and a large grassy triangle at the lane junction, which makes a good place to park.

Carry on walking up the road along which you were driving, and which leads down below some woodland. When the road bends sharp left over a stream to a farm, turn right on the grassy lane and walk up this for a few yards till you come to a gate into some woodland. Go through this onto a track. (The first ten yards or so of the track may be blocked—if so retrace your steps and enter the wood at its corner and walk up the track, turning right onto the true route opposite the gate just referred to.) This track now gently swings through the wood and crosses several others in its progress. It is possible that you will see deer on this part of the walk. Once you reach the far side of the wood, cross out of it and head to the left-hand corner of the farm on the far side of the field.

In the corner of this field pass out through a gate, and turn left in front of the stone built barn. Pass through another gate and walk up the hedge on your left to a gate at the far end. Go through this and almost immediately right through another gate onto a track which leads down into the wood and across a dam at the head of a pond. At the far end of the dam turn left over the stile and turn half left again across the field to its far side.

When you reach the hedge at the far side, turn left and walk along its length, crossing out over a stile on your right at the end. Turn immediately right through a gate and follow the fence on your left which runs almost along the hill top. About two hundred yards further on you reach a stile next to a gate. Cross this and then follow the track to the next gate and stile ahead. Over this you're on a broad track which leads gently along and then down the hill, to emerge from the woodland just above Holme Lacy House. Turn half right once out of the wood and cross over the stile onto a track. Turn right on the track and it leads you uphill and past a conifer plantation, after which it bends to the left.

However, here you take the first gate on the right and carry on straight ahead past a mound and trees on your right on the skyline and which in fact hide a fishpond. When this track turns right, around the fishpond, carry on straight ahead across the field. The path now almost exactly keeps to this same line—cross a stile on the far side of the field, and then follow a hedgerow on your left all the way down to a footbridge across the stream in the valley bottom. Head across the next field still on the same line and through a little gate into Lower Bolstone Wood. A path leads through the wood to a stile at the far end. Cross this and carry on up the fence and you come to a gate. Once through that turn right on the road to return to your vehicle.

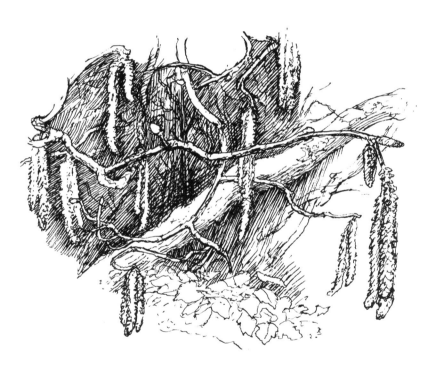

# CAPLER CAMP

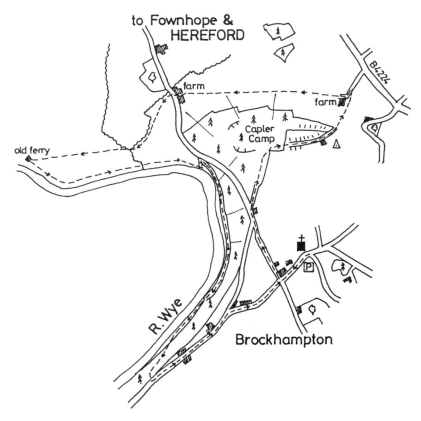

Two and a quarter hours.

A walk on paths forming part of the Wye Valley Walk around Capler
Camp, and partly on paths in the rolling countryside behind the
camp, and partly on paths and tracks along the River Wye. Some
minor road is also involved.

Park at Brockhampton Church, west of Fownhope.

Walk west along the road from the church, so that the church is to your right. At the crossroads turn right to Fownhope and Hereford. When you meet the Wye Valley Walk on the edge of some woodland, turn right up the track. Till the far side of Capler Camp you will be following the Wye Valley Walk and it is well waymarked with yellow arrows to help you. The route bears right through a young conifer plantation and right at its far end to run along the ditch between two of the fort's ramparts. At the far end it bears left past Camp Cottage, a small stone farm, and descends the hill by a series of steps. It then follows a fence on your left past a field and then round some farm buildings to emerge onto the road that leads to the farm.

Here you leave the Wye Valley Walk and turn left up the farm lane, bearing right into and through the farmyard, keeping most of the farm buildings to your left. At the far side of the yard, enter the field and walk along the hedge on your left which runs roughly parallel to Capler Camp. At the first field boundary you pass through a gate, at the next over a stile and at the third a gate. This then leads you into the middle of a field and you cross it aiming for the rails in the fence opposite, just to the left of the farm buildings in the valley below. Over these rails follow the sunken line of the track through the farm to the gate onto the road.

Cross the road and go through the gate opposite, crossing to the corner of the hedge marking the boundary of the orchard on your left. Bear round this and head for the far right-hand corner of the field. Cross the fence and follow the ditch on your right, crossing it at the stile in the corner of the field. The path now turns to the right and heads for the house across the fields, this house being the old Mansell's Ferry across the Wye. So, cross the first field to the stile ahead, then similarly the next field using the two trees as added markers. Then cross to the left of the old ferry building and to the banks of the Wye.

Turn left along the Wye, crossing the stiles you come to, eventually crossing one into the woodland at the bottom of Capler Hill. Turn left up the hillside till you meet a track on which you turn right. This track leads you back down to the Wye which you now follow round the bend ahead. When the track leads out into a grassy area, the track divides and you take the one up the hillside to meet the road at the top. Turn left on this and walk back to your vehicle.

# WOOLHOPE

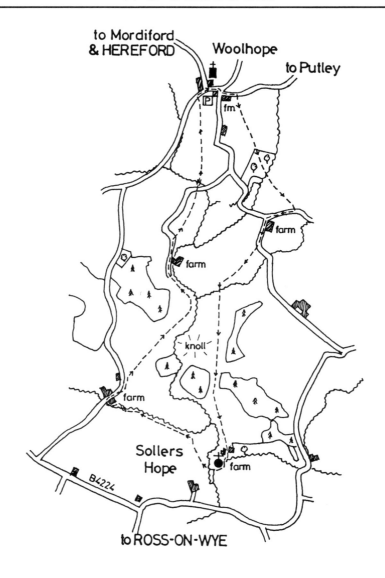

Two hours.

A walk on paths across fields between Woolhope and Sollers Hope and back again, in easy rolling countryside. The condition of many of the paths will depend upon the state of the fields, but many appear to be under permanent pasture.

Park near the Crown Inn in Woolhope.

Walk down the main road eastwards towards Putley. Immediately past the farm on the edge of the village just below the pub, cross the fence on the corner of the buildings on the right and walk down the fence on your right to the stile ahead. Once over this cross to the far left corner of the field, and pass out of it over a stile near a tin shack. At first follow the hedge on your right, then cross the field to the stile in the bottom far corner. Cross the next stile on your right and then walk through the new orchard on roughly the same line as you crossed down the last field to a footbridge across the stream. Over this, bear slightly more to the left between the newly planted trees on the bank ahead, to a stile in the far corner of the field. Cross over this on to a lane.

Turn right on this and bear left round the farm. Just past the double bend in the lane and where it has metal railings to either side, turn right through a gate into a large field. Walk across this field, aiming for the telegraph pole below the line of hedge which runs down the far right-hand side of the field. When below this line of hedge, turn left and cross the ditch in the valley bottom by the bridge provided. Walk straight over the next field to the stile ahead. Cross this and then follow the fence on your right, keeping Tack Wood on your left and a grassy knoll on your right.

This path leads to a gate at the far end. Pass through this and keep straight ahead, through a small piece of woodland, and then roughly down the middle of two successive narrow fields, with a hedge on your left and a stream to your right. At the farm buildings ahead the track bears slightly left to go through the yard with the house and most of the buildings on your right. The path then turns right and passes in front of the house, then left through the churchyard. (If you want to find out about the Whittington family, of Dick Whittington fame, then you should make a visit to the church.)

At the far side of the churchyard the path crosses a field to a bridge. Once over this, bear half right to diagonally cross the next field. Go through the gateway in the corner and bear right, keeping the hedge to your right. At the stream ahead, turn left and cross the next field boundary at the overgrown stile in the corner. Keep following the stream on your right, and once through the gate at the far side of this large field, turn right over the footbridge and then left to continue following the stream. Bear right in the farmyard and emerge onto the road to the right of the farmhouse. Turn right on the road and after just a few yards cross the rails on your right into the field past the farm buildings.

Follow the hedge on your left—the road boundary, and pass through the gate at the next field junction. Now bear slightly more to the right and downhill, sloping gently towards the valley bottom and circling round a field on your left. Pass through a gate above the stream and then head to the rails on the left-hand corner of the next field. Cross these and follow the hedge on your left to the gate at the end of the field.

You'll now find yourself on a track. Walk along this past the farm on your right and when the lane bends to the left, go through the gate indicated by a footpath sign. Follow the hedge on your right, and when it turns sharp right, turn slightly left and cross the field to the stile ahead. Once over this, cross the next field on the same line to the next stile ahead. Once over this stile cross the lane and go over the stile into the field opposite. Turn right in this field and cross the bridge over the stream. Go to the stile just opposite and once over it follow the hedge on your left. When this bears away sharp left, cross the isthmus of field and then follow the hedge on your right. Over the next stile turn slightly left and cross the next field to the stile to reach the road. Turn right on this to return to your vehicle—or the Crown.

# MUCH MARCLE

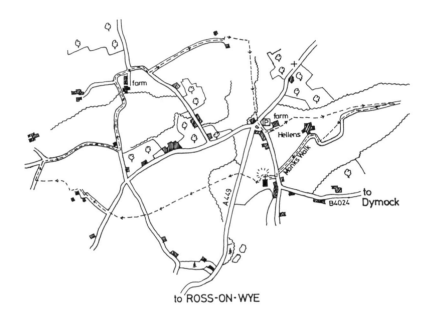

Two and a quarter hours.

Incorporates outside views of Hellens, Much Marcle Church and views over much of the countryside stretching to the Malverns.

On paths, tracks and minor roads. Many paths are in good condition but in one area, over the main road from the church and across the succeeding few fields, the farmers don't seem too keen on reinstating the paths. This may therefore mean heavy going over recently ploughed land, or difficulty in crossing wet full grown crops.

313

From the crossroads at the garage and pub in Much Marcle village, take the B4024 to Dymock. After just a hundred yards park on the wide verge near the first field gateway on your left.

Carry on walking down the B road towards Dymock, and after a further sixty yards or so, turn left up a gravelled track. Pass in front of the red brick farm on your left and continue through the gate ahead into a field. Carry on walking across the field on the same line, shadowing the hedge on your right to join the track which snakes across the field from the left. Turn right on this track and after a short distance take the smaller left-hand split and pass through a gate into another field, just to the left of a small wood. Hellens and its buildings lie to the right behind this wood. You will have better views later on.

The route now diagonally crosses the field to the far right-hand corner, and a track does make a reasonably distinct course which to follow. Pass through the gate to the left of the far corner into the next field and follow the hedge on your right, abruptly joing a major track when the hedge comes to an end. Turn right onto this track, almost retracing your steps for a while. When you reach a bend in the field boundary, cross the stile straight ahead, the path now diagonally crossing this field to the far left-hand corner. On this section you have good views of Hellens. At the far side of the field pass through a gate and walk out to rejoin the track you left earlier. Turn right on this and it will lead you to a gravelled driveway, the Monks Walk, on which you turn left to walk back to the B road.

Turn left on the B road and almost immediately right to head to the church. (For information on this refer to the gazetteer.) Walk through the gateway and follow the track round behind the church, where you cross a stile on your right. The path crosses to the right-hand bottom corner of the field where it passes out by a little gate onto the main road. Almost opposite is another small gate leading to the next path. This can be where ploughing or crops could make the walk difficult.

Look across to the field boundary opposite, a line of trees and bushes which mark the banks of a large drainage ditch. Look for the two oak trees to the left of straight ahead, themselves to the right of a small bend in the line of trees, and it is to the right of these two trees that you should aim. As a double check—you should be heading fairly well to the right of the single oak standing in the field. Confident of your course—then set off. It may of course be that others doing the

314

walk have left their track. Just to the right of the two oaks mentioned you should find a footbridge. Cross this and walk on across the next field on the same general line. You should come to the field boundary opposite at a point where it is joined by another hedge leading off at right angles up the hillside. Cross the field boundary to the right of this hedge and then follow it up the hill to the road ahead.

Just to the left of immediately over this road is a stile into the next field. If this field looks tricky to cross, then you can cut out some of the walk and turn right on the road. (If you adopt the road route, carry on reading as from the next set of brackets below.) If you're willing to press ahead, the path now turns slightly to the right of the direction you've just been following. As you cross the hillside, keep the collection of farm buildings on your left to your left, and aim for the house that appears down the next hill slope. As you cross the hill, start to bear more to the right and head to the rails which eventually appear in the far corner of the field across a small dip that runs through the field. Cross these rails and head up the track opposite, which services a couple of houses. Cross out over the stile at the end and turn left up the hedgerow, crossing the stile at the hedge ahead. Now turn right and follow the hedge on your right to the track at the far end, crossing out by another stile. Turn right on the track and follow it to the road ahead.

If you want views to the west over the Woolhope limestone to Wales, walk left up the road to the crest of the hill not far away. The walk itself turns right down the road. At the junction with another road left, turn left. (Those who omitted the last part of the walk will have to turn right down this road, being the first one they meet.)

This road winds through the limestone into which it is partially cut. It passes Lower Wolton Farm in a dip in the road and further on, round a bend, joins another road. Turn right on this, it soon turning to the right. Take the first track off to the left, just past a house on the right, to Ryemeadows. Before the gate to the Ryemeadows itself, the last house at the end of the lane, turn left through a little gate into an orchard and follow the path round Ryemeadows to a stile into the field beyond. Carry on walking on the same line, following the hedge on your right to the stile ahead. Once over this turn right, shortly crossing a plank bridge and another stile, so that the hedge that was on your right, is now on your left. Now follow this, crossing a stream, and then keeping it on your left down to the gate at the far end near the garage in Much Marcle. Bear half left to the road which you cross and so return to your vehicle.

# KEMPLEY

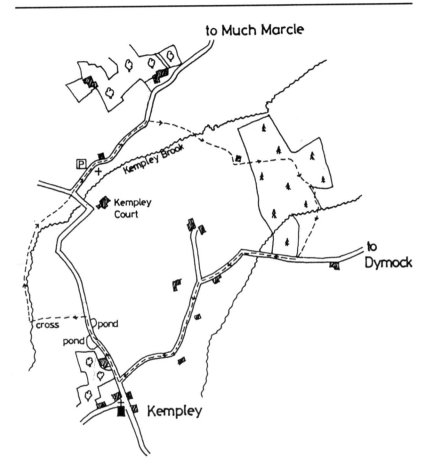

to Much Marcle

Kempley Brook

P

Kempley
Court

to
Dymock

cross    pond
pond

Kempley

One and a half hours.

A gentle walk on paths in generally good condition and on minor
roads in undulating countryside. (We've excluded some potential
paths from this walk on the grounds that they cross large fields and
don't tend to be re-instated by the farmers.)

316

Park at the old Kempley Church—St. Mary's, which you reach by turning west to Much Marcle onto the B4024 north of Dymock off the B4215. Bear left at the first junction. The church in any event is well signposted as it is in the care of English Heritage due to its murals. (See the gazetteer for further information.)

Walk back up the road you drove down till you reach the public footpath sign on the right at the first corner. This path is well waymarked for its whole length. Enter the field and bear half left, cross two stiles and then you reach a footbridge across the Kempley Brook. Here the path turns to head towards the top left-hand corner of the field, but crosses a stile on your left before you reach it. Now follow the hedge round on your right, crossing another field boundary round the corner. Here you turn left to walk round the chimney stack remains of an old cottage, crossing a narrow neck of field beyond to enter a wood. The path then heads straight through the wood, crossing another track, till you notice a field through the trees to your left. Just beyond this the route turns right, again crossing another track, beyond which at a fork in the ways, you turn left. This will bring you to a corner in the wood, and you cross a stile into the field beyond. Walk down the fence on your right, crossing back into the wood by another stile after a hundred yards or so. The path now follows the edge of the wood down to its bottom, and then round to the right. Look for the stile and bridge on your left, taking these to enter a field. Here you bear half right to cross the field diagonally to the far right-hand corner—you'll see the exit stile as you breast the ridge.

Turn right on the road over the stile, and follow it along to the T-junction at the edge of Kempley. Here turn right. After you've passed two ponds, one to the left and one to the right, look out for the next field boundary on your left not far ahead. Cross the slatted fence immediately beyond this and walk down the hedge on your left. From where it juts out slightly into the field, walk towards the oak tree and the cross erected in 1908, beyond which you cross the brook by the bridge provided. Turn right over the bridge and follow the brook. A little way ahead you cross a ditch by a small bridge, after which you cross a hedge on your right by a stile. Beyond this the path shadows the brook rather than keeping to its every wiggle, and you will eventually come to a gate into the field beyond. Here the path swings away from the brook up the bank in the field. As you ascend this you'll see St. Mary's Church ahead, and you aim just to the left of this, leaving the field by the stile provided. Walk back up the road to the church.

# SELLACK

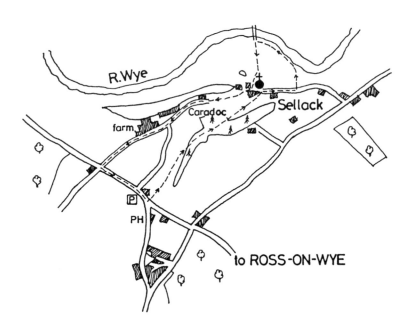

Three-quarters of an hour.

A walk on paths through a dingle, a mixture of tracks and paths by the Wye, and a track past the burnt remains of Caradoc Court and healthier looking Caradoc Farm and stables, and finally on a short section of minor road.

From Ross take the A49 to Hereford. After crossing the roundabout at Wilton, take the second road right, signposted Hoarwithy and Sellack. Travel along this road for about two miles till, after passing over a crossroads on the crest of a rise, you drop down to a valley bottom and the Loughpool Inn on your left. Either park at the pub or, if you don't fancy a drink afterwards, there is space nearby on the roadside.

Opposite the road junction near the pub a signposted footpath leads off over a stile in the direction of Sellack. Take this, crossing the fence ahead by another stile. Then follow the dingle bottom to the pond ahead, turning right up the fence in front of the pond. After thirty yards or so, turn left through the V shaped stile onto a path which leads through the woodland. This will lead you to a stile at the far end, over which you follow the fence on your left to a stile at the far end of the field.

Turn right on the lane and walk uphill till you come to a gate on your left. Turn through this and walk down the track towards the Wye, the track bearing left and converting to a path as you shadow the Wye on your right. Carry on walking till you come to the footbridge, at which point you turn left and head across the fields to the gate between the church and a house. Once through this turn right on the track and follow it along, passing Caradoc Court and Caradoc Farm on your right. When you reach the road, turn left to return to your vehicle.

# ROSS-ON-WYE

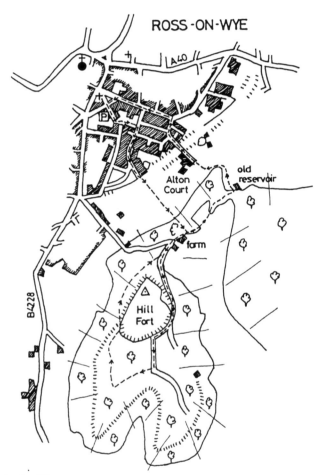

One and a half hours.

It involves a steep hill climb and is on paths and tracks largely in good order in a mixture of conifer, oak and beech woodland, with views over Ross and the surrounding countryside.

Park in Sussex Avenue, the road to the south of Alton Park.

At the far end of the road bear half left down the footpath between hedges and fences. Turn right on the road at the far end. Past the old Merrivale House and farm buildings on the left, curve to the left and head for the pair of gates over the old railway line. Cross over the line and follow the hedge on your left up to the wood ahead. Pass through the gate into the wood, turning right, and almost immediately left and work your way up the hillside to emerge above the old quarry pit. Once on the path above the quarry and at the far edge of the woodland, you are on part of the Wye Valley Walk. Turn right on this, keeping Hill Farm to your left. Carry on on the main track along the hillside when you leave the wood.

When the track splits, take the left-hand branch which runs uphill and is waymarked for the Wye Valley Walk. This leads up round the hillside, and past the old ramparts of a hillfort at the top, which now largely enclose a field. Further on you come to a clump of conifers at a split in the track and you bear right, keeping roughly level along the hillside. Further on you come to another split in the ways, and you turn right on a smaller track leading slightly uphill. A few hundred yards further on you have to keep a sharp look out for a path, well worn but still only a path, off to the left at a point where the track swings round to the right. Take this path which leads across to another corner of the hilltop field and then slants downhill through beechwood, keeping to the lowside of an open area where rocks have tumbled from the hillside. The path eventually joins a wide track, on which you turn right. This returns you to the Wye Valley Walk near Hill Farm.

Initially retrace your steps, but then rather than clambering back downhill over the old quarry, carry on along the Wye Valley path which leads you to a corner of the wood. Cross the stile and head for the wood opposite over the narrow neck of field. Once back in the wood a wide track leads you through it and to the far side, sloping gently downhill. Over the stile at the far side you turn left downhill, shadowing the wood on your left and leaving the old reservoir on your right. At the bottom left hand corner of the field, pass through a gate out onto a track which leads you out past Alton Court.

When you reach the railway track it appears there is now a path which runs along it and you could take this to regain your old route back into town. Alternatively carry on till you come to Alton Road on which you turn left.

# LLANGARRON

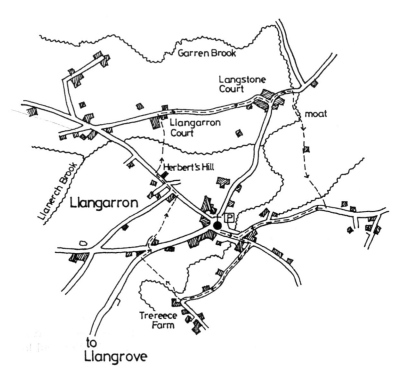

One hour.

A walk on minor roads and paths, some of the latter crossing fields, crossing streams and over fairly open rolling countryside. The walk passes a variety of farms, barns and dovecotes in a variety of styles. Boots are essential as there is a river to ford!

Park near the church.

Walk downhill along the road and cross the Garron Brook, bearing right once across the bridge. About a hundred yards further on turn right once more. When the road bends sharp right in front of Tre-reece Farm, pass through the gate into the small paddock on the right before the buildings. Walk down the sunken track and ford the brook. Once across, follow the left-hand side of the fence and hedge ahead and pass out onto the road at the top via the two gates.

Turn right on the road and presently you'll come to a junction with a road from the left. Go straight over the crossroads so formed on to the track opposite, immediately to the left of a cottage. This soon leads into a field and you follow the hedge on your right, crossing a stile at the end of the field and then following the hedge on your left to the road ahead. Turn left on this and near the crest of the road, you pass the red brick Herbert's Hill cottage on the right.

Go through the field gate on your right a few yards beyond the cottage and cross the field aiming towards the stone built Llangarron Court, on the far side of the little valley through which flows the Lla-nerch Brook. Cross the stile at the far side of the field, then go over the bridge and pass through the gate ahead, to then follow a hedge on your right up to the farm buldings. Pass out through these onto the road.

Turn right on the road and this will later lead you through the farm buildings of Langstone Court to another T-junction. Turn left here and just before you cross the stream, take the signposted footpath to the right. This is fairly well waymarked with yellow arrows and leads to the left of some stone sheds, then to a gate and bridge over the stream. On the far side the path bears slightly right to the top right-hand corner of the field, after which it follows a fence round on your left before joining a track. Continue walking along the track, and when this bends sharp right, go through the gate and stile ahead and cross the next field past the waymarked telegraph pole. This will lead you to a road on which you turn right to return to Llangarron.

# LOCATION MAPS FOR
# GAZETTEER AND WALKS

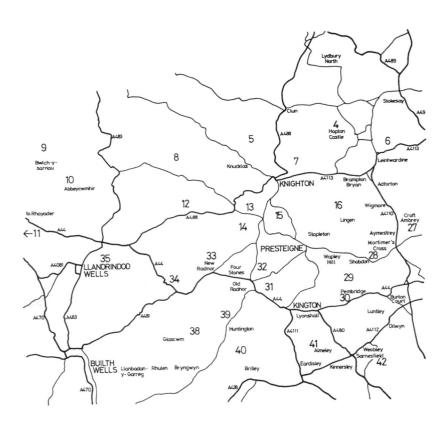

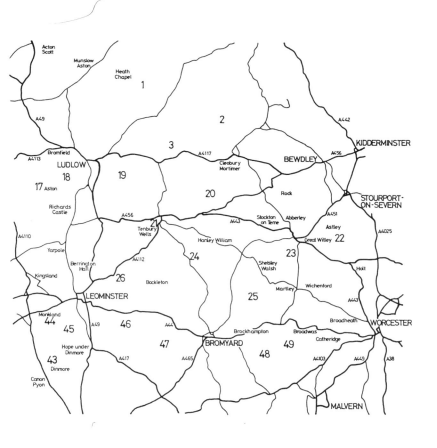

Acton
Scott

Munslow
Aston

Heath
Chapel

1

A49

2

A442

KIDDERMINSTER

3

A4117

Cleobury
Mortimer

BEWDLEY

A456

Bramfield

A4113

LUDLOW

18

19

17 Aston

20

Rock

STOURPORT-
ON-SEVERN

Richards
Castle

A456

21

Stockton
on Teme

Abberley

A451

Astley

A4025

A4110

Tenbury
Wells

A43

Great Witley

22

Yarpole

Hanley William

24

23

Berrington
Hall

A4112

Shelsley
Walsh

Holt

Kingsland

26

Backleton

25

Martley

Wichenford

A443

LEOMINSTER

Broadheath

WORCESTER

Monkland

44

45

A49

46

A44

Brockhampton

Broadwas

Catheridge

49

Hope under
Dinmore

47

BROMYARD

48

43

A417

A465

A4103

A449

A38

Dinmore

Canon
Pyon

MALVERN

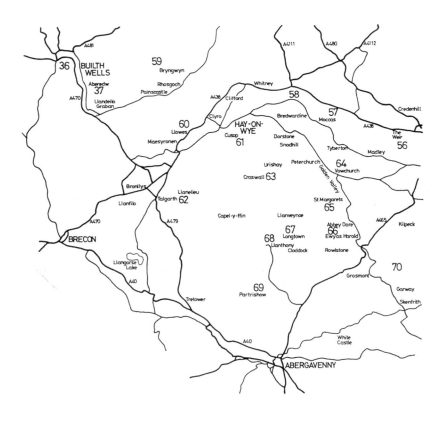

36 BUILTH WELLS

59 Bryngwyn

A481

A4111  A480  A4112

Aberedw
37
Llandeilo
Graban
A470

Rhosgoch
Painscastle

Whitney

A438 Clifford

58

Credenhill

Clyro

Bredwardine
57
Moccas
A438

The
Weir
56

60
Llowes

HAY-ON-
WYE
Cusop
61

Dorstone
Snodhill

Tyberton

Madley

Maesyronen

Urishay
Craswall 63

Peterchurch
64
Vowchurch

Bronllys

Llanelieu
Talgarth 62
Llanfilo

St.Margarets
65

A470

A479

Capel-y-ffin

Llanveynoe

Abbey Dore
66
Ewyas Harold

A465

Kilpeck

BRECON

68

67
Longtown
Llanthony
Clodock

Rowlstone

70

Llangorse
Lake

Grosmont

Garway

A40

69
Partrishow

Skenfrith

Tretower

White
Castle

A40

ABERGAVENNY

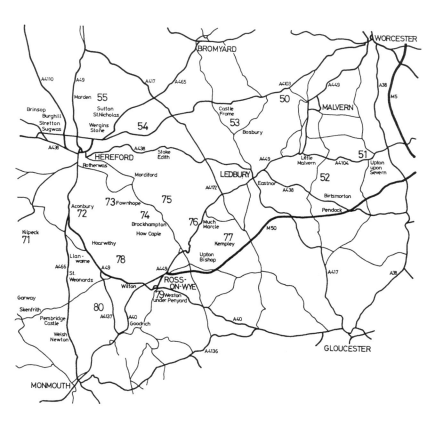

WORCESTER

BROMYARD

A4110  A49  A417  A465  A4103  A449  A38

Marden  55  50  M5

Sutton  Castle  MALVERN
Brinsop  St.Nicholas  Frome
Burghill  53
Stretton  Wergins  54  Bosbury
Sugwas  Stone

A438

HEREFORD  A438  Stoke  A449  Little  51
Rotherwas  Edith  Malvern  A4104  Upton
upon
Mordiford  LEDBURY  52  Severn

73 Fownhope  75  A4172  Eastnor  A438  Birtsmorton
Aconbury
72  74  Pendock
Brockhampton  76  Much
Kilpeck  How Caple  Marcle  M50
71  77
Hoarwithy  Kempley
Llan-  78  Upton
warne  Bishop
A466  St.  A49  A449  A417  A38
Weonards  Wilton  ROSS-
Garway  ON-WYE
Skenfrith  79 Weston
under Penyard
Pembridge  80
Castle  A4137  A40
Welsh  Goodrich  A40
Newton
A4136  GLOUCESTER

MONMOUTH

327

# WALK INDEX

Those marked with an * are the only walks which are virtually unchanged from the first edition of *Walks & More*.